P9-DTW-801

IRONIES IN ORGANIZATIONAL DEVELOPMENT

IRONIES IN ORGANIZATIONAL DEVELOPMENT

Robert T. Golembiewski

Transaction Publishers
New Brunswick (U.S.A.) and London (U.K.)

Library of Congress Catalog Number: 88-36466
ISBN: 0-88738-293-2
Printed in the United States of America

Library of Congress Cataloging-in-Publication Data
Golembiewski, Robert T.
Ironies in organizational development / Robert T. Golembiewski.
p. cm.
Includes index.
ISBN 0-88738-293-2
1. Organizational change. I. Title.
HD58.8.G644 1989 88-36466
658.4′06—dc19 CIP

To Peg,

my companion in moving toward awareness of *my* human irony, which can be expressed in such ways

—I am most myself when we are together

—I am strongest when I recognize my multiple dependencies on her

—I am most comfortably alone in her presence.

Those variants all say much the same thing: *moja kochana*.

Contents

Preface

This book contains a dozen chapters, and they are a mixture—of the old and the new, of the tried-and-true as well as the speculative, of the here-and-now with a dash or two of the by-and-by.

Some questions follow, quite naturally. Why this particular assemblage? And why now?

So some early delineation of what follows has a high priority. In a nutshell, Organizational Development (OD) practice has been quite successful, by and large. Nonetheless, there has been too little translation of that success into broader analytic frameworks that not only reflect an intellectual grasp but that can substantially enrich praxis. This expresses the basic irony motivating this book. One reader of this book perceptively expresses the barrier which this book seeks to help surmount—or perhaps better, to transform from liability into substantial asset:

> Applications have not yielded theory. The consequence of this is that too often OD successes rest on the talent and instinct of the intervenor. Generalizability of outcomes, and even more widespread application of successful techniques, will inevitably be constrained if the "science" of organizational development is not asserted in analytic frameworks.

Four emphases provide further and useful delineation for present purposes, although readers no doubt will have their multiple and additional reactions. In turn, this prefatory focus is on the chapters, then on their encapsulating context or medium, on the intended audience, and finally on the magic of *this* moment.

Chapters: Old, New, and Otherwise

To begin, the chapters have their own life histories, and four classes of them can be distinguished. First, four chapters—2, 3, 4, and 12—are published in detail here for the first time, and the first two on this list have foci that are at times distant from my normal intellectual flight paths in OD. Second, the essentials of four chapters—4, 5, 6, and 8—were published originally in sources unlikely to gain the attention of ODers, in part because I was then less clear about the significant role the pieces can play in understanding today's status of OD and, especially, in fostering tomorrow's development. Third, chapters 1, 7, 8, half of 10, and 11 were in substance published in major sources, but in at least one case outside the normal reading range of ODers. Fourth, the basic content of two chapters—3 and 4—was published originally in books that are now out of print. Those chapters can profit from being placed in the present context.

So why combine chapters with these diverse life histories into a single volume? For openers, two-thirds (or more) of the chapters probably will be news, even for the reasonably well-read ODer, and the volume as a totality can provide an upscale view of the state of the art for many possible readers—for managers, for new specialists in OD (of whom there are always legions), and for students of organizations who do not follow the twists and turns of the OD literature but whose own work is relevant to OD and can be enriched by it.

All chapters are vigorously updated and revised for present purposes. But the basic rationale for their inclusion in *Ironies* is that those chapters fit as illustrations of the book's argument, which provides useful perspective on an important area of human inquiry and practice. The illustrations are not exhaustive, but they provide a kind of launching pad for future research in OD, which is often seen as pleasantly stuck—as robust enough to support a great and growing consulting activity, but as lagging behind practice, which is far ahead of its theoretical base.

Basically, *Ironies* seems to me to enrich both theory and practice, and I believe it does so in ways that will surprise even close readers of the originals. Indeed, the fit often surprises this author. In any case, the chapters whose essentials have been published typically were written as stand-alone pieces, and some people paid less attention to the words than to what they fancied as the underlying music—that OD was seriously inadequate and stuck, even if comfortably so.

A sharp contrast seems fair enough to me. *Ironies* shows how its several component chapters can be *built upon*. Several of its chapters, as stand-alone publications, seemed to say to some, especially to those applying OD as consultants, "Your baby sure is ugly." This book corrects that perception.

Ironies as Context or Medium for Messages: The New Combination

Ironies provides a vehicle for rectifying such a misinterpretation of my view of OD, whether by critics or by friends. This book provides not only the words, and some of the music, but also reasonably precise directions for producing a better OD tune.

In addition, the theme of ironies provides a context that both unifies this even dozen of chapters and, more significantly, highlights their constructive character and, in the aggregate, even their prudent hopefulness. Individually, that is, the positions in most of the chapters pose real challenges for some OD practitioners and theorists, and encourage despondency in others. For both virginal and previously published chapters, the focus on ironies provides a developmental context and thrust that saves them from charges of mere carping, as that focus also highlights constructive aspects of positions that some saw as negative and as raining on OD's parade.

Ironically, that is, this book proposes two main arguments: that OD does quite well, in general, but that in numerous particulars it can do much better, with modest expenditures of wit and will. The theme of ironies provides a positive context for individual chapters that could be interpreted as grumpy or even malevolent—as never being satisfied or, worse still, as implying grave doubts about the integrity of the entire OD enterprise. The several chapters do encourage various "stretches" that will save us from the Dr. Feelgood–ism that sooner or later can only jeopardize vitality and growing comprehensiveness, but those stretches need to be viewed as ways to improve on a level of general performance that is far from shabby. Those stretches are not cries of despair, but they are clear directions for theoretical development that will raise the level of the conscious practice of intervention in social systems. Consulting competencies and sensitivities often have filled in the gaps in theory, but we cannot always rely on that outcome.

So this book has a simple format, although details in specific chapters will be daunting. The first eleven chapters focus on these ironies:

I. Relative Success but Pessimism about Practice (chapters 1 and 2)
II. Relative Success without a Learning Model (chapter 3)
III. Relative Success without Differentiating People (chapters 4 and 5)
IV. Relative Success without Specifying Contexts (chapters 6 and 7)
V. Relative Success While Neglecting Easy Pieces (chapters 8 and 9)
VI. Relative Success without Differentiating Change (chapters 10 and 11)

Each of the first eleven chapters contributes toward the same conclusion, and the twelfth provides the summary of that conclusion: there are handy ways to enhance success rates in OD from their already-substantial levels.

The twelve chapters constitute neither the necessary nor the sufficient catalog of relevant ironies. But they do provide a "next bite" that will sate even Rabelaisian appetites, although those chapters do not permit swallowing "the whole thing."

Right Now as *the* Congenial Moment

Finally, right now seems an opportune time to bring together the present assemblage of chapters under the rubric of ironies. And what are the characteristics of this "right now?" Two dominate. As chapters 1 and 2 establish, OD theory and practice have a solid track record, and those several estimates of success rates cannot be dismissed cavalierly. Concern was expressed about OD's efficacy even by its proponents, and a kind of minor despair set in among some afficionados before such estimates as those in chapters 1 and 2 surfaced. This newer information provides a solid base of optimism on which the constructive suggestions of chapters 3 through 11 can build. The ability to provide detailed illustrations of what can be done—either immediately, or as items on variously distant agendas—constitutes the second sense of "right now" as the opportune time.

In sum, relative optimism about success rates is here seen as providing the medium within which critical suggestions can be responded to at their own level—specifically, by reducing defensiveness or despondency. In this sense, the message of several of the chapters—perhaps especially chapters 3, 4, 5, and 10—came too soon. Their critical messages often came through as "Your baby sure is ugly" to people who saw OD as comely, even handsome. Those messages were not conditioned by accepted records of high success rates, in the first place. Moreover, it was not clear earlier what was to be done about the critical messages. *Ironies* reflects the desire to test a new combination—older message in some cases, new context in all cases.

The Intended Audiences

The intended audiences are listed earlier: OD consultants, both old hands and the large numbers of entrants that seem always with us; managers facing the challenge of continuous change and seeking a sense of value-guided methods; and those many researchers who work in organizaiton behavior and theory, including social psychologists as well as colleagues from numerous disciplines and specializations.

Some supportive readers see the real audience as largely restricted to the last-identified specialists, with but a few from among OD consultants and even fewer from among managers. As one reader concludes: "Much of [*Ironies*] is simply too sophisticated to be grasped by the practicing OD professional, and too technical to be of much practical significance or even terribly interesting to them."

This position about OD practitioners rests on some daunting realities, of course. Many ODers got their training on the job. Their initial experiences as military officers, ministers, or whatever were variously supplemented but their methodological and theoretical concerns have not been cultivated, in general. Relatedly, the common wisdom has always given preeminence to personal qualities in OD, as in the dictum that ODers' own warm bodies are their most effective tool for intervention. And rightly so. The final daunting reality on the list is that OD practitioners seem to experience a great turnover. For example, 50 percent or more of the attendees at the annual meetings of the

Organization Development Network, year in and year out, are first-timers. So early training and socialization are continuously pressing needs.

But such realities are not sufficient to deter this analysis from also targeting OD practitioners and managers. Basically, what exists provides only herniating guidance for what might become and even less guidance for closer approaches to some ideal condition. In addition, three specific points imply that the targeting of *Ironies* is not simply a kind of misguided willfulness. Like Panasonic, to begin, *Ironies* seeks to be a bit ahead of its time. The book is oriented toward where OD is going—say in five to ten years—and toward where it has been only in the sense of providing a take-off platform.

Is the proposed reach within OD's grasp? The immediate past implies an affirmative answer. The stakes have been raised greatly in the training of ODers, as in conspicuously labeled doctorate and numerous master's degree programs. Finally, what follows often requires only a bit of a stretch to enrich OD and to heighten its already-substantial success rates.

Introduction: Ironies and Consulting Competencies

This book revels in multiple ironies, and perhaps the basic one matches success with failure. To illustrate: OD theory typically reflects major analytical gaps that need filling, and yet in practice OD success rates seem to be quite high. Indeed, those success rates seem to surprise most of the OD literati, if perhaps not as much as they surprise those unconvinced of OD's reach and grasp.

Hence it should come as no surprise that two questions express the important moorings of this book, and also that this pair of queries provides the basic structure for this Introduction. These questions direct attention to what this book seeks, and why:

- How can OD have high success rates, and yet rely on formal theory that is patently fragmentary and incomplete?
- If OD has high success rates, why bother much about improving its theoretical base?

What is OD?

Before taking on these two central questions, an introductory question deserves brief note. OD here is seen as a value-loaded enterprise with an associated technology for intervening in organization and process (e.g., Golembiewski 1979, especially vol. 1). In short, I see my role as an OD intervenor as helping induce greater responsible freedom. The freedom comes in a concerted effort to meet personal needs at work, and operates in empowering as well as unfettering modes. Three basic approaches to such need-meeting can be distinguished: interpersonal and group processes, or how people relate and communicate; structural features, or how people are linked in coordinated and intendedly cooperative networks; and policies or procedures, or the rules of the game that encompass and direct both processes and structure in action.

Documenting in any depth the need-meeting potential of these three basic OD approaches would distract this analysis, but the range of issues has been raised elsewhere (e.g., Burke 1982; Golembiewski and Kiepper 1988) and a

FIGURE 1.1
Two Modes of Interaction

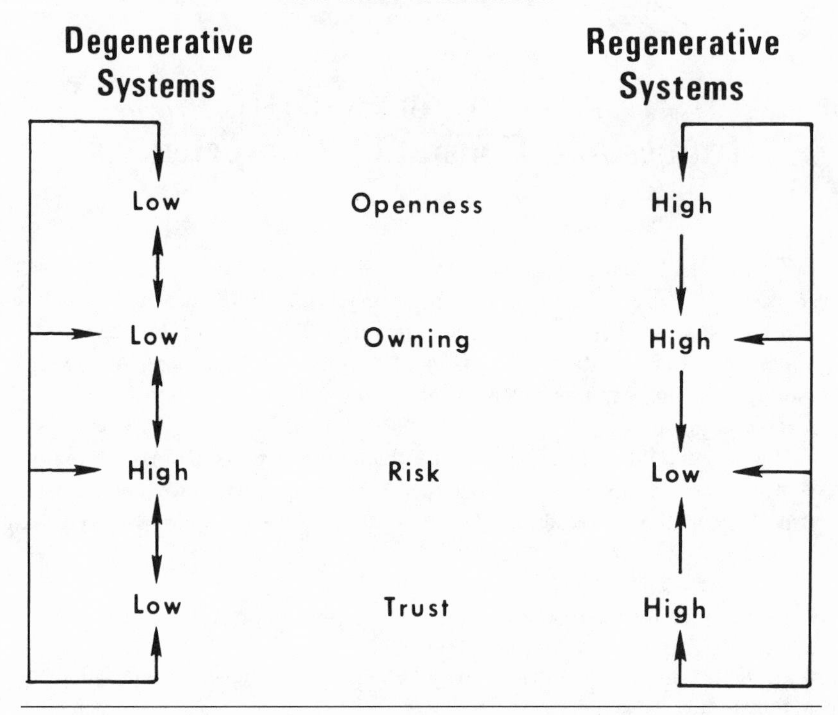

brief sketch does the job for present purposes. Consider interaction processes that are both unfettering and empowering. I like to think of regenerative and degenerative interaction in such direct terms (Golembiewski 1979, 2: esp. 162-75). See figure 1.1.

Individuals not only prefer regenerative interaction, in general, but it also generates consequences that facilitate responsible behavior in organizations. For example, individuals are less burdened with repressed materials, and real issues tend to surface that can be solved without creating greater problems in the process. Degenerative interaction, in contrast, contributes little to either freedom or its responsible manifestations. Thus, important substance or feeling can remain unexpressed and, at an extreme, norms may develop about "not rocking the boat." Degenerative interaction can lead to organizational mischief via such consequences, even when—and perhaps especially when—everyone is "trying hard." More fully, degenerative interaction will be characterized by this pattern of progressively more serious effects between people and groups:

- communication and decision-making processes become increasingly burdened
- individuals become less effective in isolating and resolving substantive issues
- the amount of unfinished business increases
- individuals feel diminished interpersonal competence and psychological failure; that is, they fail to solve problems that remain without creating other (and often more formidable) problems
- individuals become more dependent and cautious, which can lead to "don't rock the boat" attitudes and thus reinforce and deepen the tendencies outlined above
- organization norms develop that reinforce closedness, thus exacerbating normal tensions due to misunderstandings, lack of time, or conflicting missions-and-roles—e.g., line versus staff, subunit loyalties, and so on

In cousinly ways, interventions with structure and policy/procedures also can be unfettering and empowering, while also encouraging more responsible behavior—working better and smarter versus harder, giving more of self to work because it is more need satisfying, and so on. The clearest reflections-in-action of these tendencies exist at the plant level in "high-involvement organizations" (Perkins, Nieva, and Lawler 1983; Golembiewski and Kiepper 1988).

How Can OD Succeed as It Fails?

Now, this analysis gets back to the two central questions that concern this book. One need not look very far for reminders of the several inadequacies and lacunae in OD theory and research, for certain. For example, many observers point to the lack of respect in OD for the canons of pure science: assignments to treatment conditions are seldom made randomly, for example; control or comparison groups are not rare but neither are they commonplace; and long-term studies are the exception rather than the rule.

How can OD succeed in such substantial degree in practice, even as its research and theory so obviously fail to explicitly include major analytical features? This book focuses on a single but powerful explanation. Directly, intervenor competencies are running ahead of our present ability to formalize what most intervenors seem to be doing correctly most of the time. "Most intervenors" here refers especially to that substantial cadre emphasized in chapters 1 and 2 who care sufficiently, and who think deeply enough, about their practice to have committed to writing their experiences with specific learning designs, as well as their reflections on what they observed.

So intervenor competencies are seen as running ahead of our conceptualizing and theorizing about what to do and why. This proposition will require a convincing rationale, of course, and especially because no way to prove that proposition exists. But the job is not as formidable as it might initially appear. Indeed, from several points of view, this present ironic emphasis does not surprise after a bit of reflection, even though it may startle on first reading.

Consider only four perspectives consistent with the notion that OD intervenors have basic competencies that somehow provide crosswalks over—or Band-Aids on—analytic and theoretical gaps, or even chasms.

Many have emphasized that OD practice is ahead of its theory, first, and this is not particularly unusual in a growth area. The urgencies of practice may encourage the discovery of interventions that work, while at the same time discouraging the articulation of growing networks of theory that express in summary form what sensitive OD intervenors have come to know and rely upon. The effect can occur in diverse ways, with practical successes paradoxically contributing to the theoretical lag. Specifically, research with a Flexi-Time pilot study produced positive results that accorded with common-sense expectations. Management wished to extend the program throughout the organization, despite a clear lack of knowledge about why the observed effects occurred. Consultants urged a more detailed study of conditions, with only partial success (Golembiewski, Hilles, and Kagno 1974). However, management proposed to extend the good news, immediately and uniformly and by fiat, even though the success of the pilot study rested on deliberately crafted adaptations of the Flexi-Time model to local conditions via participation and involvement.

From an important point of view, then, the present collection of ironies constitutes an elaborated form of the notion that OD practice outdistances its theory because its applications have been too successful, as it were. This book thus provides chapter-and-verse illustration of some ways in which short-run success can be long-run poison. And this book also details a number of approaches to reducing the gap between practice and theory before applications too far outdistance the theoretical base, and it collapses on itself.

Second, the theoretical progress may lag behind practical achievements because of two curious interactions of complexity and convenience. Thus, I am reminded of Einstein's rationale for the theoretical elegance of physics: "Physics is easier than psychology," he is alleged to have said. Much the same may be said of OD. Electrons cannot read and hence modify their behavior in response to an experimenter's findings. In OD's action research, precisely just such inclusion of the object-of-research as the subject-of-action not only does take place, but intervenors intend it to take place.

The example at once establishes the complexity of what OD seeks to do, and also reinforces the good sense of focusing on basics—on involving broad ranges of participants, and on eliciting their commitment via participation as a workable surrogate for having a comprehensive theoretical model of what happens, when, and why. Indeed, the very power of involvement and commitment has discouraged the development of precise theoretical relationships, or at least temporarily assigned them a lower priority than making immediate use of what we do know.

This lower priority is not perverse, if we acknowledge that it is but a temporary convenience. That is, the very emphases on participation, involvement, and commitment constitute such consciousness-expanders that many are tempted to let the details take care of themselves. Moreover, what we already know—theoretical gaps and all—constitutes such an improvement over most current practice that it is worthwhile, on balance, to raise the level of current practice rather than to wait on the development of a truly comprehensive theory. Note that this does not presume an either/or. Rather, efforts to raise the level of current practice will at once help motivate the search for that comprehensive theory, as well as test the comprehensiveness of various models. In this sense, early insistence on perfection can be a major enemy of excellence.

The efficacy of the basics—participation, involvement, and commitment—may in turn rest on their human rightness, which transcends theoretical detail. It may just be, I grow increasingly convinced, that although people respond in diverse and intricate patterns, those dynamics may well be triggered by relatively direct and even elemental needs. This is the basic notion of the several "growth psychology" models of Maslow, McGregor, Argyris, Herzberg, and others. And OD rests on a related basic rationale: that most people require—or at least much prefer—environments characterized by high openness, owning, and trust, along with low interpersonal risk (Golembiewski 1979, vol. 1, chaps. 1–3). OD's power may well derive from tapping such wellsprings of human motivation, and theoretical lacunae may be troublesome but nevertheless pale in comparison with the human correctness of the OD fundaments.

Third, it appears to me that OD just might succeed in basic senses in spite of analytic deficiencies, if not exactly because of those deficiencies. Or at least this position is worth reviewing.

What can this third point of view mean? Well, much of the potency of OD lies in its values and aspirations being so right, and so generally desired as well as desirable, that OD's inherent worth often carries both intervenors and many of their clients over individual and collective inadequacies and shortcomings. In this sense, OD intervenors are valuable not only for what they do, but also—perhaps, especially—for the values they represent.

A variety of evidence supports this third viewpoint, in fact. I have been impressed with how many of those who are utterly convinced about OD's practical inapplicability nevertheless lament: "You know, it's a crying shame that we just can't do those things around here—like being open with each other. It sure would be a different and a better place if we could." Or consider some hard evidence. Well over 95 percent of the several thousands of managers and employees we surveyed had no doubt about the kinds of organizational values they prefer. For them, "Ideal" scores on the Likert Profile of Organizational Characteristics[1] typically cluster in the high-System III and System IV range—the Consultative and the Participative Group portions of the Likert system of four basic management types. That's where people want to be even when the realities are very different. "Now" or "Actual" scores typically cluster in System II to low-System III.

Perhaps the general point can be put in an elemental way. If you understand and accept a set of values, you can tolerate many glitches in attempts to realize those values in practice. Put another way, the person who accepts a *why* can tolerate almost any *how*, even halting or fumbling or long-delayed hows.

Fourth, although a general conversion to humanistic worksites does not seem to be imminent, it also appears to me that history is on OD's side. OD values more clearly and insistently apply in the kind of society and economy we seem to be becoming: more educated and with a growing range of options and personal agendas; with more complex specialties that require integration right now rather than by-and-by; and living within organization structures that at once often require high degrees of personal, immediate involvement and identification while they also put a premium on the ability to let go quickly and with minimal emotional consequences when conditions change, as they almost certainly shall.

Indeed, in many senses, OD is the only game in town oriented toward the humanistic meeting of such apparent irreconcilables. The force of their values and of historical development may keep OD proponents from stumbling over mere deficiencies in personal skills, as well as from running afoul of the analytic gaps in OD theory illustrated below.

In this case, the OD intervenor's basic capability is being on the right side of history. Being that right about a cosmic essential, it is easy enough to forgive, or at least to put into appropriate perspective, OD's shortness on particulars like theoretic or analytic completeness.

Why Try to Fix It, Since It's Not Really Broken?

The line of argument above suggests a major barrier to this book and what it represents—a dilemma, even. Since OD does pretty well, despite its several analytic deficiencies, why not leave well enough alone? Indeed, drawing attention to the several ironies below may only reduce the confidence of those who are already doing quite well, thank you. In fact, some OD intervenors have responded to several of the themes below in just this way. Put more directly: "If it ain't broken, why fix it?"

Some elements of an answer suggest themselves—quite readily, in fact—to this reformulation of the basic question: Why try to do better-than-average when average ain't at all bad? To begin, although OD success rates are lofty, they still leave plenty of room for improvement. That potential for ready improvement alone provides substantial motivation for adding the analytic enhancements that get attention later in this volume.

In addition, several of those enhancements do not require risking professional hernias. This is not true of all of the cases discussed in this book, but the generalization applies to most. A high benefit:cost ratio urges and eases the effort of making most of the analytic accommodations which this book recommends.

Finally, in this brief catalog of motivations to reduce the gap between practice and theory, OD intervenors are facing—and should *feel*—definite pressures to become more *efficient,* given that OD intervenors already appear to be tolerably *effective*.

This is a weighty point, and developing it a bit more slowly has much to recommend it. OD seems *effective,* in three senses: its values seem desired and desirable, generally; OD has evolved a family of technologies that permit approaching those attractive values in a substantial proportion of cases; and the emerging profession also boasts a substantial cadre of intervenors whose skills and sensitivities seem to extend beyond available theory.

So far, so good. Excellent, in fact.

But *efficiency* seems to be another matter. For example, individual OD intervenors working with specific teams seem to have substantial success rates in making intended things happen. But 1:1 ratios imply sharp limits on OD's reach, if only for reasons of cost.

Can some reasonable things be done to extend OD's reach, then, and to reduce the cost-per-unit? That is, can OD efficiency be increased without jeopardizing OD values?

This book basically argues that an affirmative answer is not only possible, but that reasonable next bites are already conveniently within reach. We need not invent or discover anything new, in short. We need only to make an act of the will—to apply reasonable and nonheroic skill.

The motivation for this effort is direct and substantial, because neither efficiency nor effectiveness will be much increased unless substantial attention is given to reducing the analytic deficiencies highlighted below. The conclusion applies particularly to the leverage inherent in applying the power of useful theories to guide differentiated diagnosis and prescription, especially in massive efforts—for example, for a hundred work teams. There it typically will be awkward or impossible to arrange for intervenor:team ratios of 1:1. Mass applications are a convenient way of reducing unit costs, but they can be dangerous in the absence of a comprehensive theory that can replace in part the personalized adjustments that experienced intervenors apparently make when they work with individual teams. Finally, OD in a sense has no alternative to increasing its efficiency. OD has a stake in transcending its present limitations—for example, of being available mostly to organization elites, and to small proportions of the work force, often at substantial cost. Out of enlightened self-interest, then, OD will have to increase its efficiency on several fronts. Various other motives energize such an effort at extension. Thus, pressing needs dominate in many nonelite settings, as in Third World rural settings. Failure to meet such needs may unleash formidable social and political forces.

Note

1. Those unacquainted with the instrument can consult Likert 1961.

References

Burke, W. W. 1982. *Organization Development*. Boston: Little, Brown.

Golembiewski, R. T. 1979. *Approaches to Planned Change*. New York: Marcel Dekker.

Golembiewski, R. T., and Kiepper, A. 1988. *High Performance and Human Costs*. New York: Praeger.

Golembiewski, R. T.; Hilles, R.; and Kagno, M. 1974. "A Longitudinal Study of Flexi-Time Effects." *Journal of Applied Behavioral Science* 10:503–32.

Likert, R. 1961. *New Patterns of Management*. New York: McGraw-Hill.

Perkins, D. N. T.; Nieva, V. F.; and Lawler, E. E. III. 1983. *Managing Creation*. New York: Wiley-Interscience.

Irony I

Relative Success but Pessimism about Practice

1

The Irony of Ironies: Silence about Success Rates

This chapter and the one following highlight a central irony. At one time, not so long ago, a kind of creeping pessimism invaded OD, in the absence of clear evidence of success rates and with the growing consciousness that OD theory is far from encompassing all there is to know. The pessimism pervaded almost all quarters. Indeed, the wailing and gnashing of teeth about OD's future got to be a kind of professional's game—at scholarly conferences, at meetings of the Organization Development Network, and so on.

Today, several assessment studies converge to a common conclusion: OD success rates are quite high.

The consequence? General silence. Curious, that. For ODers are women and men devotees of what should be a thoughtful and enlightened activism in connection with cooperative effort, but they have been largely mute concerning accumulating evidence that success rates in OD are not at all bad. Indeed, viewed in different ways by a range of observers, these success rates range from good to excellent. Even the relatively negative reviews are quite attractive, with the lowest success rates approximating 50 percent.

We still lack critical fine-tuning, to be sure. For example, we do not have evidence about the proportion of natural improvements—of spontaneous healings, if you will. But that implies no need to cry hunger with a loaf of bread under your arm. Even 50 percent is not bad, natural improvements notwithstanding.

Circumstances make the silence even more of a curiosity. Numerous observers over the years called for just such summary evaluations, for one thing, all the better to separate the wheat from the chaff so as to enhance the aptness and impact of OD designs and programs of change. Now the evidence is becoming increasingly available, and not only does it seem to be favorable evidence—on definite balance—but it has come at a time when some influential voices are concerned that OD is a "maturing market" and hence is in danger of falling into the shoddy practices common when the supply of resources outstrips the demand for them (Krell 1981). Native cunning urges taking advantage of the good news about success rates, of course, all the better to stimulate demand and hence to help avoid the grim dynamics of maturing markets.

And yet the silence about success rates persists. ODers clearly are not letting their faces light up as they refer to substantial success rates, and hence OD is less likely to be a beacon for those in collective distress.

This strange state of affairs may be beyond explanation, but let us give it a brief try. This section walks a narrow line, to be sure, and perhaps it would be better not to worry overly. The issues about theory and practice dealt with later will remain relevant, no matter what gets written here. Moreover, that early OD critics do not revel in public disclosure may stand without elaboration and, in any case, does not help in understanding why those observers who took no position on OD's efficacy seem underwhelmed by the success-rate literature. In addition, one could always take refuge in the proposition that OD does work or it would not be as widely used as it has come to be, whatever the reaction to success. Nonetheless, the issue of success and silence is intriguing, and some speculation follows.

Silence about Success Rates

Up front, let us admit one possibility. High success rates have a forbidding character—a thorn among the roses, as it were. Such rates heighten expectations, and hence imply greater psychological loss when failure occurs. If that is our problem, well, we will just have to learn how to live with raising the ante.

Beyond this possibility, let us focus on a single if involved point: why both OD optimists and pessimists might have given the silent treatment to the success-rate literature. The line of argument below is a bit involved, and is speculative in the bargain. But the effort needs to be made. For supporting details, see Golembiewski 1986.

Obviously, the silence might well derive from a reasonable caution that the results of success-rate studies are spurious or somehow artifactual. Observers can come to this conclusion in two different ways, however. Let us distinguish two classes of ODers responding to the growing literature on success rates: those who had an interest in the matter, but whose minds were still open as to the results of then-unavailable aggregate analysis of successes/failures in individual studies; and those who not only had made up their minds on the matter, but who also reflected a public pessimism about success rates in the absence of comprehensive evidence. This latter camp all but dominated the literature and conferences, taking two strong (if curious for ODers) positions that organizational success rates are modest, and particularly in the public service.

Parenthetically, one wonders why the pessimists kept doing what they did—that is, OD. Given really low success rates, the obvious conclusion should have been: Back to the drawing board!

But I digress.

Now, how might silence come to have been the reaction of both of these two classes of ODers? No one can say for sure, of course, but speculation is encouraged by the silence, even required by it.

Well, for openers, the open-minded ODers might be responding with conservative caution, perhaps born of unhappy experiences with too-little-restrained exuberances of the past. Sure enough, there have been "major findings" that were soon deflated, if not punctured beyond all hope of repair. Within limits, this caution is understandable and even laudatory.

This view about open-minded ODers encourages two reactions, primarily, and they both imply that the reasonable limits of caution have been exceeded. Thus, it may be edifying to contemplate such a collection of sedulous waiters-on-the-future, relying on the processes of analysis and critique to generate some substantially correct approximation of a working truth, while the world continues to turn. It may be edifying, as noted, but this view makes too much of a good thing—that is, of patience while truth values get tested, and hence get variously qualified or even rejected. Moreover, it already has been *a long time* since a second freshet of evaluation studies began appearing in late 1981, and then in greater numbers in 1982 and 1983. And it has been longer still since an earlier batch of evaluation studies appeared in the mid-to-late 1970s.

The ODers who had come to pessimistic (and public) conclusions about low success rates, and especially in the public sector, seem to constitute an easier case in some senses. But that case nevertheless poses some subtle issues.

First, how might one behave who had taken a position—often and rock-solid—that seemed to be substantially off base, to judge from several evaluative studies? Silence is a reasonable enough reaction, and for several possible motives that might be working alone or in various combinations. Hence, silence might be motivated by watchful waiting for contradictory evidence that others might supply. Or silence might simply be the outward sign of an industriousness devoted to developing a careful critique of the evaluation studies, or to generating data supporting the contrary point. Or silence for the public pessimists might simply reflect a reasonable hunkering-down—a kind of CYA by appearing to look elsewhere, hard. During this period of active neglect, the mass of ODers at least would be less likely to have the evaluative literature impressed on their minds by vigorous debate. Alternatively or complementarily, the watchful OD public might come to forget who had made which pessimistic assessments about success rates, in the absence of an enthusiasm about success-rate findings from past pessimists or, indeed, in the absence of any mention at all.

All well and good for purposes of stimulating thought, perhaps, but the pessimistic camp also encourages subtler analysis. Consider here only that nobody likes to have their baby called ugly, and any concerted attention to the emerging success-rate literature would perforce call attention to the uncomeliness of someone's baby.

Some details are useful. Without naming names, the success-rate literature raised direct questions about the pessimists' conclusions that OD success rates were quite low, and especially in the public sector. But that challenge was implicit rather than direct, and the pessimists might have decided against drawing attention to the challenge, even if they considered it poorly founded. Of course, direct and telling criticism of the evaluative literature also could blunt the implied but direct criticism, and perhaps destroy it.

These possibilities encompass a subtle wrinkle. In one case, a well-known ODer (Burke 1980) was developing the point that the record of change in large bureaucracies seemed a sorry one, with the exception of several of my publications. Burke notes:

> Robert Golembiewski is one of the more experienced consultants in the field of OD with bureaucracies, especially in the public sector. He tends to be optimistic about such consultation. . . . To the extent that he is successful as a consultant, he may be an exception to my remarks about . . . OD in the public sector. Most OD consultants find working with bureaucracies, especially public ones, to be difficult at best" (Burke 1980, 428-29).

The common extension of this position to all OD created a kind of cul-de-sac for OD pessimists in relation to the emerging success-rate literature. To put the implied point in its boldest terms, the substantial success rates left only uncomfortable conceptual territory for the pessimists. Their once-dominant view could now be cast as an exception to general practice, an exception which could have roots in the somehow peculiarly difficult situations that pessimists encountered in their practice. More directly still, this view opens the possibility that the problem for the pessimists was not in OD but in their particular approaches to it.

Such a conceptual bind might well encourage silence, for at least two reasons. Thus, it would be difficult to establish that—or to understand how—the pessimists had usually selected the non-easy pieces for intervening, in general, and hence had bad but understandable experiences, on the whole. Moreover, precious little motivation would exist among pessimists to embrace the second possibility; this nettle discourages grasping it, let alone cleaving to it.

But these are bare possibilities, and leave too much to the imagination for definite conclusions. Let us move on, knowing a bit more about the territory.

A Conceptual Context for Irony I

Thus, failing to understand the silence about success rates, we can at least describe the context that has resulted in silence. So this chapter takes us back a few years, when studies of success rates reported only a handful of cases and vocal pessimism dominated. Three subsections carry the weight of this introduction: the literature of pessimism will be reviewed; three points of major agreement will be sketched that serve as a platform for a deep-dive assessment of that pessimism; and the data base of OD applications for such an assessment will be detailed.

A pessimistic cacophony. One of the more certain topics for inspiring vigorous contention in the early days involved assessing the state of OD.[1] Debates were held, reputations were risked, and ominous warnings rumbled, both pro and con. These constitute the signs of a new and vigorous arena of thought and applications, of course.

Beginning in the mid-1970s, a curious agreement developed. Friend and foe alike tended to have real doubts about OD's future. Critics pointed to a range of problems—theoretical, methodological, and ethical (e.g., Woodworth, Meyer, and Smallwood 1980). Many historical supporters saw OD at a critical life stage—as an adolescent, with quite definite signs of lacking those qualities associated with "most likely to succeed" (e.g., Friedlander 1976, esp. 7). Other supporters saw a kind of academic and applied hardening of the arteries, with the memories of early hopes still alive but with a growing sense that the heydays were all but over (Burke 1976, 24). I have in mind an academic symposium of OD afficionados, who had for several hours zestfully played "can you top this" with pronouncements concerning the deficiencies and all-but-inevitable doom facing OD—poor research, inadequate underlying theory, etc. One practitioner had more than enough. "You people give me a headache," he noted in exasperation. "I know I do good work, but you guys have made galloping variables out of all my constants."

More current variations on this theme of OD's future provide more room for optimism. Thus Sashkin and Burke (1987) see three possible scenarios: growth and retrenchment; stability and slow but steady growth; and exciting forays into improving entire systems so as to enhance human fulfillment and system effectiveness. This book seeks to nudge OD toward that third scenario, of course.

Three minimum agreements. In the 1980s the corner may have been turned on this period of gloom and doom, as the ongoing concern with OD as a profession indicates (Golembiewski 1988). Whether this is the case or not, however, this chapter seeks to provide needed perspective for ardent supporters, convinced critics, and zestful flagellants alike—specifically by rooting this argument in three baseline minima about which broad and even universal consensus exists.

First, without doubt, OD still shows many of the signs of a burgeoning area of activity. We will be selective, but illustrations suffice to make the case. Consider only research, texts, professional activity, and programs of study as indicators. Summary volumes indicate the details of successful applications (e.g., Golembiewski and Kiepper 1988; Perkins, Nieva, and Lawler 1983). In addition, OD texts (e.g., Burke 1982; French and Bell 1978; Golembiewski 1979; Huse and Cummings 1985) and books of readings (e.g., French, Bell, and Zawacki 1975; Golembiewski and Eddy 1978) find a ready market. Moreover, professional associations with thousands of members have developed in the last decade, of which the most prominent is the Organization Development Network. It has achieved a membership of nearly five thousand in its first two decades of existence, and its energy level was reflected in its twice-yearly meetings, each lasting about a week, which it continued for over a decade. The catalog of public or business organizations having had at least a flirtation with OD is very long and growing. Finally, degree and in-service programs in OD also have proliferated. It is certainly noteworthy that the largest employers of OD perspectives, designs, and personnel include the U.S. military services, whose base values provide a very difficult target for penetration by OD perspectives and technologies.

Second, both major interpretations of this bustling cannot be correct, but both may be dead wrong. That is, the busyness implies to some that OD works. Others see a kind of market high just before an inevitable and formidable sell-off. Commonly, however, neither conclusion rests on satisfactory and comprehensive documentation of OD's efficacy, or lack thereof.

Note that this second baseline conclusion refers to satisfactory and comprehensive documentation, rather than to the absence of documentation. Documentation exists. Indeed, several comparative studies (e.g., Morrison 1978; Margulies, Wright, and Scholl 1977; Porras 1979) suggest an appreciable success rate for various OD applications, but such work has two major limitations for present purposes. The data bases for such summary studies tend to be small, on the order of scores of cases. For example, the study by Porras deals with thirty-five cases, and Morrison's methodological overview involves twenty-six cases. In addition, only a small fraction of such data bases refers to public-sector applications, which are widely regarded as posing unusually difficult problems for OD and as having low success rates. Perhaps 10-15 percent is the usual proportion of public applications in available data bases, and one-tenth of a small data base does not provide a very solid foundation for generalizations.

Third, these information gaps have not often deterred enthusiasts or critics. They seem to know, absent the required documentation. Artfully, for example, some observers see the OD intervenor as a kind of contemporary shaman (e.g., Woodworth and Nelson 1979) who features more rattle shaking than technology and theory.

Generally, in addition, the state of affairs is presented as being worse in the public sector. Drawing on his experience as both a designer and a student of OD interventions, for example, Giblin (1976) concludes that the "unique constraints imposed on public organizations appear to render them almost immune from conventional OD interventions." Others conclude that public-sector OD—if defined as something more than "tinkering with the system"—will be very difficult, if not palpably impossible, for a broad range of reasons. For example, Burke concludes: "Most OD consultants find working with bureaucracies, especially public ones, to be difficult at best. . . . Apparently, most OD consultants either become more pragmatic and realistic or they have given up when it comes to working with large, bureaucratic organizations" (1980, 429).

The present data base. What do the data imply about OD applications? Specifically, this chapter reports an effort to transcend the all-but-universal limitations of the literature, based on a very intensive search for OD applications in both business and government contexts. Five basic sources are used to develop a data base of OD applications that could support useful conclusions about effects (Proehl 1980):

- Seven specialized bibliographies
- Searches of the several relevant computerized listings (e.g., ERIC) of publications in social-science journals over the prior twenty years
- A review of the prior twenty years of studies reported in eighty-eight journals, including ten from overseas
- More than one hundred books surveyed for bibliographic items as well as for reports of interventions
- Personal letters sent to fifty well-known change agents, especially soliciting unpublished materials such as internal memos, dissertations or theses, and so on

Appropriate citations occurred as early as 1945, and the search extended into mid-1980 when it was closed to analyze data. This search process has two gaps, neither of which is seen as damning, but which all may wish did not exist. First, journals unavailable in English were searched only selectively. Even though 17 percent of the total batch of interventions come from non-U.S. settings, this leaves our data base with a dominant locus.

In addition, the search did not encompass the twice-yearly meetings of the Organization Development Network or of the OD Division of the American

- *Team-building activities,* or efforts to increase the efficiency and effectiveness of intact task groups. Variants may use T-group or sensitivity training modes, as well as one or more of the other activities listed here.
- *Intergroup activities,* which seek to build effective and satisfying linkages between two or more task groups, such as departments in a large organization.
- *Technostructural activities,* which seek to build need-satisfying roles, jobs, and structures. Typically, these activities rest on a "growth psychology," such as that of Maslow, Argyris or Herzberg. These structural or policy approaches—job enlargement, Flexi-Time and so on—often are coupled with other OD activities.
- *System-building or system-renewal activities,* which seek comprehensive changes in a large organization's climate and values, using complex combinations of the seven activities sketched above, and having time spans in the three-to-five-year range.

These eight classes of activities fit with varying precision into three basic OD modes: interaction-centered, structure, and policies or procedures. Process-analysis, skill-building, and coaching/counseling activities are basically interaction-centered. Technostructural and system-building activities emphasize structure, although not to the exclusion of the other two modes. Team-building and intergroup activities often have dominant interaction emphases, but also deal with structure and especially policies or procedures.

What is the distribution of our 574 cases among these classes of activities? Table 1.1 implies that our population covers the field of interventions. The most narrow designs—diagnostic activities and process-analysis activities—constitute the dominant intervention mode in less than 5 percent of the cases. OD interventions tend to hunt bigger game, in short. To illustrate, nearly 40 percent of the private-sector cases can be categorized as emphasizing the most complex intervention modes—system-building or system-renewal and technostructural activities. Reading the individual case reports in the public sector also reinforces this impression. The applications there seem to give substantial attention to the tough cases, on balance. Hence, the common emphases on racial tension; conflict between individuals, specialties, and organization units; community conflict between police and minorities; and basic reorganization. OD applications seem to respect this difficult prescription: *Intervene where the pain is felt!*

The 574 cases imply similar reliance on dominant OD modes in both public and business settings. In most cases, the probabilities of using the eight classes of activities vary in a narrow range only. Technostructural activities constitute the most prominent exception, perhaps because public structures/policies/procedures are more likely to be set by distal authorities, especially

TABLE 1.1
Incidence of Eight Classes of OD Activities in Public and Private Sectors

Classes of OD Design	Individual Applications Classified by Dominant Design			
	Public Sector		Private Sector	
	N	%	N	%
Process analysis activities	10	4	6	2
Skill-building activities	65	24	57	19
Diagnostic activities	14	5	18	6
Coaching/counseling activities	19	7	30	10
Team-building activities	51	19	56	18
Intergroup activities	38	14	18	6
System-building or system-renewal activities	29	11	35	11
Technostructural activities	44	16	84	28
Totals	270	100	304	100

legislatures. Therefore, these activities would more often be out of convenient reach. Even so, technostructural activities constitute the dominant OD mode in nearly one of every six public-sector cases.

In sum, the 574 cases do not constitute a collection of easy pieces, and the data base suggests no huge differences between the reliance on specific modes of OD interventions in public and business sectors. Consequently, the data base should provide a real test of the efficacy of OD techniques and perspectives, of how often and to what degree they tend to work, within as well as between the private and public sectors.

The classification of the 574 published OD reports by dominant mode of intervention has a high reliability. Two independent observers classified all cases and had a very high degree of agreement. A 10 percent sample (approximately) places that agreement at nearly 98 percent of the cases. All differences were reconciled before summation in table 1.1.

So interobserver reliability posed no major issues in this case. The efficacy of OD interventions was uniform over the full range of dominant modes.

Two Estimates of Success

How can we estimate the specific efficacy of OD interventions? Do public-sector interventions have a lower success rate than their counterparts in business organizations? Two approaches to answers will be sketched here as well as tested against business and government OD applications. The approaches may be labeled "global indicators" and "multiple indicators."

Global indicators. A few details provide needed perspective on the global evaluation of OD interventions. Two independent readers reviewed each of the 574 interventions and assigned each set of effects to one of four categories whose content the observers had discussed and illustrated in detail. The evaluative categories were:

- *Highly positive and intended effects* on the efficacy and effectiveness of some relatively discrete system, as in improving the ability of individuals to hear one another without distortion, or in reducing the degree of hostility between conflicting actors or units;
- *Definite balance of positive and intended effects,* defined in terms of mixed but generally favorable effects—e.g., most but not all intended effects are achieved on a number of variables, or major positive effects occur in one system, while some negative but not counterbalancing effects occur in another system;
- *No appreciable effect;*
- *Negative effects,* or a case in which substantial reductions occur in the efficiency and effectiveness of some subsystem or of some broader system of which it is a part.

What did this laborious rating and cross-checking reveal? Four points summarize the major findings. First, by and large, the observers saw the same effects. Specifically, the observers' ratings correlated .78, which indicates substantial agreement between raters. Almost all cases of disagreement involved the first two rating categories. Some differences were reconciled after this reliability check, but in all cases, the ratings in table 1.2 reflect the lowest contending score.

Second, given this conservative convention, one can then conclude with some confidence that *in this population of studies* more than 80 percent of the interventions had at least a definite balance of positive and intended effects.

Third, global estimates of the efficacy of OD interventions do not vary much between the public and business sectors. Table 1.2 supports this major point.

Fourth, global estimates of success vary somewhat by dominant mode of intervention. Table 1.3 summarizes the experience for private-sector interventions, which do not differ markedly from public-sector experience. Except for two classes of OD activities—process analysis and diagnostic—the efficacy estimates indicate that 83 percent or more of the cases generate at least a definite balance of positive and intended effects.

Multiple indicators. A second approach to estimating the efficacy of OD interventions relies on multiple indicators—308 variables, in fact. Proehl

TABLE 1.2
Global Estimates of the Success of 574 OD Applications

Rating Category	Individual Applications Classified by Degree of Effects			
	Public Sector		Private Sector	
	N	%	N	%
Highly positive and intended effects	110	41	122	40
Definite balance of positive and intended effects	116	43	148	49
No appreciable effect	18	7	14	5
Negative effects	26	9	20	6
Totals	270	100	304	100

(1980) coded each of the 574 cases in the present batch of studies in terms of the comprehensive set of indicators developed by Porras and Berg (1978). Proehl describes his procedure in these terms:

> [E]ach of the . . . studies in this research's data-base was searched for the 308 variables developed by Porras and Berg. When one of the variables was found, it was coded according to whether it had improved (0) or not improved (1) during the course of the change project. Once all of the variables present in each study were identified and coded, the *"percentage of positive reported change"* was calculated for each . . . level (individual, leader, group or organization) of study. This was accomplished by dividing the number of positive variables by the total number of variables in which change was desired in each organizational level of each study. For example, a change effort which sought to change five individual-level variables and reported three of them as having changed positively was given a score of 60 percent. Scores ranged from zero percent in a change effort which failed to produce any positive change in process and outcome variables to 100 percent for a case in which positive change was reported in all variables for which change was desired. (1980, p. 58).

The reliability of these assignments is estimated by a random but limited process. Three independent observers each rated two randomly selected variables, and agreement existed on 228 of 240 cases. This interobserver reliability of 95 percent is taken to be representative of the record on the other variables, and seems an acceptable level of reliability of assignments on which to base analysis.

The positive reported change is 70.5 percent, overall, when the 574 cases are scored for all of the 308 Porras/Berg variables applicable in each case. The efficacy of the 574 applications also can be arrayed according to levels of analysis, and the percentages of positive reported change are

- Individual: 78.1 percent for 243 cases;
- Leader: 68.1 percent for 173 cases;

TABLE 1.3
Global Estimates of Efficacy, Private Sector Cases

Class of OD Design	Highly Positive and Intended Effects	Definite Balance of Positive and Intended Effects	No Appreciable Effect	Negative Effects
Process analysis activities	16.7%	50.0%	16.7%	16.7%
Skill-building activities	40.4%	52.6%	3.5%	3.5%
Diagnostic activities	33.3%	44.4%	5.6%	16.7%
Coaching/counseling activities	40.0%	46.7%	6.7%	6.7%
Team-building activities	39.3%	51.8	3.6%	5.4%
Intergroup activities	44.4%	39.0%	5.6%	11.1%
System-building or system-renewal activities	45.7%	40.0%	5.7%	8.7%
Technostructural activities	40.5%	51.2%	3.6%	4.8%

Notes: Estimated effects in percent. Due to rounding, totals may accumulate to ⟩100%. N = 304.

- Group: 77.9 percent for 161 cases;
- Organization: 72.4 percent for 206 cases.

As the best-informed estimate from the standpoint of multiple indicators, then, at least seven of ten variables show that OD applications induce a balance of positive effects. In addition, no major differences characterize public versus business applications.

Greater Success by Recognizing Success Rates

By an ample margin, these results confirm a substantial success rate for a large batch of OD interventions. To be conservative, the two estimating approaches imply a success rate of at least seven in ten cases. The more ebullient observers will emphasize the global estimate of efficacy, which approximates 85 percent.

These data powerfully imply that both critics and previously pessimistic supporters of OD must sing a different tune in the future, or at least a more complicated one. That tune will have a single theme, despite numerous probable variations: greater OD success can come from recognizing that existing success rates are already substantial.

Note that the recommendation for this tune-changing does not rest on the present data alone. In both direction and degree, other studies parallel these results. Better put, *no* available comprehensive study generates a pattern of results at fundamental odds with the findings just reviewed, although these other studies use different measures of success and rely on data bases that attain only small fractions of the size of the present batch. To sample only:

- Eight percent of Morrison's (1978) twenty-six cases deal with "failures."
- In Dunn and Swierczek's (1977) seventeen cases, 65-70 percent are considered "effective."
- In thirty-five cases selected for high degrees of methodological rigor by Porras (1979), variables change in the predicted directions in about 50 percent of the cases.
- Margulies, Wright, and Scholl (1977) rate 73 percent of thirty applications as "positive," with 10 percent "mixed," 24 percent "no change," and 3 percent "negative."
- Nicholas (1982) uses quite stringent criteria of success, focuses only on "hard" criteria such as increases in objectively measured productivity, and excludes interventions, such as flexible work hours, having very high success rates while including interventions labeled as job enrichment "without participation." Nevertheless, Nicholas reports average success rates in the 50 percent neighborhood which, both absolutely and relative to his criteria, is an attractive one.

Why Success Can Lead to Greater Success

Earlier discussion tentatively speculated on why such results have not occasioned public whoops of celebration, of course, but we can be bolder about why acknowledging the high success rates can increase success, as paradoxical as that may appear initially.

Consider only four perspectives on the point. First, these favorable success rates do not mean that all OD problems have been recognized, let alone solved to such a degree that designs and perspectives can be applied following a cookbook approach. Positively, these results imply that whatever exists in the organizational world can be accommodated, most of the time, by the kind of OD intervenors who research and write up their experiences. Diagnosis is critical, and this general analysis cannot do justice to the complex dynamics underlying each of the numerous OD applications just considered in the aggregate. The key point is that some people sufficiently encompass those dynamics in unfolding situations, and with an attractive batting average.

What are the helpful implications of this positive interpretation? Basically, the success-rate literature suggests a kind of "floor" for OD practice. If an intervenor falls consistently below that floor, the major prescriptions seem direct. An intervenor must do something to improve his or her diagnosis or prescription, or try another line of work.

Both prescriptions should contribute to enhanced success rates, obviously. The general effect will be heightened and accelerated when—notice I do not write if—various OD monitoring institutions begin using the success rates to set expectations among clients and intervenors alike. I do not refer to policing activities, either exclusively or even primarily. The focus should be on education—exclusively, for a long period, and always as a priority thrust. The institutions include accrediting agencies like the now-defunct Certified Consultants International, mass-membership collectivities like the Organization Development Network, and registering agencies such as the Organization Development Institute.

Second, the present results do not imply that public-sector OD is easier than "in business," more difficult, or the same. To restate the previous point, the results here only imply that whatever the constellation of unique constraints existing in various organizations, whether governmental or business, they can be accommodated by those who have written up their experiences of appropriate OD interventions.

This is no cute conclusion. For example, we know quite a bit about how to develop such accommodations to the specific characteristics of agencies in the public sector. This is not the place, however, to detail that experience and theory; that has been accomplished elsewhere (e.g., Golembiewski 1985, 231-366). To the degree that high success rates motivate reliance on such context-relevant guidelines, patently, so also will OD success increase.

Third, the success-rate literature—whether approximately correct, or even if wildly off the mark—can improve OD success, if that literature is responded to appropriately. True believers or unreconstructed critics cannot provide such responses.

To provide some specifics, the available studies of OD success rates require testing, and that will improve OD, whether the tests are positive or negative. For example, greater specificity will be required for more finely-tuned analyses than the one attempted here. Future comparative analyses will require a more precise typology of interventions, as well as a more complex differentiation of hosts or targets for such interventions. This consciousness-raising has begun elsewhere (e.g., Bowers, Franklin, and Pecorella 1975) as well as at numerous points throughout this book (see especially chapter 7). However, much remains to be done. In the present case, interventions are distinguished only in gross terms. Targets/hosts are differentiated only as "public" and "business." A more satisfactory typology of systems hosting OD efforts will eventually take into explicit account the full range of differences and similarities usually encapsulated in the short-hand "public *versus* private"; and it seems just as clear that this typology also will encompass those equally significant differences and similarities *within* public and business sectors.

Hence, the testing of the success-rate literature will help improve OD diagnosis and intervention, in the senses illustrated here as well as in others beyond the scope of this chapter. It is that simple, and that demanding.

Fourth, and finally only for present goals, this chapter may be faulted by a major contaminant. As some observers emphasize (Mirvis and Berg 1977), published materials may be biased toward reporting positive results. If this bias characterizes the present data base, that would obviously account for some part of the high success rate. Our procedures provide only partial protection against such a bias. Note the effort to solicit unpublished materials—consultant reports, in-house memos, theses and dissertations—which seeks to counterbalance any bias toward positive results in published work. Presumably, unpublished materials would be less contaminated in this regard.

Again, we will not know until several investigators look intensively and with skill; the success-rate literature encourages—even demands—that kind of looking, by both critics and proponents of OD. In this fourth sense, then, the success-rate literature can serve to increase OD success, if approached in a concerted and balanced way.

Some research implies that the hypothesis of a positive-findings bias may apply to research on planned change, for example, but not in a powerful or consistent enough sense to negate the definite tendencies detailed above. Two early surveys of evaluative studies of OD applications (Terpstra 1981; Bullock and Svyantek 1983) generate a split decision on one version of the hypothesis: whether methodological rigor is inversely associated with attractiveness of outcomes of OD applications. Such research is troubled, however, if only in the sense that the two investigations select their cases from the same journal over the identical interval, but one population is some 80 percent larger than the other.

One of our Georgia doctorates (Sun 1988) provides related evidence of a positive-findings bias in a large batch (231 cases) of Quality of Working Life (QWL) applications. He finds a clear tendency, but not a dominant or unqualified tendency, for evaluative studies to show poorer outcomes as methodological rigor increases. There is no easy way to present the details of Sun's analysis, and two indicators must suffice here (Golembiewski and Sun 1988). Perfect support for the hypothesis of a positive-findings bias in Sun's case involves 216 predictions, of which 69 percent are realized. In general, then, as rigor increases, outcomes deteriorate for the first three of four classes of outcomes. However, only a small percentage of the variance is accounted for—approximately 7 percent. Moreover, the association is *not* linear. The vast bulk of the deviant cases involve the least successful of four classes of outcomes. Contrary to the hypothesis of a positive-findings bias, the *least* rigorous studies generate the *poorest* effects.

In sum, there seems to be more in the data than can be encompassed by the hypothesis of a positive-findings bias in planned changed.

Notes

1. An earlier version of this analysis appeared as Golembiewski, Proehl, and Sink 1982.
   The success-rate literature came into two general waves. The earlier evaluations of batches of OD applications include: Margulies, Wright, and Scholl 1977; and Pate, Nielsen, and Bacon 1977.
   The more recent wave includes larger batches of applications and/or more strict criteria of success. These studies include: Golembiewski, Proehl, and Sink 1982; Nicholas 1982; and Terpstra 1981.

References

Blumberg, A. and Golembiewski, R. T. 1976. *Learning and Change in Groups*. London: Penguin.

Bowers, D. G., Franklin, J. L., and Pecorella, P. A. 1975. "Matching Problems, Precursors and Interventions in OD: A Systematic Approach." *Journal of Applied Behavioral Science* 11:391.

Bullock, R. J., and Svyantek, D. J. 1983. "Positive-Findings Bias in Positive-Findings Bias Research." In *Proceedings* Annual Meeting, Academy of Management, 221–24. Dallas, Tex.14–17 August.

Burke, W. W. 1976. "Organization Development in Transition." *Journal of Applied Behavioral Science* 12:22–43.

______. 1980. "Organization Development and Bureaucracies of the 1980s." *Journal of Applied Behavioral Science* 16:423–438.

______. 1982. *Organization Development*. Boston: Little, Brown.

Dunn, W. N., and Swierczek, F. W. 1977. "Planned Organizational Change." *Journal of Applied Behavioral Science* 13:135.

French, W. F., and Bell, C. H., Jr. 1978. *Organization Development*. Englewood Cliffs, N.J.: Prentice-Hall.

French, W. F.; Bell, C. H. Jr.; and Zawacki, R. A. 1975. *Organization Development: Theory and Practice and Research* Dallas, Tex. Business Publications, Inc.

Friedlander, F. 1976. "OD Reaches Adolescence." *Journal of Applied Behavioral Science* 12:7-21.

Giblin, E. J. 1976. "Organization Development: Public Sector Theory and Practice." *Public Personnel Management* 5:108.

Golembiewski, R. T. 1979. *Approaches to Planned Change*. 2 vols. New York: Marcel Dekker.

______. 1985. *Humanizing Public Organizations*. Mt. Airy, Md.: Lamond.

______. 1986. "So, What about Success Rates?" and "'You Can't Be a Beacon. . . ,' I and II." *Organization Development Journal* 4(2):5–6, 4(3):5–7, 4(4):3–6.

______. 1988. *Organization Development: Ideas and Issues*. New Brunswick, N.J.: Transaction.

Golembiewski, R. T., and Eddy, W. eds. 1978. *Organization Development in Public Administration*. New York: Marcel Dekker.

Golembiewski, R. T., and Kiepper, A. 1988. *High Performance and Human Costs.* New York: Praeger.
Golembiewski, R. T., and Sun, B-C. 1988. "Testing QWL Studies for Positive-Findings Bias, II." Working paper.
Golembiewski, R. T.; Proehl, C.W. Jr.; and Sink, D. 1982. "Estimating the Success of OD Applications." *Training and Development Journal* 72:85–95.
Huse, E. F., and Cummings, T. G. 1985. *Organization Development and Change.* St. Paul, Minn.: West Publishing.
Krell, T. C. 1981. "The Marketing of Organization Development." *Journal of Applied Behavioral Science* 17:309–23.
Margulies, N.; Wright, P. L.; and Scholl, R. W. 1977. "Organization Development Techniques: Their Impact on Change." *Group and Organization Studies* 2:428–48.
Miller, G. J. 1979. *The Laboratory Approach to Planned Change in the Public Sector,* Ph.D. diss. University of Georgia, Athens, Ga.
Mirvis, P., and Berg, D. N. eds. 1977. *Failure in Organization Development and Change.* New York: Wiley.
Morrison, P. 1978. "Evaluation in OD: A Review and an Assessment." *Group and Organization Studies* 3:42–70.
Nicholas, J.M. 1982. "The Comparative Impact of Organization Development Interventions on Hard Criteria Measures." *Academy of Management Review* 7:531–42.
Pate, L. E.; Nielsen, W. R.; and Bacon, P. C. 1977. Advances in Research on Organization Development." *Group & Organization Studies* 2:449–60.
Perkins, D. N. T.; Nieva, V. F.; and Lawler, E. E. III. 1983. *Managing Creation.* New York: Wiley-Interscience.
Porras, J. I. 1979. "The Comparative Impact of Different OD Techniques and Intervention Intensities." *Journal of Applied Behavioral Science* 15:156–78.
Porras, J. I., and Berg, P. O. 1978. "Evaluation Methodology in Organization Development." *Journal of Applied Behavioral Science* 14:151–74.
Proehl, C. W. Jr. 1980. *Planned Organizational Change,* App. A of Ph.D. diss. University of Georgia, Athens, Ga.
Sashkin, M., and Burke, W. W. 1987. "Organization Development in the 1980s." *Journal of Management* 13:393–417.
Sun, B-C. 1988. *Quality of Working Life Programs: An Empirical Assessment of Designs and Outcomes.* Ph.D. diss. University of Georgia, Athens, Ga.
Terpstra, D. E. 1981. "Relationship between Methodological Rigor and Reported Outcomes in Organization Development Evaluation Research." *Journal of Applied Psychology* 66:541–43.
Woodworth, W., and Nelson, R. 1979. "Witch Doctors, Messianics, Sorcerers, and OD Consultants: Parallels and Paradigms." *Organizational Dynamics* 8:16–33.
Woodworth, W.; Meyer, G.; and Smallwood, N. 1980. "A Critical Assessment of Organization Development Theory and Practice." Working paper. Department of Organizational Behavior, Brigham Young University, Provo, Utah.

2

An Even Better Kept Secret: Success Rates in Third World Settings

The first chapter should alert readers to the author's deep fascination with success rates in planned change via OD. This interest relates not only to assessing the probability that intended consequences will follow from the application of specific OD techniques, as guided by OD values. Even more, I am intrigued by the all-but-universal lack of public reaction to the substantial (even formidable) success rates that have been reported.

If that first chapter constituted a surprise, or even a well-kept secret, this chapter no doubt exceeds its predecessor. Specifically, this chapter takes an uncommon approach to elaborating on the issue of OD's culture boundedness—a search for applications in large political jurisdictions (usually nations or countries) that may be classified as "nonaffluent." For convenience, these political jurisdictions will be referred to as Third World or developing. Operationally, the focus was on jurisdictions with a 1980 Gross National Product (GNP) of five thousand U.S. dollars or less per capita. This eliminates about the top forty jurisdictions on a list of some two hundred for which GNP data are conveniently available.

In brief, this chapter deals with an even bigger surprise, or with a better-kept secret, than does its predecessor.

A Conceptual Context for Irony I, Revisited

Evidence like that in chapter 1 urges another inquiry. What would these unfavorable conditions imply for OD efforts: impoverished countries, low-technology settings, and unsophisticated populations, for example? This is terra incognita, as far as this author knows. No comprehensive surveys exist, although a very few efforts have been directed at the success rates of single interventions (e.g., Kiggundu 1985). This stands in marked contrast with the Western literature reviewed in chapter 1, where several surveys of applications are available.

The common wisdom provides a ready answer, only a few of whose major assumptions need to be outlined here: OD evolved in developed economies with quite specific features—"high-tech" and "high-touch," to select convenient labels; OD activities can be costly and long range, in addition, and they might seem more applicable to sophisticated work forces than to labor-intensive economies. The reader can easily add length and breadth to this short list.

Third World countries do not seem hospitable hosts for OD efforts, then. Their economies are low tech with a bias toward unsophisticated work forces, and their commonly autocratic cultures suggest low (or distant) touch at work. We should expect few OD applications there, and those rarities should have far lower success rates than those estimated in chapter 1.

This assumptive line seems quite reasonable, but it suffers from two liabilities. First, no one has isolated a panel of OD applications to test the assumptions. Second, when that effort was made recently, the results did not provide strong support for the common wisdom.

Three sections detail the present test of the common wisdom about OD applications in developing or Third World settings; the test finds that wisdom lacking. The search for applications is described briefly, to begin. Then, features of the panel of applications are detailed. Third, the implications of the findings for heightening OD success rates get some attention.

Search for Applications

This search began with several bibliographies (especially Miller 1979 and Proehl 1980, but including De 1979 and Kiggundu 1985) and beyond them instituted a two-pronged search. Nearly sixty English-language periodicals dated 1957–1986 were searched for reports of relevant OD applications. Moreover, about a hundred practitioners experienced in intervening in non-affluent countries were sent personal letters soliciting both citations and copies of unpublished materials. Scholarly dissertations and theses also were sought.

A panel of one hundred OD applications was isolated by this two-pronged search, and this chapter summarizes thirteen prominent features of this panel while also testing the common position that OD applications are severely culture-bound. A complete bibliography appears at the end of this chapter, with the asterisk items indicating the 114 citations describing the hundred separate OD applications. Details about all OD designs and the specific outcomes assigned to each of them are available (Golembiewski 1989).

Twelve Features of the Panel

The usual caveats apply about the character of OD research, which is in the "natural history stage" of development. That is, most OD research is descriptive rather than theoretically based, and few studies make use of techniques common in more developed sciences such as control groups or random assignment of subjects. It seems to some observers (e.g., Bullock and Bullock 1984) that many of these techniques are *not* relevant to action research such as OD, and may be positively inimical. Whatever the case, few exceptions (e.g., Eden 1985, 1986) are found in the present panel to the label "descriptive."

The following even dozen features must inform and even tether interpretations, but they will not paralyze interpretations.

Geographic Distribution

In sum, thirty-seven jurisdictions host the OD applications in the present panel. About 65 percent of them are in large jurisdictions having a 1980 GNP under U.S. $1,310 per person, far below the present cutoff point of U.S. $5,000. India, with thirty-five applications, accounts for slightly more than one-third of the entire panel of one hundred applications, in part because a visit there put this author in touch with a range of materials having low visibility beyond that subcontinent.

Heterogeneous Settings

The panel of applications relates to a broad range of immediate settings, as four selected comparisons establish. Thus, OD applications involve:

- relatively well-off urbanites (e.g., Chattopadhyay 1972, 1973; Dayal and Thomas 1968) and impoverished villagers (e.g., Almeida et al. 1983; Belloncle 1981; De Sousa 1979; Singh 1981)
- all levels of organization in collective enterprises: at or near the top of hierarchies (e.g., Abramson 1978), at mid-levels (e.g., Armor 1986; Diesh, Sekharan, and Mohanty 1984; Eden 1985), and at workaday levels (e.g., Ejiogu 1983; Juralewicz 1974)
- learning between bitter enemies (e.g., Doob 1971, 1976) as well as between those sharing basic interests (e.g., Korten 1979, 1980; Soares 1983, 1984) or in intimate relationships (e.g., Krausz, 1985)
- agricultural (e.g., Soares 1983, 1984) and industrial (e.g., Juralewicz, 1974; Orpen 1976) participants, as well as those in administrative, managerial, or executive roles (e.g., Ramos 1971)

Within an individual study, moreover, OD applications frequently deal with heterogeneous subpopulations. This diversity may involve linkages between rich and poor, various levels of an organization, several functions in an organization, different subcultures, and so on (e.g., Halset 1967; Abramson 1978).

The present panel is not grossly unbalanced, in sum, and extends beyond the most-Westernized settings, which would be relatively affluent. Approximately one-third of the cases deal with rural villagers (e.g., Shrinivasan 1976; Almeida et al. 1983; Belloncle 1981; Chand and Soni 1981) or with industrial or construction workers (e.g., Ejiogu 1983; Orpen 1976).

Diversity of Designs

Designs associated with all four OD "stems" can be found—interaction-oriented, survey-guided, structural, and policy/procedures (French and Bell 1978). Three points support this conclusion.

Interaction-centered designs dominate, as in chapter 1. Witness the entries using team-building activities (e.g., Eden 1985; Felstehausen and Diaz-Cisneros 1985), third-party peacemaking (e.g., Lakin 1969, 1978; Levi and Benjamin 1974, 1976), intergroup confrontations (e.g., Halset 1967), and various applications of group dynamics (e.g., Ha 1986; Soares 1983, 1984; Sinha 1986). Surprisingly, about 20 percent of the applications use some direct form of T-grouping or sensitivity training (e.g., De 1971; Doob 1971; Huss 1973; Nylen, Mitchell, and Stout 1967; Ramos 1971; Sinha 1986). T-groups have been used successfully in OD, as with intact work groups (e.g., Golembiewski and Carrigan 1970a, 1970b). But most commentators report a sharp decline in recent reliance on the T-group in OD applications in Western settings.

The panel also reflects the three other OD stems. Thus, uses of survey/feedback appear (e.g., Diesh, Sekharan, and Mohanty 1984; Belloncle 1981), at times along with an expression of surprise that such a "sophisticated" approach proves useful in nonaffluent settings. In addition, structural emphases appear in a substantial subset of applications, at both system levels (e.g., Abramson 1978; Halset 1967) as well as at the level of individual jobs (e.g., Kanawaty et al. 1981).

Real-Time Relevance

The 100 applications in the panel typically challenge OD technology-cum-values to do something meaningful about inducing significant choice and change in difficult situations. This might involve empowering impoverished villagers (e.g., Chand and Soni 1981; Honadle and Hannah 1982), seeking to improve relationships between contentious neighbors with different ethnic backgrounds (e.g., Levi and Hadah n.d.), improving cooperation and collaboration in complex organizations (e.g., Halset 1967), or seeking to combat river blindness among villagers who only recently gained literacy (e.g., Belloncle 1981).

Most often, the applications constitute classical action research, or participatory research. In outline, the applications typically

- access a local felt need, or raise consciousness about such an assessment—for example, the incidence of river blindness;
- variously legitimate a program of action research directed at this need—for example, nonliterate village elders agree that newly-literate young people should learn about the remediation and prevention of river blindness;
- assess the state of the existing local knowledge base;
- as appropriate, add to or negate that knowledge base and help build skills, often with external expert resources;
- have learners put their knowledge and skills to work in an action-research mode—for example, surveys of those at various stages of river blindness are conducted, local programs of remediation and prevention are begun, and effects are assessed.

In contrast, a number of applications are explicit "experiments" or "pilot studies" (e.g., Levi and Benjamin 1974, 1976) and have narrower objectives. For example, several applications seek to show only how in an encapsulated training setting relationships between strangers, or even harsh antagonists, can be improved via learning about OD values and processes. Typically, these applications work, but they are deliberately tethered short of attempted transfers beyond the training site into the back-home worlds of participants.

At times, however, broad transfer is intended. To illustrate, several applications have lofty but tentative aspirations about a long-delayed transfer—from relatively safe learning environments to the cauldron of religious or ethnic war, for example (Doob and Foltz 1973, 1974); from learning designs for children in school contexts to the reduction of social and political conflict (e.g., Yanoov 1985); or from a gathering of elites in resort settings in the hope of building relationships that might later moderate conflicts between nations (e.g., Porter 1986). These seem to be experiments in one sense, and yet they constitute deliberate efforts to seed back-home settings in the face of acknowledgedly huge obstacles. At some future time, this seeding might achieve a critical mass sufficient to induce meaningful choice or change.

Cross-Cultural Sensitivity

The possibility of cultural differences gets frequent emphasis. For example, the panel includes demonstrations that job-enrichment applications are culturally affected (e.g., Kanawaty et al. 1981; Orpen 1976), that various cultures may find different levels of participation desirable (e.g., Ejiogu 1983; Juralewicz 1974), and so on.

In general, the bottom line is that some OD applications seem possible in all settings. However, the same degree of the same intervention might not be similarly appropriate in different cultures. Indeed, some cultural features might contraindicate a specific OD design. For example, a "culture of silence" would impede interaction-centered designs, and prior modification of that local culture might preoccupy early phases of development (e.g., Singh 1981). Thorough diagnosis is needed to identify relevant cultural features, and then to match to them specific OD designs from the available array.

In a curious way, however, some OD designs have a very broad or generic applicability. These include process-oriented activities, as in the substantial number of applications of sensitivity training (e.g., Smith 1984) or group dynamics (e.g., Ha 1986; Jedlicka 1977; Soares 1983, 1984; Tandon and Brown 1981). Such designs involve participants intimately in diagnosis, design, and implementation, and this takes local features into explicit account.

Temporal Distribution

The OD applications in the panel come from an interval of nearly three decades. Several cases have more than one supporting citation, so 114 separate citations underlay the present conclusions. Table 2.1 shows how the 114 citations are distributed over time.

One cannot speak of trends, but reliance on the OD mode does not seem to be fading. Indeed, judging from the first two years, the interval 1985–89 promises a magnum increase in OD applications in Third World settings.

TABLE 2.1
Temporal Distribution of Citations

Date	Number of Citations
No date	2
Prior to 1960	1
1960–64	0
1965–69	8
1970–74	26
1975–79	22
1980–84	31
1985–86	24

Training-Site Effects Occur

In most of the cases in the panel, one can distinguish two general sets of effects: in training, and in transfer. Transfer is summarized in the next section, while training gets immediate attention.

In most cases, expected training effects occur. This is most clearly the case in that batch of applications (e.g., Doob 1971, 1976; Doob and Foltz, 1974; Ramos 1971; Smith 1984) which rely on interaction-oriented designs to increase understanding and empathy, as well as to build skills for effective communication and problem solving. In some cases, the major issue involves consciousness raising about shared interests or potentialities (e.g., De Sousa 1979), with the goal of building group relationships where none existed. In other cases, the major goal is to remedy an unattractive relationship. These cases often involve people whose primary reference groups are in intense conflict (e.g., Doob and Foltz 1973, 1974), or they may involve differences between specific individuals (e.g., Levi and Hadah n.d.).

Variable Transfer of Effects

Transfer is by no means certain in our panel of applications, even given the high probability of training-site effects. See especially the effort to build relationships between Irish Catholics and Protestants (e.g., Doob and Foltz 1973, 1974). Pretty much, the intended workshop effects occur there for most (but not all) participants. But the intended transfer into back-home settings occurs only in attenuated and diluted forms, and some observers (e.g., Boehringer and Zeruolis 1974) report major unanticipated and negative effects. Less dramatically, one successfully trained population reentered an organization unresponsive to, if not hostile to, the thrust of the training (e.g., Cohen et al. 1977; Frits 1976). Transfer did not occur there.

Relatedly, few studies provide perspective over substantial periods of time, patently a strategic way to assess transfer. In a few cases (e.g., Ha 1986; Soares 1983, 1984) repetitions of a learning design suggest effective transfer, but do not establish it. One long learning design for Korean officials has been repeated at least yearly over a decade (Ha 1986), for example.

Several cases do provide clear models of designing for transfer, however. The design of a management development program for Sudanese middle managers can be schematized in this way (Armor 1986):

- Learners reflect their experience and understanding of management topics of direct relevance to managing a regional office;
- Expert resources introduce new theories and concepts to variously enrich this base of experience and understanding;
- The enriched base supports an effort to design a new regional office, soon to be opened;
- Recommendations are made by learners to senior officials for possible incorporation into the design of the regional office.

Process issues clearly require extensive early attention in such a design, but its time line extends far beyond the effort or process that would characterize (for example) a T-group or skill-building experience.

Transfer poses some difficult issues, normative as well as empirical. For example, what degree of probability about safe transfer is appropriate before exposing people to off-site training, however reliable its effects? In addition, problems exist for this analysis when specific transfer is not contemplated, or when transfer is stated in very general or even merely hopeful terms. A number of applications are deliberately restricted to the training site, for example, as in efforts to test whether conflicting persons or groups will respond in constructive ways in a "neutral" learning milieu (e.g., Levi and Benjamin 1974, 1976).

This analysis cannot solve the mega-problems of transfer. Typically, in assessing success rates this analysis accepts the intervenor's stated intentions about transfer, whether they be broad or narrow, and evaluates success accordingly. This suggests a conservative bias in estimating success, since major training site effects coupled with ineffective transfer would be rated a failure, even if an intervenor's intent regarding transfer is idealistic and demanding.

Success Rate Estimates

Given this convention about transfer effects, what might be a reasonable estimate of the success rate of the present panel of OD applications? Table 2.2 presents summary data, and compares them with the success rates in the broader, mostly-Western population of OD applications introduced in chapter 1.The present chapter and its predecessor both rely on the same four categories of outcomes. Note that the individual applications were each read by at least two raters, and all disagreements that could not be reconciled by discussion were resolved by assigning them to the *lowest or lower* applicable category. So the estimates here also rest on a conservative convention, in a second major sense.

Table 2.2 reflects a substantial success rate for OD applications in the Third World, especially given the difficulties typically attributed to such loci. The estimates constitute first approximations, and hence should be interpreted gently. Overall, the estimates certainly do not as a general rule discourage OD applications anywhere, even as they suggest that private-sector applications in Western settings seem to have the most favorable success rates, with nonaffluent applications having the lowest but still appreciable estimate of success.

Sociotechnical Interventions

A large cluster of cases in the present panel can be described as "sociotechnical" or "technostructural," and they focus on the design of individual

TABLE 2.2
Comparative Estimates of Success Rates

100 Applications in Third World Settings[a]	Success-Rate Category	574 Applications in Various Settings[b] Public Sector	Private Sector
16%	I. Highly positive and intended effects	41%	40%
56%	II. Definite balance of positive and intended effects	43%	49%
24%	III. No appreciable effect	7%	5%
4%	IV. Negative effects	9%	6%

[a]Three cases are relevant to OD but are basically descriptive (Ejiogu, Juralewicz, and Orpen) and hence no estimate of change is appropriate.

Kanawaty and Thorsrud review twelve separate job enrichment efforts. Three are assigned to category II, and three to category III. Six planned efforts are non-starts.

Fuchs summarizes five cases, all coded II.

Consequently, this panel deals with one hundred cases. In sum, it refers to eighty-nine cases, minus the three descriptive studies, Kanawaty/Thorsrud, and Fuchs. Since the latter two are coded as eleven cases, N = 100.

[b]See chapter 1.

jobs or of subsystems via job enrichment or "organizing around the total job." Using the same conventions as table 2.2, table 2.3 shows the estimates of success generated by the 20 relevant cases. This approximates the overall estimate in table 2.2, of course.

A Bias in Published Materials?

Since published materials may be biased toward success (e.g., Mirvis and Berg 1977), a concerted effort was made to solicit materials not published in such traditional sources as articles or books. Perhaps a fifth of the present cases qualify—several dissertations (e.g., Lagos 1972; Porras 1974), in-house consultant reports (e.g., Lynton 1986), and reports having limited circulations (e.g., Armor 1979, 1981, 1986). Moreover, particular attention

TABLE 2.3
Success Rates in Sociotechnical Interventions

Success-Rate Category	20 Sociotechnical Applications
I. Highly positive and intended effects	25%
II. Definite balance of positive and intended effects	60%
III. No appreciable effect	10%
IV. Negative effects	10%

was given to seeking multiple reports about specific OD applications, as well as to discovering multiple applications of the same or similar design at different loci. Approximately a quarter of the present applications are multiples in one or both of these two senses.

Heightening Success Rates

The present panel also suggests a reasonable way to elevate positive effects, consistent with broader OD experience (Golembiewski 1979, vol. 2). Directly, transfer of learning into back-home settings often can be facilitated when the strategy provides for reinforcing modes of OD designs. Most often, interaction-centered designs are relied upon at start-up, and these should be reinforced by design elements that emphasize structure as well as policy and procedures.

Several cases support this important conclusion (e.g., Felstehausen and Diaz-Cisneros 1985; Guess 1982; Soares 1983, 1984), which would appear to be obvious but is commonly neglected. For example, in a Latin American forestry program, success reasonably hinged on the availability of market incentives that reinforce the progress made in decision-making capacity and institution building (Guess 1982). It makes no sense to increase production, in effect, unless markets and distribution systems also exist.

This critical point may seem obvious, but the usefulness of structural and policy/procedural interventions to reinforce interaction-centered applications in development contexts is seldom fully appreciated. Consider Ruttan's penetrating question: "Why is it relatively easy to identify a number of relatively successful small-scale or pilot rural development projects but so difficult to find examples of successful rural development programs?" (1974, 10). Relatedly, numerous observers (e.g., Esman and Montgomery 1969) point up the very mixed record of attempts to transfer techniques into systems, even given all the proper ingredients in the target of transfer: "bright officials, young, technically trained, reasonably committed, and very hard working" (Moris 1976, 410).

The growing consensus emphasizes one basic explanation—perhaps the single basic explanation—of the mixed record. Observers see a managerial crisis. "It was the [administrative] system which was the problem," is Moris's representative conclusion. "It was capable of rendering any input—whether trained staff, new equipment, sensible policies, or fresh projects—ineffective" (1976, 411). And the "system" was in most cases an earlier technology transfer from Western colonial powers, as variously suffused by local conditions. As Moris notes: "The paradox we face in so many ex-colonial nations is that some of the greatest barriers to effective management consist of administrative traditions *originally derived from the colonial metro-*

pole itself" (Emphasis added.) (1976, 407). Prominent among these early managerial imports is the "hub and spoke" metaphor consistent with traditional bureaucratic thought and having (not so incidentally) the effect of reinforcing centralized colonial authority (the "hub") while encouraging the dependence of the locals (the "spokes")—locals who communicate upward to the central authorities, receive orders from them, but often are alienated from both headquarters and their clients. The overall result is a centralized decision-making system, slow acting and typically ponderous because of a narrow span of control, but dependable if expectations are low and comforting to distant powers.

OD experience and theory seem to be well attuned to this major challenge facing developing countries. Basically, OD developed as a search for alternatives to the selfsame bureaucratic principles now adversely impacting on developing areas. Those alternatives in America historically emphasize interaction-centered designs that increase responsible freedom at the worksite. It has been a prevailing OD rule of thumb, however, that more authoritarian systems respond less defensively if initial interventions deal with structures and policies/procedures. That is, interaction-centered designs often involve public power sharing as well as dynamics that are openly critical of authority figures, if not direct attacks on their legitimacy. Interventions in structures and in policies/procedures often avoid these public dynamics, and can meet employee needs without overt challenge to authority figures. Indeed, authority figures typically sponsor such interventions—as in job enrichment, flexible work hours, role analysis or negotiation, and basic structural change.

So opportunities as well as dangers inhere in this particular. As Bourgeois and Boltvinik advise (1981, 79–80), OD efforts *initially* might well emphasize interventions dealing with structures and policies/procedures in cultures that have strong autocratic traditions, which they attribute to Latin America. Early on, these interventions might be reinforced by *privatized* interaction-centered designs such as third-party conflict resolution, one-to-one counseling, and so on, as Jaeger (1984) sagely advises.

Relatedly, OD designs in the present panel relate to interventions for overbounded as well as for underbounded systems (e.g., Cummings 1980, 187-90). Overboundedness or overorganization, in general, responds to interaction-centered designs devoted to freeing up individuals. Underboundedness or underorganization often will require interventions relating to culture or to structures and policies/procedures, in contrast, as in role analysis and role negotiation. Available OD theory and experience in both genres may well serve nonaffluent settings, because they often seem characterized by complex combinations of overboundedness *and* underboundedness (e.g., Moris 1976).

In sum, the present panel of OD applications does not support the charge of narrow culture-boundedness. The batch of studies reflects a broad applicability of OD values and perspectives, and success rates are sufficiently high to encourage further applications. Moreover, convenient methods also seem to exist that may enhance success rates by being more sensitive to specific cultural features. As in chapter 1, and as will be the pattern in each chapter of this book, direct attention now focuses on details for increasing success rates.

Greater Success by Recognizing Success Rates, Revisited

As in the preceding chapter, the present estimate of success rates of OD applications in Third World settings can lead to greater success. Five points provide support for this apparently paradoxical conclusion.

More Applications and Replications

Elementally, the present estimates of success rates may motivate additional OD applications and, given sufficient wit and will, that might well enhance knowledge about which designs work best under which conditions. OD interventions tend to work more often than not, even in Third World settings. But a substantial margin for improvement patently exists. Hence, relative success up to this time might inspire greater success in the future.

Greater Reliance on Process-Oriented Interventions

The Third World record supports what common sense suggests: reliance on interaction-centered or process-oriented interventions can help increase success rates and responsiveness to cultural differences. In brief, this core OD technology focuses on the local—on interaction between specific people, acting on immediate feelings and concerns, within specific cultural and social settings. This emphasizes responsiveness to specific contexts, and hence reduces the probability that specific OD applications will falter and blunder because of a gross misfit between OD values and those characteristic of some specific setting. This refers to a Puritan in Babylon effect.

This second sense in which success can lead to greater success is always significant but is sometimes subtle, so elaboration will pay dividends. Basically, the core technology of OD involves group dynamics, and they touch on aspects of human life that are common, if not universal. Of course, the specific forms in which these dynamics appear may vary widely—for different settings, for different people, and in response to diverse individual or collective histories and experiences. Nonetheless, as one early observer noted: "Our human nature is acquired in primary groups . . ., and in the process of acquiring it we also absorb a taste for primary interaction and motivation to form and join primary groups." (Faris 1953, 166–67).

Consequently, many areas of pure and applied activity have a history of learning about the strategic leverage over choice and change inherent in small-group dynamics. These arenas include OD, therapy, and the formation of criminal gangs (e.g., Golembiewski 1979, vol. 1).

There seems little transfer of learning in this critical regard, however, and the basic lesson has been relearned, issue by issue. Consider that group forces typically are neglected in technology transfers to developing countries. As Honadle and Van Sant explain, the 1960s viewed development efforts "as a problem of national planning [which borrowed] from a European model of technocratic elites determining resource allocation to achieve economic objectives" (1985, 9). By explicit "mainstream consensus on the meaning of development" (Esman 1980, 426) such experience deals basically with

- Technology transfer rather than social transfer
- Individual vehicles for transfer rather than group vehicles
- Locally insensitive if not autocratic impositions rather than locally participative transfers
- Local populations as targets of transfer rather than as resources or as agents for transfer
- Technical experts rather than experts in group process
- Large bureaucracies as the typical vehicles for transfer
- Transfer that gives primacy to the stability of broad but fragile political institutions rather than to local participation

In sharp contrast, the development focus shifted in the 1970s to issues of equity and poverty, and here a "group focus" has gained increasing attention among subnational foci. For example, Mayfield describes a People's Participation Process, which he evaluates as "unique in its ability to generate its own sustainability" (1984). The focus is on the "poorest or the poor" as groups of specifically targeted beneficiaries. In outline:

- Beneficiaries identify membership criteria;
- Members come from an area small enough to permit convenient face-to-face meetings;
- Projects are structured around the needs and problem-solving strategies in the specification of which a "group of beneficiaries participated."

Moreover, if nothing else, group-transfer methods have attractive practical features. Jedlicka (1977, 61–62) estimates that extension-agent caseloads might well approximate 1,000–2,000 clients if group transfer is employed, while highly effective, traditional extension agents can service caseloads of only 100–150 clients.

Toward Good Fit

Despite this broad applicability of interaction-centered designs, Third World

OD applications also imply that success rates can increase if cultural particulars are taken into account. Of course, prescribing a good fit between a cultural setting and a specific OD design is as old as OD itself. Witness this basic injunction to intervenors: Begin where the client is!

How can the features of broad cultural environments be taken into account? Here, Hofstede's model of culture illustrates a "closeness-of-fit" notion that is much in the literature. It proposes that OD designs should be tailored to raise their congruence with cultural features.

Hofstede's model of cultural features. Most prominent nowadays among cultural models relevant to management and organization is Hofstede's work (1980a and 1980b). Neglecting important methodological issues for present purposes, his model builds on four purported cultural dimensions. In outline, they are (Hofstede 1980b, 45–47)

- *Power distance*, or "the extent to which a society accepts the fact that power in institutions and organizations is distributed unequally. It's reflected in the values of the less powerful members of society as well as in those of the more powerful ones."
- *Uncertainty avoidance*, or "the extent to which a society feels threatened by uncertain and ambiguous situations and tries to avoid [them] by providing greater career stability, establishing more formal rules, not tolerating deviant ideas and behaviors, and believing in absolute truths and the attainment of expertise. Nevertheless, societies in which uncertainty avoidance is strong are also characterized by a higher level of anxiety and aggressiveness that creates, among other things, a strong inner urge in people to work hard."
- *Individualism-collectivism*, an obvious pair of opposites: "Individualism implies a loosely knit social framework in which people are supposed to take care of themselves and of their immediate families only, while collectivism is characterized by a tight social framework in which people distinguish between in-groups and out-groups; they expect their in-group (relatives, clans, organizations) to look after them, and in exchange for that they feel they owe absolute loyalty to it."
- *Masculinity*, part of a purported dimension conceptually encompassing its opposite, *femininity*. Masculinity implies that the dominant values in a society emphasize "assertiveness, the acquisition of money and things, and *not* caring for others, the quality of life, or people. These values were labeled 'masculine' because within nearly all societies, men scored higher in terms of the values' positive sense than of their negative sense (in terms of assertiveness, for example, rather than its lack)—even though the society as a whole might veer toward the 'feminine' pole."

Hofstede sees societies as variously reflecting each of these four basic domains. For example, he generates 2-by-2 scatter plots for power distance–by–individualism, and power distance–by–uncertainty avoidance, locating various nation-states in quadrants defined by the two axes. "National scores" are based on responses to a questionnaire by people from a large number of countries.

Hofstede uncomfortably pairs a general concept of culture with a definite locus. Thus he reports survey responses from individuals which he aggregates by countries; and his analysis focuses on the purportedly dominant cultural features of those large political units. On the other hand, Hofstede's view of culture—as the "collective mental programming of the people in an environment"—applies to a universal and even mutually antagonistic array of groupings. He adds:

> Culture is not characteristic of individuals; it encompasses a number of people who were conditioned by the same education and life experience. When we speak of the culture of a group, a tribe, a geographical region, a national minority, or a nation, culture refers to the collective mental programming that these people have in common; the programming that is different from that of other groups, tribes, regions, minorities or majorities, or nations. (1980b, 43)

The essential issue deals with the "whole" and its "parts," of course. For a nation-state encompasses a very broad range of collectivities, some of whose "parts" are very different, and some of which may be significantly more or less influential in helping characterize the "whole" than mere numbers would suggest. To illustrate only, elite and mass opinions probably differ profoundly over a broad range of matters in any "whole" such as the countries Hofstede uses as his unit of cultural analysis. Consequently, Hofstede glides over awesome methodological issues, even if his four dimensions are appropriate for describing basic cultural differences.

Such methodological issues aside for present purposes, culture has one dominant conceptual property in Hofstede's view that makes it central to planned change, and indeed to all of life. "Culture . . . is often difficult to change," Hofstede notes in measured terms; "if it changes at all, it does so slowly" (1980b, 43). The implication drawn by most observers is a critical one. Since cultural features can change slowly and may differ markedly, most observers prescribe closeness-of-fit between specific cultures and OD designs (e.g., Blunt and Popoola 1985, 160–72).

Closeness-of-fit as decision rule. Management by objectives (MBO) illustrates the closeness-of-fit notion. Hofstede (1980b, 58–59) emphasizes the "made in U.S.A." character of MBO, and sees cultural features as prominent determinants of its reception both in the United States and elsewhere. In the Hofstede version, MBO fits the "U.S. culture"—as defined by scores derived from self-reports aggregated at the nation-state level. On at least three of his four dimensions, in outline, the U.S. culture closely fits the values presupposed by MBO:

- Power distance is "not too large" and subordinates can negotiate meaningfully with the boss;
- Uncertainty avoidance is "weak," so both superiors and subordinates are willing to risk;
- Masculinity is "high," and performance should thus be seen as more important than relationships.

Curiously, Hofstede does not include individualism in his example. U.S. respondents to his survey generate one of the two very highest of all nation-state scores on that dimension, and one could argue that MBO in America is typically a one-to-one contract and hence meets the U.S. culture in this fourth regard as well. But this may extend Hofstede beyond limits he considers comfortable.

The argument is underwhelming in several senses, in any case. Thus MBO in the United States has its share of failures, and these seem to relate at least as much to the style of application as to the concept (e.g., Golembiewski 1979, 2: 171–79). How can dominant cultural features at once encourage acceptance of the MBO technology and yet somehow often fail to appropriately guide the application of that technology? Hofstede does not tell us. At base, moreover, Hofstede settles for an indirect (and weak) proof of his essential point:

> [MBO] has been considerably more successful where results are objectively measurable than where they can only be interpreted subjectively, and even in the United States, it as been criticized heavily. Still it has been perhaps the single most popular management technique "made in U.S.A." *Therefore, it can be accepted as fitting U.S. culture* [Emphasis added.] (1980b, 58).

This formulation leaves open major questions about the impact of nation-state cultural features on MBO, of course, even if one does not dismiss the "proof."

Table 2.4 provides several other examples of closeness-of-fit of OD designs to one or more of Hofstede's dimensions. The assignments build on several sources (Bourgeois and Boltvinik 1981; Hofstede 1980b; Jaeger 1984). Overall, one point dominates. *Some* OD designs have a high closeness-of-fit, and *some* designs a poor fit, with each combination of cultural dimensions. Both features imply the serviceability of the OD inventory of designs.

Limits on Closeness-of-Fit as Decision Rule

However, the closeness-of-fit notion has sharp limits. Indeed, sometimes a poor fit is needed. Consider only three points by way of illustrating the reservations about relying on that decision rule.

First, no model of cultural features avoids the whole/part issue of social description. Some statistical techniques for isolating clusters of similarities or

TABLE 2.4
Examples of Closeness-of-Fit of OD Designs and Cultural Features

Cultural Features	Indicated OD Designs	Contraindicated OD Designs
I. High masculine high individualism	• Job enrichment of individual jobs • MBO • Task-oriented group interventions, e.g., team-building	• Job enrichment in autonomous teams
II. Low uncertainty avoidance, low power distance, low individualism	• Group confrontations • Interpersonally oriented team building • T-groups for intact work groups • Sharing 3-D images	• Interview/feedback • Survey/feedback
III. High uncertainty avoidance, medium-to-high power distance	• Flexible work hours • Role analysis • Role negotiation • Structural changes • Survey/feedback • Third-party consultation	• Public confrontations • T-groups for intact work groups
IV. High individualism, low masculine, high power distance	• 1:1 counseling • Role analysis • Role negotiation	• T-groups for intact work groups

differences in any aggregate of individuals reduce the problem, as by "attribute cluster-bloc analysis" or various forms of hierarchical decomposition. Basically, these techniques ask: How many clusters or groupings are required to simultaneously maximize differences and similarities in some population?

Hofstede forces a fit of a large number of survey respondents to their respective countries, and this approximates a worse-case example of the whole/part issue. Responses from numerous individuals must sum to a single representation of *the* culture of *a* nation-state. Such wholes no doubt contain many parts, oppositely. Thus observers may rightly point to the general inapplicability in, for example, Tanzania, of Western-style job enrichment, with its emphases on individual self-fulfillment and on psychic income, even as there will be significant pockets of employees—in the same nation-state, in the same parent organization, and even in the same jobs—who are so Westernized that the general warnings do not hold (e.g., Blunt and Popoola 1985, 160). It is not at all clear what one gets when such parts are aggregated at a macro-level such as a country or a nation-state.

Three conclusions seem appropriate. First, the whole/part issue underscores both the necessity and the difficulty of the ad hoc diagnosis of individual sites for OD applications. Repeatedly, one may well use models like Hofstede's for first-cut guidance, but unqualified reliance on the conclusions generated at the nation-state level may prove seriously misleading. Of course, one could use Hofstede's instrument to characterize various aggregates other than the nation-state—for example, organizations or even immediate work groups. Such precise targeting might aid diagnosis.

Second, choice, change, or development may require precisely what the culture disregards or even proscribes. Here reliance on the closeness-of-fit model may be reactionary as well as counterproductive. That is, OD designs might be chosen precisely because of their *degree of non-fit* to some culture. Marginal farmers might well "have to risk more to increase their yields," as Jedlicka (1977) proposes. But those farmers also often will be in cultural settings that Hofstede would score as high on uncertainty avoidance. Close-fit designs may tragically reinforce precisely what those farmers may need to reduce.

This second issue is a complex one, but two points seem clear enough. The position is not that models such as Hofstede's are useless. Rather, their usefulness should be tethered to indicating, for example, where difficulties might be expected in OD applications, as opposed to dictating the choice or rejection of a design. Or the trick might lay in developing a design that increases risk-taking even as it is simultaneously acceptable in a risk-avoiding culture. The "risky-shift" phenomenon might be a case in point, for example (Jedlicka 1977). In such cases, however, ethical issues regarding manipulation and deception are involved.

Perhaps most importantly, it remains far from clear how much non-fit is too much. Certainly, one can conceive of a design that is too much for given cultural features, even as the direction of movement intended by that design "is good for" some client. Some openness may be very useful, for example, but that does not mean that extreme openness is appropriate, or even safe, at a specific point in time. Indeed, even a little openness may be dangerous, not only in totalitarian states but even in some organizations in democratic states, at least at some times.

The theoretical issue involves determining what degree of discrepancy facilitates learning, with "discrepancy" here being defined as the difference between some learning stimulus and a subject's normal attitudinal or behavioral anchors. Opinions differ, sometimes profoundly, and no accepted learning theory yet exists. As the following chapter shows, a curvilinear relation between fit and degree of learning gets most support at this time. Designs inducing moderate dissonance seem to be best for maximizing choice or change, while low or extreme degrees of discrepancy seem to induce low choice or change, if for different reasons.

Third, as much of the preceding discussion implies, the choice of an OD design involves complex normative as well as empirical choices. Issues of the desired and the desirable require attention, from the perspective of both client and intervenor. These powerful normative issues get variously combined with empirical issues—for example, which designs tend to work under which conditions, or (much more subtly) which learning outcomes meet not only immediate needs but also relate reasonably to succeeding phases in the client's probable development (e.g., Korten 1980).

The complexity of such choices helps explain the power of relying on group processes highlighted in an earlier section. There, member participation and involvement encourage a full airing of beneficiary aspirations, as well as a good opportunity to take into account these aspirations in problem solving and program development that takes milieu details into account. This reinforces the good sense of the basic prescription that interaction-centered designs generally should constitute the front-load of OD programs, to build the foundations for later emphasis on structures, policies, and procedures.

Greater Credibility for Intervenors

As in all cultural settings, intervenor credibility is a significant factor in OD interventions—in getting them started, in hanging tough during periods of doubt, and also in ultimate success rates. Clearly, substantial success rates contribute to intervenor credibility, and hence efforts like this chapter not only survey what was, but they also can influence what will come to be.

Every intervenor knows the power inherent in credibility, which can be gained in numerous ways in addition to publicizing success rates. Typically, local cultures will influence if not determine how an intervenor gains credibility. For example, an intervenor working in an Indian village killed an attacking dog by striking it with a steel surveyor's pin, in a reflex action. Serendipitously, that led to a large uptick in the intervenor's credibility. The dog had been terrorizing villagers, but their Hindu convictions discouraged direct action. They nonetheless admired a man of action who got a useful thing done. Similarly, several interventions in our panel also rest on establishing intervenor credibility, as in the case of uncovering the actions of a corrupt police official, whose superiors were inspired to action even as the official demonstrated his repentance (Chandra and Mehta 1984; Mehta 1986).

Concluding Remarks

In sum, this analysis indicates that OD interventions can and do have a substantial if underutilized relevance in Third World settings. The inventory of OD learning designs covers a broad range of designs—interaction, policies or procedures, and structures—and builds upon a relatively specific set of values as well as upon the process analysis or interpersonal and group dynamics. This breadth permits application in many settings, and applications are encouraged from both actual and probable perspectives. Thus, success rates of available applications seem reasonably high, and several considerations suggest the usefulness of even greater reliance in nonaffluent settings on OD technology and values, especially via basic group dynamics and processes.

Note

1. This chapter extends the position in Golembiewski 1987. This earlier paper contains about seventy applications.
   Note also that a far longer and detailed version will appear in Bacharach and Magjuka, (in press).

References

*Abramson, R. 1978. *An Integrated Approach to Organization Development and Performance Improvement Planning*. West Hartford,Conn.: Kumarian Press.

*Akhilesh, K. B. 1981. *Effective Organisational Development Through Participation and Development Program*. Ph.D. diss. Indian Institute of Science, Bangalore.

*Akhilesh, K. B., and Ganguly, T. 1982. "Organization Development through Participation and Communication Programme: A Case Study." *Indian Journal of Industrial Relations* 19:549–61.

*Alevy, D. I.; Bunker, B. B.; Doob, L. W.; Foltz, W. J.; French, N.; Klein, E. B.; and Miller, J. C. 1974. "Rationale, Research and Role Relations in the Stirling Workshop." *Journal of Conflict Resolution* 18:276–84.

*An asterisk before an item indicates that it is one of the present panel of evaluative studies of OD applications.

*Allen, R. F., and Silverzweig, S. 1977. "Changing Community and Organizational Cultures." *Training and Development Journal* 31:28–34.

*Almeida, E.; Sanchez, M. E.; Sota, B.; Felix, L.; and Perez, V. 1983. "Development of a Participatory Research Center as Part of an Ongoing Rural Development Program." *Journal of Applied Behavioral Science* 19:295–306.

*Armor, T. H. 1979. "Addressing Problems of Middle Level Management." *IRD Field Report*. Washington, D.C.: Development Alternatives, Inc.

*______. 1981. "Using Organization Development in Integrated Rural Development." *IRD Working Paper No. 6*. Washington, D.C.: Development Alternatives, Inc.

*______. 1985. "Organization Development and Management Methods in Community Participation." Lead paper in *Methods and Media in Community Participation*. Uppsala, Sweden: Dag Hammarskjold Centre.

*______. 1986. "Whose Needs Are They Anyway?: From Needs Assessment to Organizational Change." Working paper.

*Atiyyah, H. S. 1986. "Management Consultation in Some Middle Eastern Countries: Process, Interactions, and Ethical Issues." Working paper.

Bacharach, S. B., and Magjuka,R., eds., (in press) *Research in the Sociology of Organizations*. Greenwich, Conn.: JAI Press, Inc.

*Bagadion, B. U., and Korten, F. F. 1980. "Developing Viable Irrigators' Associations: Lessons from Small Scale Irrigation in the Philippines." *Agricultural Administration* 7:273–87.

*Belloncle, G. 1981. "Toward a New Method in Rural Development in West Africa: Lessons from Niger, Senegal, and Mali." *Rural Africana* 10:1–7.

*Benjamin, A., and Levi, A. M. No date. "High School Seniors Resolve the Conflict: The SDOT Yam Workshop." Unpublished ms.

*Berlew, D. E., and LeClere, W. E. 1974. "Social Intervention in Curacao." *Journal of Applied Behavioral Science* 10:29–52.

*Bhagat, R. S., and McQuaid, S. J. 1982. "The Role of Subjective Culture in Organizations: A Review and Directions for Future Research." *Journal of Applied Psychology* 67:653–85.

*Bhattacharyya, S. K. 1980. "Making Organizational-Design Changes Effective: An Approach Based on Indian Experience." *Group and Organization Studies* 5:418–37.

Blunt, P. 1980. "Bureaucracy and Ethnicity in Kenya: Some Conjectures for the Eighties." *Journal of Applied Behavioral Science* 16:336–53.

Blunt, P., and Popoola, O. 1985. *Personnel Management in Africa*. London: Longman Group Limited, Longman House.

*Boehringer, G. H., and Zeruolis, V. 1974. "Stirling: The Destructive Application of Group Techniques to a Conflict." *Journal of Conflict Resolution* 18:258–75.

Bourgeois, L. J. III, and Boltvinik, M. 1981. "OD in Cross-Cultural Settings." *California Management Review* 73:75–81.

Brown, L. D., and Tandon, R. 1983. "Ideology and Political Economy in Inquiry." *Journal of Applied Behavioral Science* 19:277–94.

Bullock, R. J., and Bullock, P. F. 1984. "Pure Science versus Science-Action Models of Data Feedback." *Group and Organization Studies* 9:7–28.

*Carney, J. A. Jr.; Honadle, G.; and Armor, T. H. 1980. "Coordination and Implementation at Bula-Minalabac." *IRD Field Report*.Washington, D.C.: Development Alternatives, Inc.

*Chand, A. D., and Soni, M. I. 1981. "The Pachod Health Programme." In *Participatory Research and Evaluation*, edited by W. Fernandes and R. Tandon, 127–50.

*Chandra, N., and Mehta, P. 1984. *People's Self-Action for Development*. New Delhi: National Labour Institute.

*Chattopadhyay, G. P. 1972. "The Use of a Group Dynamics Laboratory in Consultation: A Case Study Set in the Bank of Calcutta, I." *The Journal of Management Studies* 9:314–36.

*______. 1973. "The Use of a Group Dynamics Laboratory in Consultation: A Case Study Set in the Bank of Calcutta, II." *The Journal of Management Studies* 10:15–24.

*Chattopadhyay, S., and Pareek, U. 1984. "Organization Development in a Voluntary Organization." *International Studies of Man and Organization* 14:46–85.

*Chetkow-Yanoov, B. 1985. *The Pursuit of Peace: A Curriculum for Teachers*. Haifa, Israel: Partnership.

*Chroscicki, Z. 1986. "Conceptualization of OD Process Management." Working paper.

*______. 1986a. "Factors in the Performance of Task Forces in Innovation Programs." Working paper.

Clegg, I. 1971. *Worker's Self-Management in Algeria*. London: Allen Lane, The Penguin Press.

*Cohen, S. P.; Kelman, H. C.; Miller, F. D.; and Smith, B. L. 1977. "Evolving Intergroup Techniques for Conflict Resolution: An Israeli-Palestinian Pilot Workshop." *Journal of Social Issues* 33:165–89.

*Cordova, E. 1982. "Workers' Participation in Decisions within Enterprises: Recent Trends and Problems." *International Labour Review* 121:125–40.

Cummings, T. G. 1980. *Systems Theory for Organization Development*. New York: John Wiley.

*Dayal, I., and Thomas J. M. 1968. "Operation KPE: Developing a New Organization." *Journal of Applied Behavioral Science* 4:473–512.

*De, N. R. 1971. "Organizational Development: An Interim Balance Sheet." *Economic and Political Weekly* 6:M–42–M–57.

*______. 1979. "India." In *New Forms of Work Organization*, International Labour Office, 2:26–61. Geneva: International Labour Organization.

*De Sousa, P. 1979. "IRD and the Agent of Change." *Indian Journal of Social Work* 39:425–30.

*Diesh, K.; Sekharan, C. C.; and Mohanty, G. I. 1984. "Toward Organizational Development in Government: An Empirical Study." *International Studies of Man and Organization* 14:30–45.

*Doob, L. W. 1971. "The Impact of the Fermeda Workshop on the Conflicts in the Horn of Africa." *International Journal of Group Tensions* 1:91–101.

*______. 1976. "A Cyprus Workshop: Intervention Methodology During a Continuing Crisis." *Journal of Social Psychology* 98:143–44.

*Doob, L. W., and Foltz, W. J. 1973. "The Belfast Workshop: An Application of Group Techniques to a Destructive Conflict." *Journal of Conflict Resolution* 17:489–512.

*______. 1974. "The Impact of a Workshop upon Grass-Roots Leaders in Belfast." *Journal of Conflict Resolution* 18:237–56.

*Doob, L. W.; Foltz, W. J.; and Stevens, R. B. 1969. "The Fermeda Workshop: A Different Approach to Border Conflicts in Eastern Africa." *Journal of Psychology* 73:249–66.

*Eden, D. 1985. "Team Development: A True Field Experiment at Three Levels of Rigor." *Journal of Applied Psychology* 70:94–100.

______. 1986. "Team Development: Quasi-Experimental Confirmation among Combat Companies." *Group and Organization Studies* 11:133–46.

*Ejiogu, A. M. 1983. "Participative Management in a Developing Economy: Poison or Placebo?" *Journal of Applied Behavioral Science* 19:239–48.

Esman, M. J. 1980. "Development Assistance in Public Administration: Requirements for Renewal." *Public Administration Review* 40:426–31.

Esman, M. J., and Montgomery, J. 1969. "The Role of Developing Administration." *Public Administration Review* 29:507–39.

Faris, R. E. L. 1953. "Development of the Small-Group Research Movement." In *Group Relations at the Crossroads*, edited by M. Sherif, and M. O. Wilson, 155–84. New York: Harper.

*Felstehausen, H., and Diaz-Cisneros, H. 1985. "The Strategy of Rural Development: The Puebla Initiative." *Human Organization* 49:285–92.

Fernandes, W., and Tandon, R. eds. 1981. *Participatory Research and Evaluation*. New Delhi: Indian Social Science Institute.

French, W. F., and Bell, C. H. Jr. 1978. *Organization Development*. Englewood Cliffs, N.J.: Prentice-Hall.

*Frits, J. 1976. "Results of Motivational Training in Ecuador." *Development Digest* 14:81–90.

*Fuchs, C. J. 1985. "Organizational Development under Political, Economic, and Natural Crisis." Paper presented at Fifth OD World Congress. Zeist, Netherlands.

Golembiewski, R. T. 1962. *The Small Group*. Chicago: University of Chicago Press.

______. 1979. *Approaches to Planned Change*, vols. 1 and 2. New York: Marcel Dekker.

______. 1987. "OD Applications in Non-Affluent Settings." Paper presented at the International Conference on Organization Behavior and Development, Indian Institute of Management. Ahmedabad, India.

______. 1989. "OD Applications in Non-Affluent Settings: Four Perspectives on Critical Action Research." In Bachrach and Magjuka (in press).

Golembiewski, R. T., and Carrigan, S. B. 1970a. "Planned Change in Organization Style Based on Laboratory Approach." *Administrative Science Quarterly* 15: 79–93.

______. 1970b. "The Persistence of Laboratory-Induced Changes in Organization Styles." *Administrative Science Quarterly* 15:330–40.

*Guess, G. M. 1982. "Institution-Building for Development Forestry in Latin America." *Public Administration and Development* 2:309–24.

*Gupta, R. 1986. "Programmed Team Building" *HRD* 4:5–7.

*Gupta, R. K., and Gangotra, V. 1986. "OD in a Marketing Office." In *Recent Experiences in Human Development*, edited by T. V. Rao and D. F. Pereira, 329–61. New Delhi: Oxford.

*Ha, M. 1986. "'Self-Overcoming Training' in Korean Public Organizations." Seminar paper. University of Georgia.

*Hall, R. W. 1969. *Putting Down Roots*. New York: Celanese Corporation.

Halset, W. G. 1967. "Organizational Development and Its Application to the East Pakistan Water and Power Development Authority." In *Problems of Public Enterprises*, edited by Abramson, R.; Beg, M.A.K.; and Ahmad, I., 129–49. Lahore, Pakistan: National Institute of Public Administration.

Hofstede, G. 1980a. *Culture's Consequences*. Beverly Hills, Calif.: Sage.

______. 1980b. "Motivation, Leadership, and Organization." *Organizational Dynamics* 9:42–63.

*Honadle, G. H., et al. 1980. "Implementing Capacity Building in Jamaica: Field Experience in Human Resource Development." *IRD Field Report*. Washington, D.C.: Development Alternatives, Inc.

*Honadle, G. H., and Hannah, J. P. 1982. "Management Performance for Rural Development: Packaged Training for Capacity Building." *Public Administration and Development* 2:295–307.

Honadle, G. H., and Van Sant, J. 1985. *Implementation for Sustainability*. West Hartford, Conn.: Kumarian Press.

*Hopper, J. R. 1972. "Management Training in Developing Countries: A Sectoral Approach." *Training and Development Journal* 26:6–10.

*Huss, C. 1973. *Planned Organizational Change in the Structure and Functioning of Indian Hospitals*. Ph.D. diss. Delhi University.

Jaeger, A. M. 1984. "The Appropriateness of Organization Development outside North America." *International Studies of Man and Organization* 14:23–35.

______. 1986. "Organization Development and National Culture: Where's the Fit?" *Academy of Management Review* 11:178–90.

Janis, I. 1972. *Groupthink*. Boston: Houghton Mifflin.

*Jedlicka, A. D. 1977. *Organization for Rural Development*. New York: Praeger.

Jones, G. N. 1966. "Change Catalyst in Managed Organizational Change." *Indian Journal of Public Administration* 12:717–42.

*Juralewicz, R. 1974. "An Experiment on Participation in a Latin American Factory." *Human Relations* 22:627–37.

*Kamani, P. R. 1971. "The Birth of a New Management Philosophy." Calcutta: Indian Institute of Management.

*Kanawaty, G.; Thorsrud, J. P.; Semiono, J. P.; and Singh, J. P. 1981. "Field Experiences with New Forms of Work Organization." *International Labour Review* 120:263–77.

*Kiggundu, M. N. 1985. "Sociotechnical Systems in Developing Countries: A Review and Directions for Future Research." Working paper. Carleton University School of Business. Ottawa, Canada.

*Korten, D. C. 1979. "The Pilot Project: Formal Experiment or Learning Laboratory?" Unpublished ms. Manila, Philippines: The Ford Foundation.

*______. 1980. "Community Organization and Rural Development." *Public Administration Review* 40:480–511.

*Krausz, P. 1985. "Israel: Eastwards? Westwards? Negotiations? Confrontations? Shalshelet's Antidote to Dilemmas." *Organization Development Journal* 3:33–38.

Kurian, G. T. 1984. *The New Book of World Rankings*. New York: Facts on File Publications.

*Lagos, C. R. 1972. *An Experiment in Laboratory Training in a Chilean Public Organization and Its Implication for Organization Development*. Ph.D. diss. University of Pittsburgh.

*Lakin, M. 1969. *Arab and Jew in Israel*. Washington, D.C.: NTL Institute for Applied Behavioral Science.

*______. 1978. "Arab and Jew in Israel: A Case Study of a Training Approach to Intergroup Conflict." In *The Small Group in Political Science: The Last Two Decades of Development*, edited by Golembiewski, R.T., 368–92. Athens,Ga.: University of Georgia Press.

Leonard, D. K. 1977. *Reaching the Peasant Farmer*. Chicago: University of Chicago Press.

*Levi, A. M., and Benjamin, A. 1974. "Jews and Arabs in Israel Rehearse Geneva: A Pilot Study in Conflict Resolution." Unpublished ms. Israel: University of Haifa.

______. 1976. "Jews and Arabs Rehearse Geneva: A Model of Conflict Resolution." *Human Relations* 29:1035–44.

*______. 1977. "Focus and Flexibility in a Model of Conflict Resolution." *Journal of Conflict Resolution* 21:405–25.

*Levi, A. M., and Hadah, D. No date. "Around the Mulberry Tree: Method Supporting Skill in Conflict Resolution." Unpublished ms. Israel: University of Haifa.

*Lynton, R. 1986. "End of Assignment Report: The Training Component, 1983–1986." In-house report. Jakarta, Indonesia: University of South Carolina and Management Sciences for Health, Contractor.

Mathur, H. M. 1981. "Cooperation in Administrative Training among Developing Countries: Experiences with Sharing Indian Expertise." *Indian Journal of Public Administration* 27:981–92.

*Maule, H. G. 1965. "The Application of Industrial Psychology to Developing Countries." *International Labour Review* 92:283–97.

Mayfield, J. B. 1984. "The Rural Development Center: A New Strategy for Rural Development in the Phillipines." *International Journal of Public Administration* 6:367–88.

*Mehta, P. 1983–1984. "Participatory Education for Rural Workers." *National Labour Institute Bulletin* 9:199–218.

*______. 1986. "Organising for Empowering the Poor." Paper delivered at the International Conference on Organizational and Behavioural Perspectives for Social Development. Ahmedabad, India.

*Miller, E. J. 1975. "Sociotechnical Systems in Weaving, 1953–1970: A Follow-up Study." *Human Relations* 28:349–86.

Miller, G. J. 1979. *The Laboratory Approach to Planned Change in the Public Sector*. Ph.D. diss. University of Georgia.

Mirvis, P. H., and Berg, D. N. 1977. *Failures in Organization Development and Change*. New York: John Wiley.

Moris, J. R. 1976. "The Transferability of the Western Management Tradition to the Non-Western Public Service Sectors: An East African Perspective." *Philippine Journal of Public Administration* 20:401–27.

______. 1981. *Managing Induced Rural Development*. Bloomington, Ind.: International Development Institute.

Morrison, P. 1978. "Evaluation in OD: A Review and An Assessment." *Group and Organization Studies* 3:42–70.

Mozumdar, S. N. 1963. "Training in Community Development." *Indian Journal of Public Administration* 9:182–88.

Mukherji, P. N. 1970. "A Study in Induced Social Change: An Indian Experiment." *Human Organization* 29:169–77.

*Murrell, K. L., and Valsan, E. H. 1985. "A Team-Building Workshop as an OD Intervention in Egypt." *Leadership and Organization Development Journal* 6:11–16.

*Myrtle, R. C. 1986. "Management Capacity Building in Third-World Countries: A Case Study." Working paper. University of Southern California.

*Nylen, D.; Mitchell, J. R.; and Stout, A. 1967. *Handbook of Staff Development and Human Relations Training*. Washington, D.C.: NTL Institute for Applied Behavioral Science.

Okpala, D. C. L. 1980. "Towards a Better Conceptualization of Rural Community Development: Empirical Findings from Nigeria." *Human Organization* 39:161–69.

*Orpen, C. 1976. "Job Enlargement, Individual Differences, and Worker Responses: A Test of Black Workers." *Journal of Cross-Cultural Psychology* 7:473–80.

*Padaki, R. 1984. "How Enriched Is Your Job?" *Journal of the Textile Association* 45:54–62 and 87–94.

Pareek, U. 1975. "The Concept and the Process of Organization Development." *Indian Journal of Social Work* 36:109–25.

*Porras, J. I. 1974. *A General Research Model for the Measurement of the Impact of an Organization Development Project: An Argentine Experience*. Ph.D. diss. University of California at Los Angeles.

______. 1979. "The Comparative Impact of Different OD Techniques and Intervention Intensities." *Journal of Applied Behavioral Science* 15:156–78.

*Porter, L. 1986. "International Tension-Reduction through the Person-Centered Approach: An Interview with Larry Solomon." *OD Practitioner* 18:1–7.

Proehl, C. W., Jr. 1980. *Planned Organizational Change*. Ph.D. diss. University of Georgia, Athens, Ga.

*Ramos, C. P. 1971. "The Use of Modern Management Techniques in the Public Administration of Developing Countries: The Philippine Experience." *Philippine Journal of Public Administration* 15:12–20.

Rao, T.V., and Pereira, D. F., eds. 1986. *Recent Experiences in Human Development*. New Delhi: Oxford.

Redl, F. 1943. "Group Psychological Elements in Discipline Problems." *American Journal of Orthopsychiatry* 13:77–82.

*Rice, A. K. 1958. *Productivity and Social Organization: The Ahmedabad Experiment*. London: Tavistock Publications.

*Rogers, C. R. 1984. "The Rust Workshop: A Personal Overview." *Journal of Humanistic Psychology* 26:23–45.

*Carl Rogers Peace Project. 1986. "Brief Report of Peace Meeting—Rust, Austria, November 1–4, 1985." La Jolla,Calif.: Center for the Study of the Person.

Ruttan, V. 1974. "Rural Development Programs: A Skeptical Perspective." New York: Agricultural Development Council, Inc., June 26.

*Sajo, T. A. 1970. "Sensitivity Training: A Report on an Application of a Change Technique in the Philippine Bureaucracy." *Philippine Journal of Public Administration* 14:284–97.

*Salinas, A. D. R. 1978. "An OD Experience in the Latin American Public Sector through an Instrument of Collective Organizational Programming." *Public Personnel Management* 7:272–78.

*Seal, J. B. Jr. 1971. "Managing for Development: The Kenyan Approach to Management by Objectives and Organizational Development." In *Organization Development: Improving Governments' Delivery Systems*. Papers from the Eighth Annual Conference on Management Analysis in State and Local Government, 11–12 November, Albany, N.Y. The Development Administrators Training Program, Institute of Public Service, University of Connecticut in conjunction with the Committee on Management Analysis in State and Local Government.

*Seashore, C. 1965. *An Evaluation of Staff Development and Human Relations Workshops Conducted by the Ford Foundation in West Africa, 1961–1963*. Washington, D.C.: National Training Laboratories.

*Sherif, A. F. 1971. "New Approach to Training for Improved Performance in Public Corporations," 7–8 April, and "Improving Performance of East African Community Corporations," 23–24 October. *Public Administration Newsletter*. New York: U.N. Public Administration Division.

*Shrinivasan, C. 1976. "Guatemala: Approach to Relief." Paper presented at the United Nations World Conference on Habitat, 1 June 1976. Vancouver.

Singh, J. P. 1983. "QWL Experiments in India: Trials and Triumphs." *Abhigyan* 23–37.

*Singh, M. 1981. "Literacy to Development: The Growth of a Tribal Village." In *Participatory Research and Evaluation*, edited by W. Fernandes and R. Tandon, 162–71.

Singh, R. 1952. "An Introduction of Green Manuring in Rural India." In *Human Problems in Technological Change*, edited by E. Spicer, 55–69. New York: John Wiley.

*Sinha, D. P. 1986. "Training the Top: Building New Administrative Cultures." Paper delivered at International Conference on Organizational and Behavioural Perspectives for Social Development. Ahmedabad, India.

*Sinha, J. B. P. 1974. "A Case of Reversal in Participative Management." *Indian Journal of Industrial Relations* 10:179–88.

*Smith, M. L. 1984. "Human Relations Training for African Public Officials." *Small Group Behavior* 15:349–60.

*Soares, K.C. 1983. "Development of the Informal Sector through Participation." Paper prepared for presentation at a meeting sponsored by the Department of Labor and the Agency for International Development, "Productivity, Participation, and Ownership."

*______. 1984. "Improving the Quality of Life in Caribbean Villages: Participatory Approaches in Development." *Organization Development Journal* 2:5–11.

*Solomon, M. J. 1985. "An Organizational Change Strategy for Developing Countries." Washington, D.C.: Development Program Management Center, U.S. Department of Agriculture.

Stauffer, R. B. 1977. "The American Development Model: Hidden Agenda for the Third World." *Philippine Journal of Public Administration* 21:123–40.

*Straszak, A., and Maslyk, E. 1984. "OD Practice and Research in Poland." *Organization Development Journal* 2:7–13.

Tainio, R., and Santalainen, T. 1984. "Some Evidence for the Cultural Relativity of Organizational Development Programs." *Journal of Applied Behavioral Science* 20:93–112.

*Tandon, R., and Brown, L. D. 1981. "Organization-Building for Rural Development: An Experiment in India." *Journal of Applied Behavioral Science* 17:172–89.

*Thorsrud, E. 1968. "Socio-technical Approach to Job Design and Organization Development." *Management International Review* 8:120–31.
*Torczyner, J. 1972. "The Political Context of Social Change." *Journal of Applied Behavioral Science* 8:287–317.
Vengroff, R. 1974. "Popular Participation and the Administration of Rural Development: The Case of Botswana." *Human Organization* 33:303–9.
*Vittitow, D. 1983. "Applying Behavioral Science to Third World Development." *Journal of Applied Behavioral Science* 19:307–18.
*Walton, R. E. 1970a. "A Problem-Solving Workshop on Border Conflict in Eastern Africa." *Journal of Applied Behavioral Science* 6:453–501.
*______. 1970b. "Strategic Issues in Designing Workshops." In *Resolving Conflict in Africa*, edited by L.E. Doob, 136–61. New Haven, Conn.: Yale University Press.
*Wedge, B. 1971. "A Psychiatric Model for Intercession in Intergroup Conflict." *Journal of Applied Behavioral Science* 7:733–61.
*Yanoov, B. 1985. *The Pursuit of Peace*. Haifa, Israel: Partnership.
Zander, A. 1982. *Making Groups Effective*. San Francisco: Jossey-Bass.

Irony II

Relative Success without a Learning Model

3

An Optimum Discrepancy: A Critical Feature of OD Designs

This second irony in OD may be stated boldly. To increase its predictive and applied usefulness, work in OD must become increasingly specific about what effects can be expected under which circumstances. To be sure, general agreement exists that learning typically occurs in response to some hitch or incongruence between what we expect or believe and what we come to know or experience. This can be viewed as a gap between "ideal" and "actual." And reasonable OD advice proposes intervening where trauma exists, or where hurt is present. The trauma or hurt, in effect, generates energies that may be used to motivate choice or change—that is to say, learning.

But what is the optimum hitch—small, medium, or large?

Despite the substantial success rates sketched in the preceding chapters, we have a long way to go in being usefully specific about the kind of ideal/actual discrepancy that best induces learning, choice, or change. Assume we wish to effectively bring to someone's attention some piece of feedback. What is the recommended strength of the dosage? Should the feedback, consistent with essential honesty, be mild, tough, or somewhere in between?

Several varieties of the common wisdom propose rules of thumb concerning such specificity, but little relevant research exists. Hence this chapter contributes to one aspect of the required specificity, and this by dealing with one issue—the different degrees of motivational force that can be attributed to varying degrees of discrepancy between an individual's preferences about desirable organizational climate and perceptions of the actual situation. The present research seeks to relate degrees of change following an OD intervention to the prior ideal/actual discrepancies of individuals reporting on the climate of their immediate work unit. In sum, how much discrepancy is too much?

A Conceptual Context for Irony II

The design in OD of appropriate discrepancies patently must deal with the properties of individual learners as well as with the characteristics of the organizations from which they come. Major early signs of concern about the point (Bennis 1969, 44–55; Harrison 1965) were expressed, but two largely unexplored issues still loom large despite recent confirming evidence that the early concerns are right-on (e.g., Bowers 1973; Bowers and Hausser 1977; Pasmore and King 1978). These two central issues may be phrased in the form of questions:

- What properties of individuals or organizations affect outcomes of OD learning designs?
- What degree of discrepancy between existing design properties and OD values is too much, or too little?

We are not very far down the trail toward having detailed answers to these two questions, however. Opinions about such key questions abound and tend to be strongly held. Not only does little research address these questions, however, but the research that does address them seems to be methodologically vulnerable. Witness the criticisms of Bowers's major effort to differentiate interventions appropriate for different hosts (e.g., Torbert 1973; Pasmore 1976). And my own narrower work on a related theme (Golembiewski 1970) can also be faulted on methodological grounds.

Some progress is possible despite the enormity of the unknowns about optimum discrepancies, and that possibility motivates this chapter to address aspects of the two largely unexplored questions posed above. The data come from a mass team-building experience at one site for personnel from thirty-three sales regions of a national marketing organization, including all first-line managers and all salesmen reporting to them. The data here are self-reports about behavior, which are interpreted as reflecting changes in organizational climate and, if by inference only, changes in behavior as a result of an OD intervention. Respondents initially described the organizational climate of their immediate work units as falling short of their ideal, which was basically consistent with the values underlying OD. The intervention thus had two tasks: to induce attitudes supporting the possibility of reducing the gap between ideal and actual organizational climate, and, especially, to increase the performance of behaviors appropriate to reducing that gap. Impressionistically, the experience was considered successful—by the consultants and by several levels of management, as well as by most other observers. More rigorous efforts to document effects generally support this global and impressionistic evaluation (Golembiewski 1979a, 132–36), albeit with significant reservations.

Is There an Optimum Discrepancy?: Three Alternative Models

Conceptually, this chapter focuses on the issue of an optimum discrepancy for learning. That is, a discrepancy can exist between how a person behaves or what he or she believes and some challenging stimulus. Motivating energy is often attributed to such discrepancies, with change in attitudes or behaviors being a convenient way to reduce a discrepancy and thus to satiate a motivational urge. If I believe I am about the proper weight, but my sweetheart believes I am a bit pudgy—well, that discrepancy might motivate some direct action. Some call this the "dilemma/invention model" of change.

Hypothetically, the simple models in figure 3.1 sketch three alternative but not exclusive discrepancy/change linkages. The models are analogues of ones that have received much attention in studies of attitudes. They are used here as a tentative starting point, and the qualifier "tentative" is appropriate for several reasons. For example, the models obviously homogenize the complex mix of behavioral and attitudinal changes generated by an OD intervention. In addition, the present approach is also too simplistic to extend to Heider's (1958) balance model, which has a variety of attractive features. These are inelegant limitations, but unavoidable at this early stage of research. See also the comments concluding this chapter, as well as chapter 10.

Model I in figure 3.1 is called "accelerating" because it proposes that the greater the discrepancy between the stimulus of an OD intervention and an individual's anchors, the greater will be the tendency to move those anchors toward that stimulus. That is to say, the individual reduces dissonance between self and stimulus by making adjustments in self, in direct proportion to the magnitude of the dissonance. Model I shares a basic conceptual thrust, then, with approaches such as Festinger's theory of cognitive dissonance. He proposes that "the discrepant reality which impinges on a person will exert pressures in the direction of bringing the appropriate cognitive elements into correspondence with that reality. . . . The strength of the pressures to reduce the dissonance is a function of the magnitude of dissonance" (1957, 18).

Model II is "decelerating," in direct contrast. Essentially, it implies that change in OD programs occurs more by assimilation than by contrast. High degrees of discrepancy, consequently, will tend to restrict the degree of change, or negate it entirely. Model II is consistent with a variety of experimental research by the Sherifs (1967), who argue that Model I describes attitudinal change only where "ego involvement" is low. There, learning occurs by contrast. Model II implies that learning or change in OD programs—where high ego involvement is intended, and often will exist—will tend to occur by assimilation. Hence, low discrepancies will be associated with larger changes, if Model II describes reality.

FIGURE 3.1
Three Alternative Models of the Relationship between Discrepancy and Degree of Change toward That Discrepancy

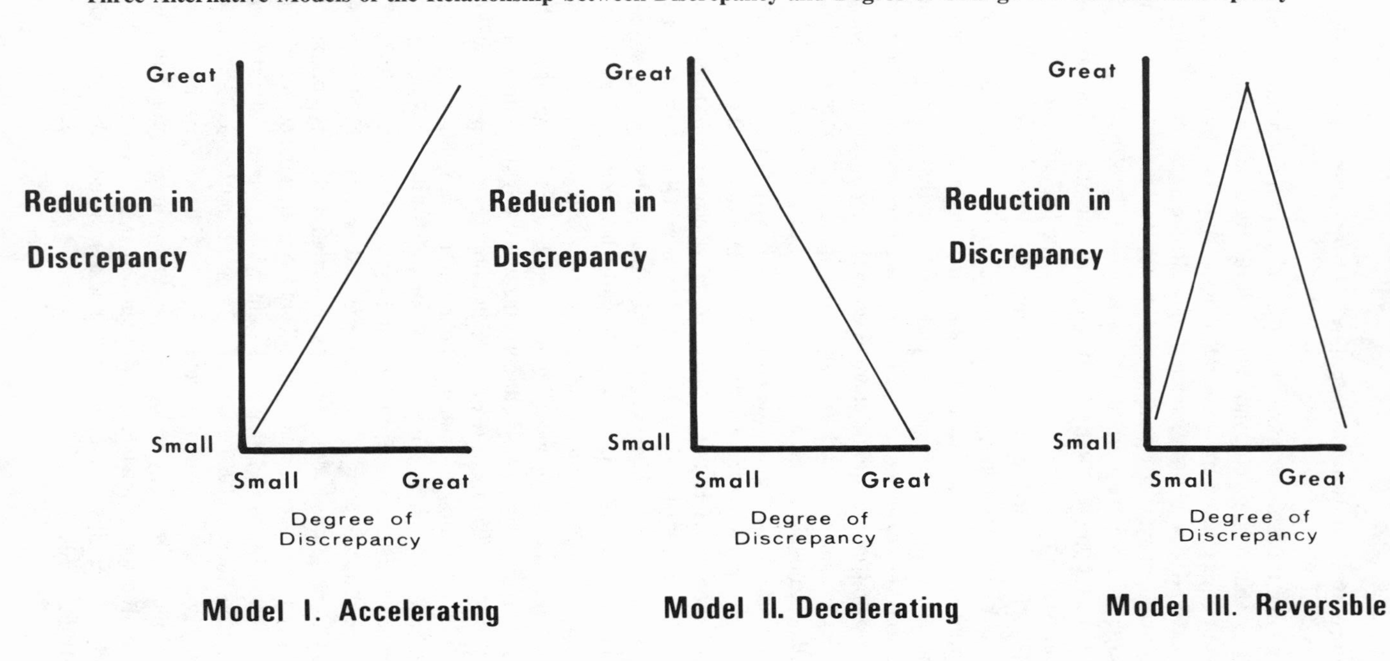

Model III in the figure above is perhaps dominant in OD theory (e.g., Bennis 1969; Harrison 1965). Model III, in effect, provides an accelerating effect for low-to-intermediate discrepancies, and adds to it decelerating change for intermediate-to-high discrepancies. To illustrate, in the case of choosing a suitable strength for a piece of significant feedback to an individual, too little may fail to get the message across, and too much may be so threatening to the target that the message is misheard or rejected. For example: the stimulus is an individual who sees self as mentally healthy but who persistently resorts to dramatic outpourings of language that describe a fearful fantasy. One could express a concern about this behavior with any of these three statements:

- Gee, you tell a good story.
- When you talk so long, and use such rich metaphors, it is hard for me to follow you. And I often don't know where you are going, even though I want to understand you.
- Pretty clearly, you are concerned about schizoid tendencies in yourself. You sound sick to me. You have real reason to be fearful.

In the context of Model III, the first alternative may be "too little" to encourage attention to the other's behavior, and the third alternative is almost always "too much."

OD Learning and Discrepancies: Individual Preferences and Organizational Climate

One particular discrepancy gets attention here—an "optimum prior discrepancy"—as does its association with the degree of learning or change attributed to an OD program. This optimum prior discrepancy refers to the most effective degree of difference for stimulating change, with the difference referring to the gap between what an individual says he would like his organization's climate or style to be, and how he perceives that climate *before* an OD experience. "Discrepancy" here has both attitudinal and behavioral components, in sum. In effect, the OD intervention in this case provides most participants with an experience that legitimates moving toward their preference as to organization climate, which is distinctly different from the climate they attribute to their real organization, in general. Directly, the OD intervention highlights this prior discrepancy while it also encourages skill practice with behaviors appropriate for more closely approaching the preferred climate. The key question is: How much prior discrepancy is optimum for learning?

Operationally Measuring Discrepancy

The present approach to measuring prior discrepancy uses respondent self-reports on the Likert (1967) Profile of Organizational Characteristics, form E.

For an overview of the profile and its features and uses, see also Likert's later work (1977). Form E consists of the twenty-four items that measure aspects of an organization's comprehensive climate or style, rated both as: *Now*, or the way the respondent sees his organization on each item, and *Ideal*, or the way the respondent would like his organization to be.

Differences between Ideal and Now ratings before the OD intervention provide the operational measure of prior discrepancy. Ideal scores measure personal preferences about organization climate, in sum, and Now scores measure actual organization conditions as perceived by the respondents.

The twenty-four Likert items are not reproduced here to conserve space, but they are intended to tap a broad phenomenal range. In capsule, seven basic organizational processes are said to be tapped by the profile items:

- Items 1 and 2 deal with leadership;
- Items 3–6 deal with motivation;
- Items 7–13 deal with the character of communication;
- Items 14–17 deal with interaction and influence;
- Items 17–20 deal with decision making;
- Item 21 deals with goal setting;
- Items 22–24 deal with the character of control.

The profile has another useful property. Each item is measured along a 20-point scale of equal-appearing intervals with four major segments, each of which is anchored by a brief descriptive statement. Likert conceives of these four segments as qualitatively different "systems of management," that is, as distinct managerial climates or styles. The systems are:

- System 1: Exploitative-authoritative (1–5 on the scale)
- System 2: Benevolent-authoritative (6–10 on the scale)
- System 3: Consultative (11–15 on the scale)
- System 4: Participative group (16–20 on the scale)

Systems 1 and 4 are taken to be the anti-goal and goal, respectively, of OD applications based on the laboratory approach. Almost all respondents saw their organization as too far removed from high-System 3 or System 4, toward which they desired to move.

Massive Team Building as the Goal

Overall, the OD design in this case intends to enhance movement of the climate or style of thirty-three regional sales units in the direction of Likert's System 4, the Participative Group System. In effect, the design has three purposes. First, it seeks to legitimate looking at possible discrepancies between individual preferences and organization style. Second, the design intends to make participants aware of actual discrepancies, where consciousness is lacking. Third, the design provides a model for reducing any discrepancies via a learning experience with appropriate values, attitudes, and behavioral skills.

The design lasted two days, and follow-up experiences were possible for individual units. This undermines a view of the team building as a one-shot effort. The data reported here were gathered before any region had a follow-up experience.

The details of the design have been elaborated elsewhere (Golembiewski 1979a, 132–33), consequently brief notice here will suffice. By intent, the design is of modest intensity and basically seeks to develop skills as well as attitudes consistent with OD values and especially regenerative interaction. Practice was also emphasized, with contagion effects being important in a large ballroom where learners were exposed to high-tech graphics and to one another's excitement. A team of six facilitators was available. Their help could be requested by any regional assemblage which raised a flag at their table. The design's motif was: Tell it like it is. This won no style points, but contributed to the sense of an elevated and up-tempo mood.

Each of the design's five major components takes a common approach to increasing the quantity and improving the quality of job-relevant feedback available to members of each region. Thus, brief cognitive inputs in large general sessions attempt to help participants organize their experiences as team members. The dual purposes are to aid participants in seeing themselves and others more clearly in job-relevant activities, and to begin building more effective and satisfying relations at work.

After each input, commonly, individual regions spent an hour or two applying the sense of each input to their relationships at work. For example, task and maintenance roles were introduced, and participants then were given lists of behaviors consistent with such roles and asked to identify specific team members whom they saw as having performed one or more of the behaviors attributed to each role type. These perceptions were shared, providing not only some experience with openness and cross-checking of perceptions, but also often indicating a deficit of maintenance behaviors that inspired action planning to remedy the deficit. Action planning appropriate for each region followed, as a scheduled event.

Analysis of the Results of Team Building

The present data are generated by a simple research design: Observation 1–OD intervention–Observation 2 in form, where Observation 1 is a pre-test with the Likert profile which preceded the OD intervention by a month, and

Observation 2 is a post-test which was administered approximately three months after the intervention. The four-month interval between the two administrations was a guesstimate about the length of time required for any attitudinal or behavioral changes to be tested in the regional units, whose members came together only episodically. This sought to focus on behavioral changes, as opposed to the good intentions that might well directly follow the OD experience but also might quickly evaporate back in the real world. Both administrations were by mail, sent from the firm but returned to the author's university address. For convenience, data from the first administration are identified as "Now 1" and "Ideal 1," or combinations thereof, and data from the second administration carry the labels "Now 2" and "Ideal 2."

Response rates. The response rate for salespersons falls somewhere between 75 and 85 percent, depending upon the denominator one chooses. At Day 1, that is, respondents numbered 430. Of these, 406 responded to the first Likert administration, and 341 to the second one some four months later. The sample here is the 329 salespersons who responded both times, or some 76 percent of the original 430. By Day 120, due to turnover, approximately 345 respondents remained. So the response rate could also be calculated at somewhat over 83 percent. In either case, no major sampling errors seem probable. Normal attrition accounts for about one-third of the difference between the numbers of respondents to the two administrations, but the bulk of the missing cases involve those who responded once but not twice.

Strategy for organizing data. Two major points suggest the range of alternatives for organizing the data, and they also sketch a rationale for the eventual comparisons. These comparisons involve individual respondents, the four Likert systems, and individual Likert items.

First, the level of analysis here is the individual respondent. In effect, this opts against analysis at two other levels: by the thirty-three regions, or by the individuals within regions.

Several factors motivate this compound choice. Paramountly, the issue of optimum discrepancies for change by individuals has been a major and continuing focus for research and speculation, as in the cognitive dissonance literature. We continue in this tradition by testing for a regularity between prior discrepancies reported by individuals and changes in their self-reports after an OD intervention. This choice also avoids well-known measurement and conceptual problems at the regional level of analysis. For example, convenient operations for estimating regional climate—much as averaging the self-reports of all members of a region—imply severe interpretive difficulties. If self-reports are equally weighted, as is usual, that may undervalue the reports of opinion leaders, hide significant individual differences in self-canceling aggregations, and so on. Finally, analysis at the individual level avoids a variety of troublesome statistical issues with unequal sample sizes and differential response rates in the thirty-three regions, as well as with the small numbers of salespersons per region.

Second, the analysis will focus on individual Likert items for each of the 329 respondents. In effect, this opts against two other possible ways of treating responses to the profile: using a total score based on each individual's response to all items, or aggregating each individual's responses in terms of the seven dimensions into which Likert subdivides the profile items.

The decision to focus on individual items reflects some difficult judgments. Thus, a principal components analysis strongly implies that it is not reasonable to view the Likert profile as having seven dimensions. Specifically, the first principal components of Now 1 and Now 2 scores account for 41.10 and 58.00 percent of the variance, respectively. (See table 3.1 for details.) If anything, given that the *lowest* item loading on the two first principal components for Now 1 and Now 2 scores is a substantial .53, table 3.1 provides more support for calculating one total Likert score than for distinguishing scores on seven dimensions. Support for such an approach also derives from the fact that aggregating items thought to tap a common phenomenal realm can increase reliability via the randomization of unique variance and the pooling of common variance.

Why focus on individual items, then, rather than on a total Likert score? Several reasons dominate. Although all twenty-four Likert items load substantially on a single principal component which accounts for over 40 percent of the variance in pre-test scores, it was deemed premature to conclude that the Likert scale therefore taps a single phenomenal domain. Moreover, the present approach in effect permits highlighting any unique variance between items, which is critical and lacking information for uses of the profile (Munzenrider 1976).

In sum, the comparisons below focus on three classes of targets: 329 respondents, four Likert systems, and twenty-four Likert items. If those comparisons yield a consistent and statistically significant pattern, that outcome is consistent with a dominant covariation of individual discrepancies and changes in self-reports about organization climate. Readers should be cautious in interpreting tables 3.2 and 3.3, however, because they clearly do not refer to tests of twenty-four separate phenomenal domains.

Trends in data. Table 3.2 provides some preliminary data about individual respondents and their self-reports, with this summary supporting three generalizations. First, 239 of the 329 respondents rate their region's Now 1 climate as System 1, 2, or 3, which implies that most individuals see their organization unit as falling short of OD ideals. The differences between the four clusters of Now 1 scores attain extremely high levels of statistical significance.

Second, Ideal 1 scores in table 3.2 indicate a very strong preference for

TABLE 3.1
Principal Component Analysis of Likert Scores, O_1 and O_2

Likert Item	Loadings on Principal Components: Likert Now 1 Scores				Likert Now 2 Scores		
1	.73	−.34	−.12	.01	.77	−.15	−.21
2	.66	−.45	−.16	−.05	.78	−.27	−.32
3	.63	−.14	−.32	.13	.75	.04	−.33
4	.64	.01	−.34	.03	.76	.10	−.08
5	.57	.27	.01	.17	.70	.11	.31
6	.66	−.13	−.26	.06	.78	−.08	−.01
7	.73	−.09	.11	−.05	.79	.00	.08
8	.69	−.22	−.10	−.01	.81	−.19	−.15
9	.65	−.08	.23	.36	.77	−.35	.20
10	.65	−.01	.32	.34	.70	−.44	.30
11	.53	−.14	.48	.39	.65	−.14	.52
12	.72	−.40	−.06	−.07	.83	−.06	−.32
13	.72	−.22	.09	−.05	.83	−.20	−.11
14	.72	.11	.14	.06	.77	−.06	.10
15	.68	.18	.09	−.14	.80	.12	−.09
16	.66	.04	.14	−.30	.75	.15	−.08
17	.53	.21	.35	−.51	.74	.10	.07
18	.66	.07	.30	−.24	.76	.14	.19
19	.73	.13	−.05	−.23	.83	.19	.02
20	.60	.09	−.19	−.10	.73	.19	−.07
21	.58	.33	−.23	.07	.70	.32	.08
22	.58	.51	−.13	.15	.73	.37	.13
23	.53	.53	−.15	.20	.73	.42	−.04
24	.64	.10	−.11	−.09	.78	−.06	−.01
Eigen root	10.10	1.49	1.16	1.03	13.92	1.11	1.00
Percent variance	41.10%	6.23	4.82	4.30	58.00%	4.61	4.17
Cumulative variance		48.33%	53.15	53.15		62.61%	66.78

mid-System 4, which is to say that respondents attitudinally prefer an organization climate consistent with the normative thrust of OD. Essentially, then, the challenge to the OD program was dual: convincing participants that they could safely behave in ways that approach their preferences as to organization climate, and providing them with sufficient skill-practice with appropriate attitudes and behaviors.

Third, respondents who initially rate their regions in System 1 have the highest prior-discrepancy scores by far, while System 4 respondents approximate a mean discrepancy of half-a-point. Row 4 in table 3.2 suggests this regularity (which column 5 in table 3.3 establishes more directly). Tests of the differences between the means of the discrepancy scores, classified in terms of the four Likert systems, achieve huge F-levels.

TABLE 3.2
Some Summary Data from Member Self-Reports about Climate of Regional Units as Measured by Likert Profile

	Initial Likert System of Management by Individual Respondent			
	System 1	System 2	System 3	System 4
(1) Average number of respondents rating their region on Now I as	12	63	164	90
(2) Mean Now 1 scores[a]	3.1	8.1	12.8	17.2
(3) Mean Ideal I scores[b]	16.5	16.5	17.4	17.6
(4) Mean discrepancy scores, or Ideal 1–Now 1[c]	13.4	8.4	4.6	0.4
(5) Mean Now 2 scores[d]	9.8	11.6	13.6	15.0
(6) Mean Now 2–Now 1 scores[e]	6.8	3.7	.8	−2.2

Notes: Overall F-values for rows 2–6 were statistically significant in all cases.

As is conventional when overall F-values are significant, each paired comparison in rows 2–6 was tested for statistical significance using Duncan's Multiple-Range test. The test permits comparisons of each of the six possible pairs of the four Likert Systems on each of the twenty-four items, or 144 comparisons in all for each row.

[a]All 144 possible pairs of differences far surpass the .01 level.

[b]Seventy of the 144 possible pairs of differences do not attain the .05 level. Fifty-one of the 72 comparisons involving only Systems 2, 3, and 4 do reach the .05 level.

[c]All 144 possible pairs of differences surpass the .05 level.

[d]126 of the 144 possible pairs of differences surpass the .05 level.

[e]132 of the 144 possible pairs of differences surpass the .05 level.

The Ideal 1–Now 1 discrepancies in table 3.2 (i.e., row 4) provide the takeoff point for the central concern of this article. Specifically, which model of change in figure 3.1 best accounts for the actual pattern of movement in Now 2 scores?

The accelerating model of discrepancy/change gets strong support from the data—in fact, it gets almost unqualified support. (See rows 4 and 6 in table 3.2, for general support.) As the mean discrepancy score decreases, in sum, so do respondents report less change in pre- versus post-intervention Likert self-reports. For the lowest prior-discrepancy scores, in fact, the mean change has a *negative* value.

Table 3.3 provides far more detail on the applicability of the accelerating model to the present data, via a breakdown by each of the twenty-four Likert items which establishes a pattern of massive consistency. Table 3.3 also reflects more sophisticated data treatment, an analysis of variance which—among other virtues—permits the use of covariance techniques to control for differences in the initial levels of prior discrepancies reported by individuals. That is, the two measures of post-intervention self-reports—Now 2 and Now 2–Now 1 scores—are adjusted for differences in the levels of Ideal 1–Now 1 discrepancies. The control is a vital procedure, assuring as it does that any post-intervention differences are not simply an artifact reflecting differences

TABLE 3.3
Size of Initial Discrepancy and Two Measures of Learning or Change

			Mean Scores, Classified by System					
	1	2	3	4	5	6	7	8
	Likert System	Number of respondents	Now 1	Now 2	Prior discrepancy, or Ideal 1–Now 1	Now 2–Now 1	F-ratios for differences in levels of Now 2 scores, adjusted by differences in Ideal 1–Now 1 discrepancies	F-ratios for differences in levels of Now 2–Now 1 scores, adjusted by differences in Ideal 1–Now 1 discrepancies
	1	7	3.1	6.0	12.9	2.9		
	2	38	8.0	12.4	8.2	4.4		
Item 1	3	154	12.8	14.3	4.3	1.5	23.88[b]	12.31[b]
	4	130	17.2	16.2	1.0	−1.0		
	1	7	2.9	6.4	15.0	3.5		
	2	55	8.0	11.0	11.1	3.0		
Item 2	3	168	12.7	14.5	5.1	1.8	12.89[b]	11.39[b]
	4	99	17.9	16.2	0.7	−1.7		
	1	37	3.5	9.3	13.3	5.8		
	2	120	8.2	10.9	8.6	2.7		
Item 3	3	137	12.6	12.6	4.4	0.0	5.04[b]	12.04[b]
	4	59	17.4	14.5	1.3	−2.7		
	1	4	3.5	10.2	13.5	6.8		
	2	51	8.2	12.3	7.2	4.1		
Item 4	3	215	12.8	13.5	4.4	0.7	5.01[b]	21.04[b]
	4	59	17.4	15.0	0.7	−2.4		

	1	4	3.5	10.2	13.5	6.8		
	2	51	8.2	12.3	7.2	4.1		
Item 5	3	215	12.8	13.5	4.4	0.7	2.50	20.32[b]
	4	59	17.4	15.0	0.7	−2.4		
	1	6	3.5	8.2	12.0	4.7		
	2	42	8.4	12.2	8.9	3.8		
Item 6	3	217	12.9	13.6	5.1	0.7	3.74[a]	19.34[b]
	4	64	17.0	15.0	2.0	−1.9		
	1	16	3.3	10.6	13.6	7.2		
	2	79	8.3	12.0	8.6	3.7		
Item 7	3	135	12.8	13.7	5.0	0.9	3.77[b]	10.70[b]
	4	99	16.9	15.3	1.7	−1.7		
	1	5	2.2	7.0	13.4	4.8		
	2	78	7.9	11.4	9.1	3.5		
Item 8	3	147	12.8	14.2	5.0	1.3	10.89[a]	9.93[a]
	4	99	17.3	15.4	1.4	−1.9		
	1	2	4.5	15.0	14.5	10.5		
	2	34	8.1	11.9	9.3	3.8		
Item 9	3	148	12.9	13.8	4.9	0.9	11.15[b]	8.31[b]
	4	145	17.1	15.7	1.7	−1.4		
	1	2	2.5	18.5	15.5	16.0		
	2	19	7.8	12.0	9.3	4.2		
Item 10	3	172	13.2	13.7	5.1	0.5	10.32[b]	15.50[b]
	4	136	17.3	15.4	1.3	−1.9		
	1	5	2.8	12.8	12.2	10.0		
	2	60	8.2	12.3	6.0	4.2		
Item 11	3	145	13.0	13.7	3.6	0.6	8.57[b]	25.83[b]
	4	119	17.3	14.9	1.0	−2.4		

TABLE 3.3 (Continued)
Size of Initial Discrepancy and Two Measures of Learning or Change

	Mean Scores, Classified by System							
	1	2	3	4	5	6	7	8
	1	17	3.4	7.1	11.2	3.6		
	2	72	8.2	11.2	6.1	3.0		
Item 12	3	141	12.8	13.3	3.4	0.5	22.55[b]	10.26[b]
	4	99	17.6	16.2	1.1	−1.4		
	1	6	3.0	11.5	13.7	8.5		
	2	43	8.3	10.7	8.0	2.3		
Item 13	3	177	12.8	13.2	4.4	0.4	12.74[b]	9.21[b]
	4	103	16.8	15.1	1.8	−1.7		
	1	5	2.4	11.6	16.0	9.2		
	2	37	8.2	11.4	8.9	8.9		
Item 14	3	164	12.7	13.9	5.2	1.1	10.1[b]	8.32[b]
	4	124	16.9	15.3	1.6	−1.6		
	1	18	3.8	10.1	12.8	6.3		
	2	92	8.1	12.3	7.5	4.3		
Item 15	3	150	13.0	12.8	3.7	−0.2	7.04[b]	13.36[b]
	4	69	17.1	14.7	0.6	−2.4		
	1	15	2.8	18.6	11.4	5.7		
	2	106	7.9	10.8	8.3	2.9		
Item 16	3	15	12.6	12.7	4.5	0.0	2.37	30.31[b]
	4	50	17.1	13.2	1.2	−4.6		
	1	9	2.7	11.8	15.3	9.1		
	2	68	8.3	11.2	9.3	2.9		
Item 17	3	199	12.8	13.1	5.0	0.3	5.37[b]	9.86[b]
	4	53	16.9	13.6	1.6	−3.3		

	1	26	3.2	9.0	14.5	6.1		
	2	91	8.1	11.3	9.4	3.2		
Item 18	3	145	12.4	12.5	5.6	0.1	4.21[b]	8.10[b]
	4	67	16.8	15.0	2.1	−1.9		
	1	16	3.2	8.7	14.1	5.5		
	2	70	7.8	11.7	9.2	3.9		
Item 19	3	183	12.5	12.9	4.9	0.4	4.15[b]	14.87[b]
	4	60	16.7	14.1	2.1	−2.7		
	1	19	2.1	7.1	14.4	5.0		
	2	81	7.2	11.4	9.1	4.3		
Item 20	3	137	11.9	13.2	5.9	1.2	11.2[b]	9.05[b]
	4	92	16.6	15.2	1.6	−1.5		
	1	6	1.8	3.8	12.2	2.0		
	2	43	8.0	11.9	7.2	3.8		
Item 21	3	213	12.9	13.8	3.7	0.9	25.33[b]	15.38[b]
	4	67	17.1	15.0	0.4	−2.1		
	1	7	1.9	8.4	15.1	6.6		
	2	52	8.1	12.1	8.6	4.0		
Item 22	3	156	12.7	13.4	4.6	0.7	3.06[b]	16.14[b]
	4	114	17.1	14.7	1.3	−2.4		
	1	23	2.9	9.2	10.9	6.3		
	2	108	8.1	10.6	7.1	2.5		
Item 23	3	148	12.7	13.0	3.5	0.3	6.90[b]	11.40[b]
	4	50	16.9	13.6	0.3	−3.3		
	1	17	5.3	9.8	14.0	7.5		
	2	59	7.8	11.9	9.0	4.1		
Item 24	3	165	12.7	13.4	4.6	0.7	5.20[b]	12.44[b]
	4	88	17.1	15.2	1.4	−1.9		

Notes [a] designates that P 〈 .05. $F_{.05} = 2.62$ for 3, 324 d.f. [b] designates that P 〈 .01. $F_{.01} = 3.85$ for 3, 324 d.f.

between the standards of individuals in designating their various levels of discrepancies. This approach permits substantial confidence in the results in table 3.3.

That the accelerating model also best accounts for discrepancy/change interaction in table 3.3 can be established by a two-stage analysis, the first stage of which suggests that prior discrepancy does not seem to be associated with learning or change. Consider columns 4 (Now 2) and 7 (F-values) in table 3.3. Note that twenty-two of the twenty-four differences between Now 2 means for the four Likert systems still achieve usually accepted levels of statistical significance, using analysis of covariance techniques whose F-ratios are reported in column 7. The OD intervention, in sum, did not eliminate the major differences in Now 1 scores.

Second, however, this suggestion of quite uniform change between T_1 and T_2 does not stand up to the acid test. Specifically, columns 6 and 8 in table 3.3 imply that the greater the initial discrepancy, the greater the relative change toward System 4. Indeed, the individuals who initially perceive their organization climates as being System 4 not only change the least in the expected direction, but on the average, they learn negatively, as it were. In sum, the apparent similarities in relative Now 1 and Now 2 scores hide more than they reveal.

The accelerating model of discrepancy/change in figure 3.1 applies to over 90 percent of the cases in column 6 and 8 of table 3.3, in sum. Two cases—Items 1 and 21—are deviant. They follow the reversible model in figure 3.1. All F-ratios for Now 2—Now 1 scores, as adjusted, far surpass usually accepted levels of statistical significance for all twenty-four items. That is to say, all twenty-two cases fitting the accelerating model reflect statistically significant between- versus within-variance for the four Likert systems. The two cases of the reversible model also attain statistical significance. Consistently, although autocorrelation effects are possible, average $r = .46$ for Now 2–Now 1 scores and Ideal 1–Now 1 scores on the twenty-four Likert items.

Greater Success by Specifying a Learning Model

The data above generate a number of implications which, if necessarily tentative, touch profound concerns in OD programs as well as in such areas as budgeting and advertising. Clearly the determination of an optimum discrepancy will affect the answers to two questions:

- What implications for enhanced OD success rates do the present data suggest?
- Can the literature help us test the present perspective on a learning model featuring discrepancies?

Direct Implications for Enhanced Success

Under this first heading, four points get attention. They all relate to the probability of greater success in OD efforts that specify in detail the properties of their learning theory, and derive from the results just presented.

Most dramatically, first, the data urge major attention to the tailoring of OD designs to the characteristics of change targets. This does not outrage common sense, and it also gets support from research resting on different designs and methodologies (e.g., most prominently, Bowers and Hausser 1977) as well as from emerging prescriptive formulations (Bowers, Franklin, and Pecorella 1975). The above data imply that the prior discrepancies between perceived and ideal organization climate are massive covariants of change.

What do the present results imply for designing OD interventions? Only illustrations are possible here, but they can help. For example, high discrepancies might well respond to different kinds of designs than low discrepancies. In the latter case, for example, the primary goal might focus on raising expectations about what can be aspired to—a kind of consciousness raising about ideals that are not so lofty as to make them seem like pie-in-the-sky, by-and-by. Various "visioning" designs seem applicable in such cases (e.g., Lindaman and Lippitt 1979), as do activities focusing on developing a broad "culture statement" or a "mission statement" at an operational level (e.g., Walton and Hackman 1986).

For organizations whose members have high prior discrepancies, on the other hand, the primary focus would be on raising the perceived or actual level of functioning. A broad range of conventional designs seems applicable here. For example, preparing and sharing three-dimensional images (Golembiewski 1979a, 318–23) seems to have high success rates in alerting persons to unsatisfactory relations or conditions between superior and subordinates or between work units, depending upon the target to which the design is applied. Role negotiation designs have a similar impact on actual or perceived functioning, with real but subsidiary effects on the ideal (e.g., Harrison 1972).

The data above imply the usefulness—if not the necessity—of making constructive response in OD designs to differences in ideal/actual discrepancies. Consider the post-design regression in Likert scores reported by the average low-discrepancy respondent. What causes that major trend? One might argue that the OD design simply worsened the objective situation for the low-discrepancy respondents. That certainly would account for the trend. But other plausible explanations also demand attention. Perhaps low-discrepancy respondents were biased in their original perceptions. In this case, the public team-building design would have impressed on them the unrealism of their initial assessments of their units' climate. This is a benign effect, as effects go, and probably beneficial. But it does suggest that separate subdesigns might have to be developed for those whose prior discrepancies are low.

Other possibilities similarly encourage reliance on two-stage learning designs. For example, "social desirability" (Crowne and Marlow 1964) might be related to the reporting of low prior discrepancies, with some persons having a strong tendency to see and report what is socially acceptable or desirable, as contrasted with what exists. Available evidence shows such an effect (e.g., Golembiewski and Munzenrider 1975), and this encourages more intensive diagnosis in the pre-intervention phases of OD applications. See also Irony III below, which deals with the impact on OD success rates of differentiating people and their properties. A two-stage design in the case of high social desirability would first focus on sensitizing people to their sunny bias, and then perhaps on moderating that bias. Conventional confrontation designs seem to have both effects (e.g., Golembiewski 1983), and these effects also have been associated with T-groups or sensitivity training (e.g., Golembiewski 1972, 252–71). The second stage would then rely on this preparation to enhance operational problem solving.

Whatever the case, the next step is patent. Research using different OD designs for individuals and groups at different takeoff points is indicated. For example, low-discrepancy respondents might profit from a more impactful design than the present one. Or perhaps it is better to leave well enough alone, as when respondents report that relationships in their organization are more or less where they prefer them to be.

The second implication for enhanced success derives from the suggestion in the data that prior discrepancy is directly associated with the change or learning in the present design. Qualifications, however, are appropriate. Thus, a more impactful design—such as a week-long family T-group—might generate a different pattern of change or learning. It is credible, for example, that a high-impact design might threaten high-discrepancy respondents so as to inhibit or preclude attitudinal behavioral change. On the other hand, even the largest discrepancies in the present data batch may not have been big enough to trigger effects more consistent with Models II and, especially, III. Fortunately, this hypothesis not only needs attention but is researchable. The sparse evidence available (e.g., Golembiewski 1970, esp. 23–34) does not permit unqualified interpretation, but it implies that the accelerating model also best explains the effects of even more impactful interventions than are focal here.

Third, as is the case with all research reporting changes in extreme scores, it is possible that the data above reflect correlation effects, or regression toward the mean (Campbell 1963). Table 3.3 in part controls for such effects by adjusting both Now 2 and Now 2–Now 1 scores for differences in prior discrepancies, but such statistical manipulations clearly do not eliminate the alternative hypothesis that correlation effects are more operative than experimental effects.

Fourth, most OD intervenors probably tend to favor Model III, or the reversible model. So the present results may surprise. Indeed, they may hold only for measures like the Likert Profile. Some measures of prior discrepancy are open ended, as it were, and beyond some point escalating differences between anchor and stimulus might lose credibility or even become grotesque. In such cases, Model II might not apply. Hitler's "big lie" technique would not work, in short. His advice was that—if one is going to tell a lie with the intent of changing someone's behavior—one should tell the biggest whopper conceivable.

Theoretical Leads Toward Enhanced Success

The present research design has significant limitations, but the literature also contains some directions for improving the reach and grasp of the search for an optimum discrepancy, if one exists. In short, the results above may motivate research on a broader range of possible models, and in the long run that will lead to greater success in OD applications. Thus enlarged, the conceptual range of discrepancies will relate to crucial aspects of choice and change: for example, to fitting OD designs to existing conditions, to determining the kind and intensity of feedback appropriate for eliciting hearing and learning, and so on.

Model I: greater discrepancy, greater change. What does the literature tell us about optimum discrepancies for inducing learning or change, beyond the results and the trio of models depicted in figure 3.1? To review, Model I is no doubt the most popular view. Basically, it predicts that the greater the discrepancy between a stimulus and an individual's internal anchors, the greater the probable change in attitudes and opinions so as to reduce that discrepancy. The tension induced by discrepancy acts as a motivator, propose such syntheses as Festinger's theory of cognitive dissonance. As he notes: "the discrepant reality which impinges on a person will exert pressures in the direction of bringing the appropriate cognitive elements into correspondence with that reality. . . . The strength of the pressures to reduce the dissonance is a function of the magnitude of dissonance" (1957, 18).

Native cunning raises strong questions about Model I, however, and this encourages putting the results above in a special perspective. In OD terms, for example, Model I may not provide an optimum discrepancy under degenerative interaction—where risk is high, as well as where openness, owning, and trust are low. The OD learning design in the present case may have faced only a mildly degenerative system, to put it directly. Hence the results above favoring Model I may not apply universally, but only to the special environments where OD values already exist or can be vivified easily.

Model II: greater discrepancy, lesser change. To continue the review, Model II proposes a stark alternative. This view gets no prominent theoretical support, but practice is another matter. Many of us act this way, much of the time, as in tethering short our feedback to others. The underlying expectation is that people can bring massive forces to bear to fend off even incisive thunderbolts of feedback—as by denial, misinterpretation, or whatever. So the common guide often is: Easy as she goes.

In sum, one can argue that Model II is more appropriate for degenerative conditions—that is, for what often exists in relationships between individuals and groups. Under regenerative interaction, in contrast, Model II might provide an overcautious and tiptoeing guide for discrepancies.

Model III: reversible when ego involvement varies. To complete the review of figure 3.1, Model III encourages introducing an intervening variable in the progression from discrepancy to change linkages—"ego involvement," or the condition when a person feels strongly about an issue that is seen as a central one.

Two conditions can be envisioned. When ego involvement is low, Model I obtains. That is, the reasonable course of least resistance is for an individual to move attitudinally toward the discrepant stimulus or to perceive it as less discrepant than it is. In sum:

	Discrepancy		**Probable Effect**		**Change Toward Discrepant Stimulus**
Low Ego	(1) Small	→	Assimilation	→	Small
Involvement	(2) Great	→	Assimilation	→	Great

When ego involvement is high, however, different dynamics may be expected. For example, beyond some point, growing discrepancies may induce high ego involvement—that is, "That's outrageous; I can't accept that." Or ego involvement may be high for some other reason. In either case:

	Discrepancy		**Probable Effect**		**Change Toward Discrepant Stimulus**
High Ego	(3) Small	→	Assimilation	→	Great
Involvement	(4) Great	→	Contrast	→	Small

That is, increases in discrepancy will generate increasing change only up to a point, some students propose. As Whittaker explains: "Small discrepancies

References

Bennis, W. G. 1969. *Organization Development*. Reading, Mass.: Addison-Wesley.

Bowers, D. G. 1973. "OD Techniques and Their Results in 23 Organizations: The Michigan ICL Study." *Journal of Applied Behavioral Science* 9:21–43.

Bowers, D. G., and Hausser, D. L. 1977. "Work Group Types and Intervention Effects in Organizational Development." *Administrative Science Quarterly* 22:76–94.

Bowers, D. G.; Franklin, J. L.; and Pecorella, P. A. 1975. "Matching Problems, Precursors, and Interventions in OD." *Journal of Applied Behavioral Science* 11:391–410.

Campbell, T. 1963. "From Description to Experimentation." In *Problems in Measuring Change*, edited by C. W. Harris, 212–42. Madison, Wis.: University of Wisconsin Press.

Crowne, D. P., and Marlow, D. 1964. *The Approval Motive*. New York: Wiley.

Festinger, L. 1957. *A Theory of Cognitive Dissonance*. Evanston, Ill.: Row, Peterson.

Golembiewski, R. T. 1970. "Organizational Properties and Managerial Learning." *Academy of Management Journal* 13:13–31.

______. 1972. *Renewing Organizations*. Itasca, Ill.: F. E. Peacock.

______. 1979a. *Approaches to Planned Change: Orienting Perspectives and Micro-Level Interventions*. New York: Marcel Dekker.

______. 1979b. *Approaches to Planned Change: Macro-Level Interventions and Change-Agent Strategies*. New York: Marcel Dekker.

______. 1983. "Social Desirability and Change in Organizations." *Review of Business and Economic Research* 18:9–20.

Golembiewski, R. T., and Munzenrider, R. 1975. "Social Desirability as an Intervening Variable in Interpreting OD Effects." *Journal of Applied Behavioral Science* 11:317–32.

Harrison, R. 1965. "Group Composition Models for Laboratory Design." *Journal of Applied Behavioral Science* 1:409–32.

______. 1972. "Role Negotiation." In *The Social Technology of Organization Development*, edited by W. W. Burke and H. Hornstein, 84–96. Washington, D.C.: NTL Learning Resources.

Heider, F. 1958. *The Psychology of Interpersonal Relations*. New York: Wiley.

Likert, R. 1967. *The Human Organization*. New York: McGraw-Hill.

______. 1977. "Past and Future Perspectives on System 4." Paper presented at Annual Meeting, Academy of Management, 16 August 1977.

Lindaman, E., and Lippitt, R. 1979. *Choosing the Future You Prefer*. Washington, D.C.: Development Associates.

Munzenrider, R. 1976. *Organization Climates*. Ph.D. diss. University of Georgia, Athens, Ga.

Pasmore, W. A. 1976. "The Michigan ICL Study Revisited: An Alternative Explanation of Results." *Journal of Applied Behavioral Science* 12:245–51.

Pasmore, W. A., and King, D. C. 1978. "Understanding Organizational Change." *Journal of Applied Behavioral Science* 14:455–65.

Sherif, M., and Sherif, C. eds. 1967. *Attitude, Ego-involvement and Change*. New York: Wiley.

Torbert, W. R. 1973. "Some Questions on Bowers' Study of Different OD Techniques." *Journal of Applied Behavioral Science* 9:668–71.

Walton, R. E., and Hackman, J. R. 1986. "Groups under Contrasting Management

Strategies." In *Designing Effective Work Groups*, edited by P. S. Goodman et al., 168–201. San Francisco: Jossey-Bass.

Whittaker, J. O. 1967. "Resolution of the Communication Discrepancy." In *Attitude, Ego-involvement and Change*, edited by M. Sherif and C. Sherif.

Irony III

Relative Success without Differentiating People

4

One Person, One Vote: Performance Appraisals and Survey/Feedback Results

Survey/feedback may not be the general design of choice in efforts to develop large systems that are more efficient and effective, more productive, and more humane. But it comes as close to that status as any design. Not only have substantial success rates been reported, but the design seems to have been more potent than a number of historically favored designs such as the use of interpersonal process analysis or T-grouping (e.g., Bowers 1973 a and b). And a spate of how-to books clearly signals the arrival of survey/feedback (e.g., Bowers and Franklin 1977; Golembiewski and Hilles 1979; Nadler 1977).

This burgeoning status disguises but does not eliminate Irony III: that the relative success of survey/feedback designs has been achieved without specifying important differences between people. Generally, little attention has been directed to the conditions under which specific versions of that design are indicated and contraindicated, or to how survey results can be interpreted with greater fidelity and insight by distinguishing between respondents.

How to do better? This chapter deals with one narrow but significant issue in interpreting survey results—specifically, the usefulness of differentiating responses in terms of the performance appraisals of respondents. Empirically, a large subpopulation (1,474 respondents), classified into three different categories by performance appraisals, was surveyed for differences of opinion on fifty-three variables.

These words may scan easily, but do not neglect their uniqueness and even the temptation (if not the danger) that they pose. Unreflectively but nonetheless decisively, a "one person, one vote" assumption commonly guides interpretations of survey results. In contrast, specifying performance appraisals here proves useful not only in distinguishing clusters of significantly different responses, but also in suggesting *where and whether* ameliorative action seems appropriate.

And what of the temptation (if not the danger) in this chapter? Normative and ethical considerations help explain the common acceptance of the one person, one vote assumption in survey/feedback designs. These considerations urge caution in whether and how to differentiate survey respondents in terms of such factors as differences in performance appraisals. In short, knowledge can hurt the careless or uninformed.

A Conceptual Context for Irony III

The long-substantial and now-burgeoning reliance on survey/feedback in OD (French and Bell 1973, 25-29) has not generated a corresponding concern with when and how that design is most useful.[1] Bowers's (1973a) mammoth comparison of several standard OD designs in many organizations exemplifies the state of the literature. His results suggest the special potency of survey/feedback interventions, but caution seems appropriate. Bowers's research has generated much critical comment (Torbert 1973; Pasmore 1976); serious methodological questions can be raised as to whether the results have any presently interpretable meaning (Golembiewski, Billingsley, and Yeager 1976); and Bowers himself (1973a, 41-42) guesses that important intervening variables determine when (for example) laboratory training is more appropriate than survey/feedback, despite the huge advantage his data accord the latter design.

The common assumption that a respondent is a respondent constitutes perhaps the greatest point of unspecificity in survey/feedback designs. To be sure, survey respondents often will be differentiated in terms of various demographics: age, race, sex, organization unit, and so on. Beyond these categoric variables, however, survey/feedback interventions basically reflect a behavioral-science version of one person, one vote. Whether the issue is assessing an organization's climate or evaluating employee acceptance of some practice or policy, far more rather than less, a survey respondent is a survey respondent.

Ideology reinforces the analytic convenience of the assumption that respondent A is equal to respondent B, and this easy coupling helps explain why the assumption has been so little challenged as well as why it will be difficult to supplant. Like the U.S. Supreme Court's prevailing political philosophy—one person, one vote—the OD version rests on democratic, even populist, values. Or perhaps better said, OD values imply populist predispositions liberally amalgamated with elitist tendencies. The latter derive from the OD technocracy, as well as from the power-wielders who commonly sponsor applications of the technology. This metaphysical pathos, in Gouldner's (1955) sense, powerfully reinforces analytic convenience and the tendency to let well-enough alone.

Albeit little tested and difficult to analyze, the one person, one vote assumption seems to rest on shaky empirical foundations. Admittedly sparse empirical evidence as well as common sense imply that such unspecificity regarding survey/feedback interventions cannot be tolerated over the long run. For example, one study demonstrates that people who differ in basic personality predispositions will report seeing different aspects of reality (Golembiewski and Munzenrider 1974). Survey results, in short, tell us something about the respondent as well as about the stimulus reality. Interpretation of survey results consequently will be chancy in the absence of knowledge about differences between the specific persons who provide the data.

This chapter tests this conclusion by assessing differences across a broad range of indicators between survey respondents who differ in their performance appraisals. Despite their problems (McGregor 1960, esp. 77–89), performance appraisals do stand as a major tangible expression of the organizational value placed on specific individuals. This significant fact motivates the test here of differences in appraisals, of how they may influence responses to surveys, and interpretations of results vary with differences between people.

This effort implies numerous questions—empirical and normative, ethical and practical. Empirically, it will be possible to test whether employees with high versus low appraisals differ significantly on a wide range of attitudinal scales and items. Where such empirical differences exist, important ethical issues with serious practical implications must be addressed. For example, what should be done if survey research reveals a major problem, but major only to those with low appraisals? Most survey/feedback designs finesse such questions because the designs do not make distinctions between respondents—e.g., as high versus low distinctions on performance appraisals.

But on to an empirical analysis. We will return later to the normative issues that empirical analysis will stimulate.

Research Design

This study focuses on differences in the performance-appraisal ratings of 1,474 respondents to a broad QWL survey, whose data come from all hierarchical levels and major functions in a soft-goods firm.[2] In all cases, the appraisal closest in time to the date of the QWL survey was coded for each individual. Matches of specific appraisals to QWL respondents proceeded in absolute isolation from company officials. To scotch suspicion that the linking of survey and appraisal data might be used punitively, in addition, appraisal data were not made available to the researcher until eighteen months after the QWL survey.

Officials of the host organization much preferred rigidly safeguarded anonymity for individual respondents. They agreed only with great reluctance to a complicated provision whereby willing respondents could identify them-

TABLE 4.1
Data about Appraisals in Study Population

Firm's Appraisal Category	N	%	Study's Appraisal Categories
Exceptional	103	6.95	1 = Superior
Excellent	1,046	71.00	2 = Modal
Good	251	17.00	
Acceptable	67	4.55	3 = Sub-Modal
Unacceptable	7	0.50	
	1,474	100.00%	

selves to the consultant/ researcher while their identity was withheld from the employing organization, within which the coding and keypunching were done.[3] This convention permitted basic research without contaminating the survey results of interest to the client.

Performance Appraisal Classes

The firm used five appraisal rankings, but these are collapsed for present purposes into three categories. (See table 4.1 for details.) Basically, a Good appraisal or worse in this firm seriously affects employees, as in the length of the period they must wait for a normal salary review as well as in the maximum percentage salary increase available to them. The details would be burdensome, but they massively reinforce the decision here to classify a Good appraisal or worse as Sub-Modal. Exceptional and Excellent appraisal ratings were tapped as Superior and Modal, respectively.

The distribution of appraisals in table 4.1 closely corresponds to organizational practice in recent years. Approximately 80 percent of all ratings awarded have been Exceptional or Excellent, with about 70 percent in the latter category. This compares with 77.95 and 71 percent, respectively, in the present subpopulation of 1,474. More specific comparisons—such as those distinguishing major operating centers—also support this conclusion.

Four Kinds of Comparisons

The three appraisal categories are used to distinguish subgroups of respondents on four clusters of measures. These clusters include fifty-three variables, distributed in the following ways:

- Three bottom-line measures of employee perceptions of the firm
- Seventeen multi-item scales dealing with a range of managerially relevant variables
- Twelve single items referring to various management practices
- Single-item evaluations of twenty-one benefits, programs, and practices in the firm

Each cluster of measures is treated similarly. F-ratios test for significant overall variance between the three appraisal categories on each measure. Where significant overall variance exists, statistically significant differences between all possible pairs of appraisal categories are isolated using the modified Least Significant Differences (LSD) procedure. This procedure has the virtue of providing an exact value when sizes of cells are unequal (Nie et al. 1975, 427–28), the condition that obviously exists here. The overall F-ratios might detect nonrandom differences, of course, while the LSD test fails to isolate any statistically significant pairs of differences. Hence, the LSD procedure provides the definitive test of the magnitude and regularity of covariation between differences in performance appraisal and the fifty-three target variables.

Differences on three bottom-line measures. The three items shown in table 4.2 are considered to tap important employee perceptions of their firm and imply that differences in performance appraisals can enrich analysis. Table 4.2 shows that the average employee in each appraisal subgroup similarly perceives the firm as "among the best" places to work ($\bar{X}$ approximates 2.0 on a 7-point scale); and employees in each appraisal subgroup generally expect long tenure in the firm ($\bar{X} = 1.5$ on a 5-point scale, where 1 = "until retirement" and 2 = "more than 5 years"). Significant differences do show up on the item providing an overall evaluation of the quality of management now versus three years ago, at which time a significant management change occurred. Sub-Modals provide the lowest evaluation (3.1), but even that average score implies that management is "about the same." The mean (2.4) for employees with Superior appraisals, in comparison, approaches the next verbal anchor for respondents, which is that management got "better" over the three-year interval.

Single-item measures imply interpretive problems but, with that caution in mind, does specifying differences in performance appraisals enrich the analysis of the three bottom-line measures? The answer seems affirmative. Without that specification, the data in table 4.2 imply only that the firm is a good place to work, pretty much as all employees see it. This may be comforting news, but it seems misleading in at least one major particular: when appraisal differences are specified, the responses of Sub-Modals suggest that even their poor appraisal experiences have not proved alienating, at least at a gross level.

This may be welcome news for some managements, but this good news suggests one major potential point of unreality. Even employees with the poorest performance appraisals *expect* to remain with the firm for long periods, in most cases until retirement. This suggests a number of potentially serious issues, centering around the probability that any tightening of performance appraisals in future will be seen as violating widely (but perhaps not wisely) held expectations. As the business grows more complicated, profit

TABLE 4.2
Differences in Appraisals and Three Bottom-Line Measures of Employee Attitudes toward Firm

	Item Means, Classified by Appraisal Category				Test for Significance of Differences between Pairs of Means (where √ designates a difference achieving .05 level by modified LSD procedure)		
	1 Superior	2 Modal	3 Sub-Modal	Overall F-Probability	1 vs. 2	1 vs. 3	2 vs. 3
How firm rates as a place to work?	2.0	2.1	2.1	.898			
Firm management better now than three years ago?	2.4	2.9	3.1	<.000	√	√	√
Years employee expects to work for firm?	1.5	1.6	1.5	.650			

margins shrink and competition increases; that is, satisfactory performance today might be seriously inadequate tomorrow.

The storm clouds were clearly on the horizon at the time of the research, and major personnel actions in the firm were taken somewhat later. Generally, the firm moved its basic emphasis from loyalty toward competence. Sub-Modals may have been poorly prepared for this outcome, the enriched survey data suggest, despite having received some clues that boded no particular good for their careers in the firm.

In sum, specifying differences in appraisals raises a warning not apparent in the overall results. In fact, the overall results encourage a too-sanguine interpretation of the responses on this first cluster of three items. The warning signal takes on added significance because of management's special interest in the three bottom-line measures in table 4.2.

Differences on seventeen managerially relevant scales. Differences in appraisals become even more salient in analyses of the seventeen managerially-relevant scales shown in table 4.3. That is, despite suggestions in table 4.2 that Sub-Modals have not been grossly alienated by their appraisal experience, impressive evidence suggests that they clearly differ in major particulars from those with Superior and Modal appraisals. Specifically, this study focuses on seventeen scales:

- The eighteen-item scale Job Descriptive Index (JDI)-Work (Smith, Kendall, and Hulin 1969).
- The eighteen-item scale JDI-Supervision (Smith, Kendall, and Hulin 1969)
- The eighteen-item scale JDI-Coworkers (Smith, Kendall, and Hulin 1969)
- The nine-item scale JDI-Promotions (Smith, Kendall, and Hulin 1969)
- The nine-item scale JDI-Pay (Smith, Kendall, and Hulin 1969)
- The seventy-two-item JDI-Total (Smith, Kendall, Hulin 1969)
- A set of fourteen items tapping Efficacy of Upward Communication (Roberts and O'Reilly 1974)
- A two-item measure of Upward Mobility (Roberts and O'Reilly 1974)
- A measure of Supervisory Influence (Roberts and O'Reilly 1974)
- A three-item measure of Trust and Confidence in Immediate Supervisor (Trust I on table 4.3) (Roberts and O'Reilly 1974)
- A five-item measure of Composite Trust and Confidence in All Levels of Supervision (Trust II on table 4.3)
- A five-item scale tapping Participation in Decision Making (White and Ruh 1973)
- A nine-item scale measuring Job Involvement (White and Ruh 1973)
- A five-item scale tapping Motivation to Do the Job (White and Ruh 1973)
- A two-item scale measuring Identification with Firm (White and Ruh 1973)
- A four-item measure of Willingness to Disagree with Supervisor (Patchen 1965, 48–51)

- A fourteen-item measure of Job-Related Tension (Kahn, et al. 1964, 424–25)

Patterns in this panel of measures will be consequential, for the measures seem both sound and significant. Confidence in the instruments seems well placed, to begin. Alpha coefficients for each scale are given in table 4.3. Except in three cases, those coefficients reach levels that permit optimism that the scales deal with significant dimensions of reality. Moreover, sometimes-voluminous research testifies to the validity and reliability of most of the scales. Hence, any consistent pattern of results on these seventeen scales must be taken seriously.

Several technical notes usefully precede discussion of the data. The scales are so coded that, in all but two cases, high scores imply more of the attitude/behavior in question than low scores. The two Trust scales have reversed scores. Note that the direction of questionnaire items was often varied to inhibit response set.

The pattern of variation between the seventeen scales and appraisal differences is almost monolithic. Table 4.3 reveals statistically significant overall variation between appraisal categories on fourteen of the seventeen scales, with random differences existing only for JDI-Promotions, Upward Communication, and Identification with Firm. Promotion was a major problem throughout the firm, due to its growth history, which may explain why those in all performance appraisal categories see it in approximately the same light. The other two deviant scales have low alpha coefficients, so table 4.3 may reflect only technical problems in those cases.

The differences are regular as well as robust, moreover, and send a clear and constant message. Those with Superior appraisals have the most positive profile, with the Sub-Modals reflecting the least positive profile. Specifically, nonrandom differences exist between twenty-eight of the forty-two possible pairs, or nearly 67 percent of the cases. This suggests formidable differences.

Table 4.3 poses no interpretive puzzle, then. Sub-Modals see their environment as being significantly less attractive. For example, those with Sub-Modal appraisals report less satisfaction on five of the six JDI dimensions; they are lowest on Trust, Motivation, Involvement, Participation, and so on. Sub-Modals also rate their immediate supervisors as highest on Influence, while being least inclined to Disagree with Supervisor. These suggest a reasonable reaction to the low appraisal of the Sub-Modals, in which their immediate supervisors played the most prominent role.

Table 4.3 is mute on some important questions, patently. That table obviously does not reveal whether the low appraisals lead to the negative attitudes, for example, or whether the low appraisal is more of a dependent variable. Perhaps the relationship is interactive, but causality cannot be inferred.

TABLE 4.3
Differences in Appraisals and Seventeen Managerially Relevant Scales

	Means, Classified by Appraisal Category					Test for Significance of Differences between Pairs of Means (where √ designates a difference achieving .05 level by modified LSD procedure)		
	Alpha Coefficient	Superior	Modal	Sub-Modal	F-Probability	1 vs. 2	1 vs. 3	2 vs. 3
JDI-work	.8056	38.5	36.7	34.0	<.000		√	√
JDI-supervision	.8705	45.8	42.8	40.7	<.000	√	√	√
JDI-coworkers	.8889	42.5	41.8	40.2	.046			
JDI-promotions	.9000	13.2	12.4	12.4	.448			
JDI-pay	.7786	19.5	18.1	16.8	<.000		√	√
JDI-total	.9239	190.3	180.3	170.6	<.000	√	√	√
Efficacy of Upward communication	.5723	12.8	13.3	13.7	.269			
Upward mobility	.8660	9.3	10.3	9.5	<.000			
Supervisory influence	.6866	6.6	7.2	7.7	.038		√	
Trust I (R)[a]	.8551	4.6	6.2	7.4	<.000	√	√	√
Trust II (R)[a]	.7459	6.7	7.7	8.2	.001	√	√	√
Participation in decision making	.7932	14.7	13.4	11.7	<.000	√	√	√
Job involvement	.8237	26.7	25.9	24.2	<.000		√	√
Motivation	.5897	18.8	18.2	17.7	<.000	√	√	√
Identification with firm	.5985	6.7	6.5	6.5	.351			
Willingness to disagree with supervisor	.6685	12.2	11.9	10.2	<.000		√	√
Job-related tension	.8153	16.5	18.3	17.9	.044	√		

Note: [a]R designates a reversed score; i.e., a high Trust I or Trust II score indicates low trust.

No doubt exists, however, about whether the relationship is marked and regular. It makes a major difference which employees provide self-reports on the present seventeen scales. Differences in performance appraisals co-vary significantly and regularly, on definite balance, with how employees see their worksite.

Knowledge of this pattern of variance could be important, even critical, in influencing possible managerial responses to the survey data. For example, efforts to do something about promotion procedures and policies could be motivated by the fact that they pose problems for all employees, regardless of their appraisal, judging from JDI-Promotions as well as from much confirming survey evidence not reviewed here.

Conversely, a proposal to "increase participation" would get a longer look. Those with Superior and Modal appraisals already score high on participation, that is, relative to both Sub-Modals as well as with respect to the highest possible score on the scale. To increase participation for Sub-Modals, moreover, might be constrained by their lower Job Involvement, Motivation, and Willingness to Disagree with Supervisor, as well as by higher Job-Related Tension. Efforts to increase participation, that is to say, might be reasonable only after some success in increasing (for example) one's willingness to disagree with supervisors. There may even be a darker reality. Prior improvements in appraisal ratings might be required.

Differences on twelve management practices. Differences in performance appraisals also seem to co-vary significantly with the twelve single-item measures of various management practices shown in table 4.4, which provides details. Except for the first variable, for which the table provides the response stems, all other items utilize a 5-point scale: (1) Strongly Agree, (2) Agree, (3) Not Sure, (4) Disagree, and (5) Strongly Disagree.

Table 4.4 reflects a dominant pattern. Significant covariation exists on ten of the twelve items. Moreover, for the thirty pairs of comparisons between appraisal categories involving the ten items whose overall variation is almost certainly not random, eighteen pairs (or 60 percent) achieve statistical significance.

To be sure, the reliance on single-item measures does not permit certainty about the multidimensionality of the phenomena tapped by table 4.4. Whether those single items measure twelve dimensions, or one dimension twelve times, however, appraisal differences clearly must be accorded major potency. (Note that the discussion of table 4.5 employs factor analysis to illustrate how the dimensionality issue can be dealt with in the present data. A similar analysis was performed on items in table 4.4, but is not reprinted here to conserve space and because table 4.5 presents more interesting problems.)

Specifying appraisal categories for such management practices as those in table 4.4 can serve at least three purposes in tailoring responses to the data

TABLE 4.4
Differences in Appraisals and Twelve Management Practices, Classified by Appraisal Category Item Means

	1 Superior	2 Modal	3 Sub-Modal	Overall F-Probability	Test for Significance of Differences between Pairs of Means (where √ designates a difference achieving .05 level by modified LSD procedure) 1 vs. 2	1 vs. 3	2 vs. 3
Dominant supervisory mode:							
1. Primarily reward							
2. Mostly reward							
3. Reward and punishment	1.7	2.1	2.2	.002	√	√	
4. Mostly punishment							
5. Primarily punishment							
Managers insist on high standards	1.7	1.8	1.7	.870			
Management creates crisis atmosphere	2.9	2.8	2.9	.540			
Last merit pay increase left employee dissatisfied	3.9	3.5	3.1	⟨.000	√	√	√
Management standards are consistent	2.6	2.8	2.7	.025			
Satisfaction with information available	2.2	2.4	2.3	.036			
Generally understand reasons for management policies	2.3	2.5	2.5	.035	√	√	
Management criticizes more quickly than praises	3.5	2.9	2.6	⟨.000	√	√	√
Employees treated like children	3.6	3.2	2.9	⟨.000	√	√	√
Work involves learning new things	2.3	2.2	2.4	.017			√
Employee feels overqualified for present job	3.9	3.8	3.5	⟨.000		√	√
Employee should evaluate supervisors	2.7	2.4	2.2	.001		√	√

from a survey/feedback design. First, whatever their performance appraisal, employees see things similarly on two items. Crisis Atmosphere constitutes a high-leverage target on which ameliorative action would be widely welcome, and High Standards taps a practice pretty much seen as already in good shape.

Second, employees with different appraisals see some items in significantly different ways, and these differences merit managerial attention in decisions about whether, and when, to take corrective action. Consider the greater (and reasonable) enthusiasm of Sub-Modals for a program by which subordinates could evaluate supervisors.

What should management do? The data help in moving toward an answer. Subordinate evaluations do not seem to have a high priority. Those with Superior appraisals approach an average response of Not Sure; and not even the Sub-Modals' average response is Agree. Moreover, some observers might be concerned that some Sub-Modals only reflect a desire to get even.

Third, table 4.4 also contains some surprises. For example, it implies that Sub-Modals seem satisfied with their last salary increase. Given that appropriate policies put them at a significant disadvantage in regard to the timing and amount of such increases, the mean response implies a substantial satisfaction with processes about which Sub-Modals could reasonably have negative feelings. From one perspective, the data thus provide some welcome evidence about the perceived fairness if not benificence of management practices and policies with regard to performance appraisal. Specifying appraisal differences, patently, highlights the perhaps-surprising generality of this perceived fairness and benificence. From another perspective, more somber interpretations of the data should be considered. For example, management might wish to consider whether the salary increments and the appraisal differences to which they are attached convey a consistent message to employees. And management might also consider whether the received message is the one intended.

Differences on twenty-one benefits, programs, and practices. Survey/feedback designs often seek to elicit data about how a range of benefits, programs, and practices are perceived by organizational members. Such data can motivate ameliorative action, or can confirm suspicions that well enough should be left alone. Table 4.5 summarizes the results of one such overview of twenty-one benefits, programs, and practices, each of which respondents scored on a 5-point scale including these response-stems: (1) Excellent, (2) Good, (3) Fair, (4) Not Very Good, and (5) Poor.

Overall, table 4.5 suggests that employees see the firm in question quite positively. Beyond that, specifying performance appraisals enlightens analysis in several ways.

Paradoxically, to begin, performance appraisals do not seem to co-vary significantly with differences on specific items and this provides useful in-

TABLE 4.5
Differences in Appraisals and Twenty-one Benefits, Programs, and Practices, Classified by Appraisal Category Item Means

	1 Superior	2 Modal	3 Sub-Modal	Overall F-Probability	Test for Significance of Differences between Pairs of Means (where √ designates a difference achieving .05 level by modified LSD procedure)		
					1 vs. 2	1 vs. 3	2 vs. 3
Retirement plan	2.4	2.4	2.4	.853		√	
Savings plan	2.7	2.5	2.4	.018			
Vacation policy	1.7	1.8	1.9	.112			
Sick leave policy	1.7	1.8	2.0	<.000		√	√
Dispensary and first aid	2.4	2.3	2.3	.578			
Medical insurance	2.5	2.5	2.5	.969			
Parking lots	2.5	2.8	2.9	.018		√	
Absence policy	1.9	2.1	2.5	<.000	√	√	√
Career development	2.6	2.8	2.6	.007			√
Employee promotions	2.6	3.0	3.0	.007	√	√	
Tuition payments	1.9	2.0	2.0	.361			
Local phone policy	3.2	3.2	3.1	.853			
Affirmative action programs	2.3	2.4	2.6	.119			
Severance pay policy	2.5	2.4	2.5	.386			
Life insurance program	1.9	1.9	2.0	.146			
Disability insurance program	2.1	2.2	2.1	.801			
Security practices	2.5	2.4	2.3	.087			
Maternity leave policy	2.0	2.1	2.1	.875			
Lounges	3.0	2.9	2.6	.003			
Elevators	2.7	2.6	2.4	.017		√	√
Restrooms	2.5	2.5	2.3	.022		√	

formation that would otherwise be unavailable. Specifically, differences in appraisals do not seem relevant in twelve of the twenty-one cases. Some of these cases seem to be high-leverage opportunities for possible ameliorative action (for example, Local Phone Policy), and others (for example, Vacation Policy) suggest that no urgent need for change is seen by any employees.

Nonetheless, differences in performance appraisals seem associated with nonrandom variation in evaluations of nine of the twenty-one benefits, programs, and practices. On these nine significant items, thirteen of the twenty-seven possible paired comparisons of appraisal categories show noteworthy differences.

None of these statistically significant items can be interpreted definitively, but some suggest major grist for the mill. Consider a few interpretive puzzles. For example, Sub-Modals score lowest on Lounges, Elevators, and Parking Lots. Does that merely reflect a general malaise—an emphasis on hygiene factors in the absence of motivators like recognition and achievement? Or what? At least for parking lots, speculation about the more negative attitudes of Sub-Modals seems safe enough. Company parking spaces are scarce in the host firm, and are awarded on two grounds: hierarchical status and tenure. Patently, employees with Sub-Modal appraisals are less likely to gain either.

Intriguing patterns also can be teased out of other items on which differences in appraisals seem important. Note that Sub-Modals are least positive about Sick Leave Policy and Absence Policy. Does this mean that some supervisors make too much in their appraisals of two of the most concrete measures available to them? And does it mean that employees perceive that productivity gets too little attention, while too much attention goes to a few days more or less of sick leave or absence? Or, far worse still, do some truly sick employees come to work, unaware of or uncertain about firm policy, afraid to report sick for fear that they could never again do much right in the eyes of the myopic supervisors? Should other evidence suggest such dynamics are operating, the following program of corrective action might be appropriate:

- Supervisory training about appropriate policies
- Emphasis on nonthreatening management styles
- More carefully informing employees about the sickness and absenteeism policies applicable to them
- More effective monitoring of supervisory behavior
- Policy changes, such as flexible work hours, that can reduce hassling about short-term absences or indisposition

Factor analysis permits a more searching interpretation of the data summarized in table 4.5. Basically, that interpretation deals with the troublesome issue of how many dimensions of reality are tapped by the twenty-one variables represented there. In the extreme case, the twenty-one variables might measure the same single dimension twenty-one times. For many important particulars—for example, choosing targets for ameliorative action—it is necessary to establish the specific multidimensionalities underlying a data set.

Table 4.6 reports the results of a factor analysis of the twenty-one variables using principal components with iterations, followed by Varimax rotation to a terminal solution. The choice of the number of factors is dictated by the number of eigenvalues greater than 1.0. The structure in table 4.6 is quite clean, with only a few variables having even modest loadings on more than one factor. Table 4.6 reports all loadings of .3 or higher.

With some confidence, then, we conclude that the twenty-one variables tap at least five dimensions of reality, which may be thought of as potential targets for managerial action in four significant ways. First, the percentages of total variance accounted for by each of the five factors may be thought of as estimates of their relative significance to respondents in the host organization at the time of the survey. Table 4.7 shows specific percentages of variance for each of the five factors.

Second, the individual loadings provide some guidance as to the relative impact of specific variables contributing to a factor. In sum, these loadings help identify variables that provide special leverage for inducing change on a specific factor. For example, the loadings on Worksite Amenities suggest that the character and quality of elevator service, lounges, and restrooms dominate in the factor which accounts for most variance in the data. Ameliorative action in their cases might be especially cost-effective.

Third, information about the interaction of performance appraisals and responses on the twenty-one items also provides further guidance to management. Recall that table 4.5 indicates nine cases in which differences in appraisals co-vary significantly with differences in responses to survey items—those nine cases are indicated by an "S" in table 4.6. In the case of Factor I, for example, those respondents with the highest appraisals had the most negative scores on elevator services and restrooms. This implies a relatively unconflicted choice for management. Not only does Factor I account for the largest portion of the variance in the twenty-one relevant variables, but the two highest loadings on that factor relate to variables on which those with the highest appraisals also have the greatest concern. The situation is more complicated for Factor III, where those with the lowest appraisals are significantly less favorable on the two key target variables—sick leave and absence policy.

The data in table 4.6 cannot decide for management, patently. Just as clearly, however, the analysis does highlight central issues for choice.

Fourth, available knowledge does not permit definite prediction of the consequences of ameliorative action on any of the factors. Will production increase if resources are expended to improve Factor I? The best guess is,

TABLE 4.6
Summary of a Factor Analysis of Twenty-one Personnel Benefits, Programs, and Practices

	Factors, or Dimensions of Reality, Isolated by Factor Analysis				
	I Worksite Amenities	II Proximate Financial Support	III Policies re Time Off	IV Career Development	V Long-Run Financial Security
Retirement plan					.6151
Savings plan					.4880(S)
Vacation policy			.3536		
Sick leave policy			.6517(S)		
Dispensary and first aid	.4204				
Medical insurance		.4549			
Parking lots	.6458(S[a])		.3361		
Absence policy			.6683(S)		
Career Development				.5653(S)	
Employee promotions				.7546(S)	
Tuition payments		.3664			
Local phone policy	.4164				
Affirmative action programs	.3696			.3504	
Severance pay policy					.3063
Life insurance program		.6975			
Disability insurance program		.5298			
Security practices	.4749				
Maternity leave policy	.3182	.3104			
Lounges	.5563(S)				
Elevators	.6016(S)				
Restrooms	.5628(S)				

Note: [a]An "S" designates a variable which when classified by appriasal category achieved a statisically significant overall difference in table 4.5

TABLE 4.7
Percentages of Variance Accounted for by Five Factors

Factor	% of Variance	Cumulative % of Variance
I Worksite amenities	26.1	26.1
II Proximate financial supports	8.3	34.4
III Policies re time off	6.1	40.5
IV Career development	5.7	46.2
V Long-run financial security	4.8	51.0

probably not, because Factor I seems to be a hygiene rather than a motivating factor, in the vocabulary popularized by Herzberg, Mausner, and Snyderman (1959). In their schema, motivators tend to be built into the work itself, and derive from elements such as the potential in work for fulfillment, achievement, recognition, and so on. In table 4.6, Factor IV probably comes closest to being a motivator in Herzberg, Mausner, and Snyderman's language.

Greater Success by Specifying Important Differences between People

This one approach to Irony III reinforces the virtues of specifying differences between people, with the likelihood that OD will become more successful in making intended things happen. Both the data, as well as illustrations of how they might be used, strongly suggest the usefulness in survey/feedback designs of specifying differences in performance appraisals. Pretty clearly, major practical and normative issues get neglected in equally weighting each survey response by aggregating individual responses which are differentiated, if at all, only in terms of common demographic variables.

Three questions take stage center, and attention will be given to each in turn. The questions are:

- What are the attractions of giving survey responses equal weight?
- Are there any general developmental trends that seem likely to raise the attractiveness of differentiating individuals?
- Are there any trends in OD itself that will encourage differentiating individuals?

In general, the answers to the second and third questions imply that the attractions elicited in response to the first question will have a reduced salience in the near future. Hence, improving OD success rates via differentiating respondents will face reduced challenges.

Why Weight Responses Equally?

Numerous attractions encourage weighting each survey response equally, despite the evidence above of the usefulness of differentiating respondents. Consider five varieties of such attractions: existential, motivational, philosophical, mensural, and stylistic.

Existentially, the implicit basic rationale in survey/feedback resembles that in political democracy. Those who wear the shoes know best if they pinch. Hence the reasonableness of a guarantee to each shoe wearer of an equal voice, if only episodically as via a vote or a survey, so that no major pinching goes unremarked for very long. The orthodox rationale in political philosophy supporting this guarantee emphasizes the danger if such pinching continues without redress, and especially so in the case of the masses of system members. For all systems ultimately depend upon mass support but, for many pressing reasons, mass opinion may be slow to form and often ineffectual even long after it does coalesce. Since mass opinion nonetheless will be ultimately determinative, the alternative to incremental amelioration is periodic but massive outbursts of pent-up frustration that may indiscriminantly damage many innocents, and perhaps long after the possibility of timely action has passed.

Motivationally, in addition, the promise of equal weighting might encourage participation in survey/feedback designs, especially by those who normally are disadvantaged in other modes of influencing their system. That survey/feedback is not "the same old crap" may support the efficacy of the intervention, especially for low-power members who might become dangerously alienated from their systems without the benefit of some arrangements for some real influence, at least some of the time.

Philosophically, many good things in our social and political systems rest on a belief in some kind of ultimate equality, such as equality before the law. Reality often falls far short of the ideal.

Mensurally, in addition, "one person, one vote" variants avoid some ticklish and even dangerous issues. We can sample only. What are the criteria for unequal treatment? And who determines and enforces them, with what effects on the freedom of which participants in a system?

Take the present case, which selects performance appraisal as the criterion. The rationale is uncomplicated. Appraisals exist; they provide one important measure of the perceived value of the individual to the organization; and appraisals influence who gets what in organizations. However, appraisals are not carved in stone; individuals can progress or regress; and appraisals may be said to be unreliable, to reflect more prejudice, lock-step thinking, and perhaps malice than to reflect tough, dispassionate analysis.

The linkage of appraisal data and survey data also could result in an unfortunate concentration of power, as in the risk of a management purge of the Sub-Modals because of their lower level of support for the organizational regime. The danger will be especially great where informed consent is lacking, as when members innocently provide questionnaire responses that are linked to other data which might motivate action against specific individuals, without sufficient appreciation by those providing the data of the awkward possibilities of their action. In effect, insidious managements might entrap respondents into providing unwitting evidence against themselves or others.

Style attractions, finally, also can encourage equal weighting of opinions in survey/feedback designs. Some OD professionals prefer a style that is unrelievedly helpful versus even potentially hurtful or punitive. Differentiations of the kind illustrated above may not be their cup of tea. For differentiation raises tough questions, whose answers may be helpful to the system while punishing to some members. These questions include: Who really counts in System X? Who do we want most to keep, and who is more dispensable?

Of course, such questions get raised and answered in all systems, in one way or another. But facing such questions explicitly and directly is no easy matter, especially since objective answers seldom exist. And just because someone will raise and answer such questions does not mean that OD specialists will do so, or should.

These constitute powerful reasons for weighting all survey respondents equally, but counterforces are growing. The next two subsections illustrate this tendency, and also reframe the differentiation argument in terms of various developmental features. Broadly, differentiation is not a yes/no issue, as this subsection suggests. Rather, progressive differentiation can enhance OD success rates as two classes of developments mature.

Trends in Three Developmental Areas

Some major components in the antidifferentiation rationale have lost substantial force in recent days. Consider the revolution in access to computers. Not long ago, data-processing problems militated against routinely differentiating respondents, even in large organizations. Now, the required technology is within the convenient reach of all interested observers, even though beliefs about analytical problems still persist. Patience and care definitely are required, but elaborate libraries of computational programs and hardware now serve all but the most casual users. Developments in the computational arena, in short, reduce the practical force of the antidifferentiation rationale.

In addition, the extension and maturation of OD activities tend to reduce the credibility of a second major reason for not differentiating individuals. Consider the objection that employees who know that appraisals or similar information will be integrated with survey data might provide bogus responses. Such linkages typically require that survey respondents be identified and—even given a trusted and discreet third party—the potential for, and temptation toward, mischief inhere in anyone's ability to match names and responses.

Since there seems no convenient way out of the dilemmas of identifying respondents, some observers conclude that this precludes differentiation. Devious approaches that permit secret linking of survey and other data are ruled out by OD values, as well as by ethical standards and law. Alternatively, asking respondents to supply their own appraisals as one of their responses to the survey questionnaire probably will not do.[4] This approach does not require identifying individuals, but experience with asking individuals for some recall data—like family income—reflects major reliability and validity problems.

This second class of components of a rationale against differentiation, however, can be looked at in developmental terms. In effect, such objections resolve into this truism: Where OD values do not exist, one can expect behaviors and attitudes to reflect anti-OD values. Stated positively, differentiation will be more accepted as an organization develops regenerative systems—high openness, owning, and trust, along with low risk. And differentiation can both contribute to regenerative interaction and be legitimated by it. As OD is extended, in short, so will differentiation be more probable. In this sense, OD success rates enhance its credibility which, in turn, will legitimate differentiation. And that will further raise success rates.

As a final point concerning developments bearing on the issue of differentiating respondents in survey/feedback designs, many observers have emphasized the probable resistance from employee associations or labor unions. Adversarial relations have tended to dominate in the labor/management arena; OD has not given fulsome attention to unions, in general; and the labor movement has not been very positive toward management-initiated surveys to begin with. Especially in industries where costs are easily passed on to consumers, management may be motivated to avoid negative reactions from professional or union officials, or any other source. So who needs data?

Developmental trends favoring differentiation appear even in this arena of historical "hard ball" between labor and management. Most signally, cooperation between these historical adversaries has become increasingly common, as in the QWL movement (e.g., Sun 1988). Competition from abroad and loss of jobs have proved powerful reinforcers of those who believe in the gospel of joint labor/management initiatives as a matter of principle.

Trends in OD Tensions

The bias against differentiating respondents gets additional support from certain historical tensions within OD as an area of professional activity. The basic question is whether OD practice is elitist (Ross 1971) or populist (Bass 1967, esp. 221–25). The fact of the matter seems to be that OD practice not only does, but must, encompass aspects of both orientations. OD practice will have strong elitist features, if only because clients often will be figures in authority. At the same time, OD practice needs a populist thrust in order to generate credible data for analysis, and to develop motivation for implementing any action plans. In short, lack of balance has costs.

Guaranteeing respondent anonymity is a convenient way to achieve the required working balance of elitist and populist orientations, at least early in the game. That is obvious.

Developmental trends in this critical professional particular are mixed, but the trend seems unmistakable. ODers are increasingly sensitive to the complex character of their profession, and balance seems more the order of the day than procrustean in/out distinctions (e.g., Browne, Cotton, and Golembiewski 1977). Moreover, managements seem to understand more and more that OD's basic value inheres in its multiple in-betweennesses, and hence resists forcing choices as to whether "you're with us or against us" (e.g., Golembiewski and Kiepper 1988, esp. 216–26).

In such a developmental context, reasonably bounded differentiation can develop. Sharp elitist/populist orientations favor nondifferentiation.

Conclusion

Three points summarize this analysis, then. There seem to be multiple advantages in specifying differences between respondents to survey/feedback designs. However, this approach contains potential for mischief. This potential helps explain why survey/feedback designs have seldom differentiated their respondents, and encourages the prediction (and the prescription) that such differences will (and should) come only after careful deliberation, reinforced by effective guarantees of individual anonymity and/or high levels of mutual trust and confidence. Finally, several developmental tendencies encourage the view that reasonable progress toward differentiation can and will be made.

A Personal View

President Truman once noted that he needed more "one-handed" advisors. Like the present analysis, many of Truman's advisors were good at generating multiple alternatives: "on the one hand . . . , but on the other hand. . . ." Truman wanted fewer hedged opinions and more specific recommendations for action.

So what is my one-handed view, once the alternatives are stated for the record? My goal in this chapter is to suggest the virtue of a principle or operating guide. Whenever you can safely do so, I propose, differentiate respondents, or have them do so. Also try to do more of that as time goes by, and recognize that the present approach to specificity about personal differences is illustrative only. The discussion of the several developmental tendencies should encourage the reader toward the conclusion that differentiation does not merely mean swimming up a torrential stream.

When circumstances seem to encourage unspecificity or anonymity, I suggest two actions: reevaluate to discount the possibility that you are simply taking the easy way out; and then, if your initial sense of the situation remains, be mindful of what may be lost, or even surrendered, because of the lack of specificity.

In short, this chapter has a consciousness-raising character—a sense of what can be, even though conditions might tether one short, in a specific place at a certain time. In the long run, progress gets defined as the tension between what can be and what has to be. This chapter seeks to contribute to that tension, but without prescribing indiscriminately for the diverse settings that are encountered in specific settings in the world of work.

Moreover, this chapter reinforces the rationale for seeking to develop and heighten regenerative interaction in organizations: to increase trust, openness, and owning, while reducing risk. Such settings raise the probability of constructive specification of individual differences. Indeed, in the long run, it is only when numerous differences are specifiable that advanced regenerative interaction is possible.

Notes

1. An earlier version of this material appeared in Golembiewski et al. 1977. See also Golembiewski and Hilles, 1979, pp. 243–67.
2. Total respondents to the QWL questionnaire numbered 2,671, which represents a voluntary response rate of some 70 percent of the total employment. All respondents were located at headquarters or several nearby sites, representing the full range of functions from Research and Development through Manufacturing to Marketing. Of the respondents, 770 chose not to identify themselves, and 376 were excluded because they were in-the-field salesforce and posed different analytic problems. This left 1,525 cases for the present study. Performance appraisals were not available for 51 "identifiers." Hence the present N of 1,474.

   Elaborate comparisons on a large number of demographics establish that the 2,671 voluntary respondents constitute a close replica of the total employment.

   The 1,525 cases considered here are merely an interesting subpopulation, however, and no implied or expressed claim about their representativeness will be made. Convincing evidence (Golembiewski and Billingsley 1976) does establish that identifiers provide survey responses that are clearly more favorable or optimistic about their organizational experiences and attitudes. Here, however, it will not be possible to test whether appraisal differences among the non-identifiers generate patterns similar to those described in the text for identifiers.
3. Specifically, all respondents were asked to enter a self-chosen, nine-digit code on their response sheets, which were to be deposited in large boxes scattered throughout the organization. If they wished, respondents also could enter that code number

plus their name on a separate sheet, which they sent directly to the consultant/ researcher in a stamped, self-addressed envelope. A letter to respondents explained that this procedure would permit analyses like the present one, and also might later facilitate efficient resurveys to test for trends.

4. In at least one case, only minor differences existed between performance appraisals gathered by self-reports and then checked against archival data. See Golembiewski, Munzenrider, and Stevenson 1986, 87–101.

References

Andrews, F. M.; Morgan, J. M.; and Sonquist, J. A. 1973. *Multiple Classification Analysis*. Ann Arbor, Mich.: Institute for Social Research.

Bass, B. 1967. "The Anarchist Movement and the T-Group." *Journal of Applied Behavioral Science* 3:211–27.

Blalock, H. M. 1960. *Social Statistics*. New York: McGraw-Hill.

Bowers, D. G. 1973a. "OD Techniques and Their Results in 23 Organizations." *Journal of Applied Behavioral Science* 9:21–43.

Bowers, D. G. 1973b. "Back to Bowers on OD Techniques." *Journal of Applied Behavioral Science* 9:671–72.

Bowers, D. G., and Franklin, J. L. 1977. *Data-Based Organizational Change*. La Jolla, Calif.: University Associates.

Browne, P. J.; Cotton, C. C.; and Golembiewski, R. T. 1977. "Marginality and the OD Practitioner." *Journal of Applied Behavioral Science* 13:493–506.

French, W. L., and Bell, C. H. Jr. 1973. *Organization Development*. Englewood Cliffs, N.J.: Prentice-Hall.

Golembiewski, R. T., and Billingsley, K. 1976. "A Critical Decision in Survey/ Feedback Designs: To Identify Respondents or No." *Group and Organization Studies* 1:448–54.

Golembiewski, R. T., and Hilles, R. 1979. *Toward the Responsive Organization*. Salt Lake City: Brighton Publishing.

Golembiewski, R. T., and Kiepper, A. 1988. *High Performance and Human Costs*. New York: Praeger.

Golembiewski, R. T., and Munzenrider, R. 1974. "Social Desirability as an Intervening Variable in Interpreting OD Effects." *Journal of Applied Behavioral Science* 10:503–32.

Golembiewski, R. T.; Billingsley, K.; and Yeager, S. 1976. "Measuring Change and Persistence in Human Affairs: Types of Change Generated by OD Designs." *Journal of Applied Behavioral Science* 12:133–57.

Golembiewski, R. T.; Munzenrider, R.; and Stevenson, J. 1986. *Stress in Organizations*. New York: Praeger.

Golembiewski, R. T.; Yeager, S.; Hilles, R.; and Carrigan, S. B. 1977. "Toward Increasing the Specificity of Survey/ Feedback Designs: Costs/Benefits of Differentiating Respondents in Terms of Performance Appraisals." Paper presented at the Annual Meeting, Academy of Management. Orlando, Fla.

Gouldner, A. 1955. "Metaphysical Pathos and the Theory of Bureaucracy." *American Political Science Review* 49:496–507.

Herzberg, F.; Mausner, B.; and Snyderman, B. B. 1959. *The Motivation to Work*. New York: Wiley.

Kahn, R. L. Wolfe, D. M.; Quin, R. P.; Snoek, J. D.; and Rosenthal, R. A. 1964. *Organizational Stress*. New York: Wiley.

McGregor, D. 1960. *The Human Side of Enterprise*. New York: McGraw-Hill.
Nadler, D. A. 1977. *Feedback and Organization Development*. Reading, Mass.: Addison-Wesley.
Nie, N. H.; Hull, C. H.; Jenkins, J. G.; Steinbreener, K.; and Bent, K. H. 1975. *SPSS: Statistical Package for the Social Sciences*. New York: McGraw-Hill.
Pasmore, W. A. 1976. "The Michigan ICL Study Revisited: An Alternative Explanation of Results." *Journal of Applied Behavioral Science*, 12:245–51.
Patchen, M. 1965. *Some Questionnaire Measures of Employee Motivation and Morale*. Ann Arbor, Mich.: Survey Research Center, University of Michigan.
Roberts, K. H., and O'Reilly, C. A. III 1974. "Failures in Upward Communication in Organizations: Three Possible Culprits." *Academy of Management Journal* 17:205–15.
Ross, R. 1971. "OD for Whom?" *Journal of Applied Behavioral Science* 7:58–85.
Smith, P. C.; Kendall, L. M.; and Hulin, C. L. 1969. *The Measurement of Satisfaction in Work and Retirement*. Chicago: Rand McNally.
Sun, B-C. 1988. *Quality of Working Life Programs*. Ph.D. diss. University of Georgia, Athens, Ga.
Torbert, W. R. 1973. "Some Questions on Bowers' Study of Different OD Techniques." *Journal of Applied Behavioral Science* 9:668–71.
White, J. K., and Ruh, R. A. 1973. "Effects of Personal Values on the Relationship Between Participation and Job Attitudes." *Administrative Science Quarterly* 18:506–614.

5

Personal Slack for Choice and Change: Individual Burnout and Physical Symptoms

Common sense tells us that individuals will differ in the degree of their personal slack—the physical and emotional reserves that different individuals can mobilize—and the research reported in this chapter confirms common sense. The focus is on the relationship of an individual's experienced strain with normal coping limits. That strain can variously challenge those coping limits, or even overwhelm them.

The specific focus is on burnout, with the goal of testing several critical points. The clinical and anecdotal literatures on burnout suggest that noxious effects accompany and exacerbate high levels of strain. Building on these general observations, this research uses a paper-and-pencil instrument to assess degrees of burnout in a large population, and relates those differences to a panel of nineteen self-reports of physical symptoms. Burnout proves to have direct and marked associations with a broad range of physical symptoms, as expected.

The findings add urgency to dealing with stress at work, as in corporate wellness programs, and the results also underscore the conceptual myopia of much of the OD literature. That literature tends to neglect differences between the targets of OD interventions, in general as well as in the specific case of the degree to which individuals have physical and emotional slack to choose or to change.

This neglect of individual differences has a long tradition. For example, selection of participants became an issue in the use of T-groups due to reports of psychiatric casualties (e.g., Yalom and Lieberman 1971), but the filters have been for gross in/out decisions, such as cautions that individuals not consider the experience a substitute for therapy, rather than for determining which individuals are likely to profit from specific designs. Some exceptions exist, but they are few and far between (e.g., Harrison 1965). Similarly, team-building designs seldom take explicit account of personal differences, despite some suggestions of the myopia of this general practice. (See also the next chapter on this point.)

The results presented in this chapter require seeing this neglect of individual differences as a significant weakness. Again, this chapter provides another perspective on the theme that the substantial estimates of OD success rates can be enhanced in direct ways by enlarging OD's theoretical base to encompass individual differences, such as those in burnout.[1]

A Conceptual Context for Irony III, Revisited

The burgeoning literature on psychological burnout suggests that a range of noxious effects accompany high levels of strain. Thus Cherniss (1980, 15–16) expects that greater incidences of a long catalog of psychophysical disturbances will be associated with increasing burnout; Freudenberger (1980) emphasizes that great personal distress is a common concomitant; and Maslach and Jackson report that their studies of burnout (e.g., 1981, 99–101) lead them to expect high rates of headaches, lingering colds, backaches, gastrointestinal disturbances, and other indicators of impaired physical functioning.

Most of these reports are anecdotal or involve small populations, however. Hence this effort to identify physical covariants of differential burnout in a large population using a paper-and-pencil instrument. Details follow about the host organization and conventions for measurement.

Host Population

The present data come from one division of a federal agency, which has about fifty similar offices throughout the country performing the same set of people-helping activities. Details are available elsewhere (Golembiewski, Munzenrider, and Stevenson 1986), and only a general sense of the population will be provided here. The division has a total employment of approximately 2,600, with the effective response rate for different items approximating 55–60 percent. Division missions-and-roles center around direct contact with clients, under conditions that can be emotionally arousing and hostile. The population might best be described as a "middle slice" of a federal bureaucracy, with the bulk of the present respondents falling in position classes GS-5 through GS-12. The full federal employment schedule includes eighteen grades, plus a senior executive group.

This survey received support at three levels. Headquarters provided the initial encouragement, and general design and questionnaire format were later approved by the division's union. Field managers proved to be a more difficult target, and a presentation was made at a national managers' meeting that emphasized the character and organizational consequences of burnout. Three of the fifty-plus field managers refused to have their employees participate, and several others took lukewarm stances toward the research project.

Measures Utilized

This study utilized two basic measures—of burnout and of physical symptoms. They will be described briefly.

Five burnout measures. Psychological strain is estimated by the Maslach Burnout Inventory, or MBI (Maslach and Jackson 1982, 1986), which contains twenty-five items and is modified for present purposes (Golembiewski, Munzenrider, and Carter 1983). The items tap three subscales:

- *Depersonalization,* high scores on which indicate that respondents tend to distance themselves from others—to reify human contacts and to view them as categories or things
- *Personal Accomplishment (reversed),* low scores on which imply that individuals are doing well on jobs they consider worthwhile
- *Emotional Exhaustion,* high scores on which imply that individuals are strained beyond their comfortable coping limits—that they are nearing, or beyond, the "end of the rope," emotionally and psychologically speaking.

The MBI items generate five kinds of scores, each of which derives substantial support from the available literature. Four of the scores come from the three subscale scores and a total score. The subscales seem to reliably isolate highly similar domains in different settings—in a product-line division of a multinational firm, in a people-helping division of a large federal agency, at high levels of organization, and at low (Golembiewski, Munzenrider, and Carter 1983). Subscale and total scores in other studies both correlate in predictable ways with a large panel of descriptors of worksites, with statistically significant associations observed in seventy-five of eighty-two cases that account for an average of 8.7 percent of the common variance (Golembiewski and Munzenrider 1981). In the present case, the measurement properties of these four burnout scales also seem acceptable. That is, factor analysis again isolates three domains that closely resemble the original three subscales. Moreover, the factors also are highly congruent with those extracted from independent analyses of the MBI items, which assess the congruence of the pattern as well as the magnitude of pairs of factorial structures (Munzenrider and Golembiewski 1987). More narrowly, the four aggregate MBI measures generate these acceptable alpha coefficients: Depersonalization, 0.76; Personal Accomplishment, 0.72; Emotional Exhaustion, 0.86; and Total Score, 0.86.

The MBI items also generate a fifth and more complicated measure of burnout—a phase model. It considers the three subscales prepotent in the order given above, and basically proposes that increases in Depersonalization characterize the earliest and least virulent stages of burnout. Up to a point, some depersonalizing may not adversely affect performance—indeed, may

TABLE 5.1
Phases of Psychological Burnout

	Phases of Psychological Burnout							
	I	II	III	IV	V	VI	VII	VIII
Depersonalization	Lo	Hi	Lo	Hi	Lo	Hi	Lo	Hi
Personal accomplishment (reversed)	Lo	Lo	Hi	Hi	Lo	Lo	Hi	Hi
Emotional exhaustion	Lo	Lo	Lo	Lo	Hi	Hi	Hi	Hi

even enhance it. Beyond that presently indeterminate point, however, increases in Depersonalization can negatively impact Personal Achievement. Sufficient increases in the two subscales, in turn, can trigger high levels of Emotional Exhaustion.

This simple decision rule generates an eight-phase model, when respondents are distinguished as High versus Low on the three MBI subscales. High versus Low assignments are made in terms of median cuts in the present population, which constitutes the largest available population from a single organization with a relatively homogeneous set of missions and roles. Subscale norms have been reported elsewhere (Golembiewski and Munzenrider 1984). The phases are defined in table 5.1.

Physical symptoms. Self-reports concerning physical well-being derive from responses to a conventional list of possible complaints (Quinn and Shepard 1979, esp. 30). Respondents had available four possible response stems for describing their experience of each symptom: Often, Sometimes, Rarely, and Never. The response stems relate to the following nineteen indicators of well-being, with the scoring being uniform so that Often is coded "4" and Never "1".

1. cramps in my legs
2. pains in my heart
3. tightness or heaviness in my chest
4. trouble breathing or shortness of breath
5. swollen ankles
6. pains in my back or spine
7. pains in my stomach
8. headaches
9. coughing or having heavy chest colds
10. stiffness, swelling, or aching in my leg muscles and joints
11. becoming very tired in a short period of time (fatigued)
12. having trouble getting to sleep
13. having trouble staying asleep
14. finding it difficult to get up in the morning
15. feeling my heart pounding or racing
16. hands sweating or feeling damp and clammy

17. feeling nervous or fidgety and tense
18. being completely worn out at the end of the day
19. having a poor appetite

Note that Cronbach's alpha for Total Symptoms is 0.89.

Findings

In general, the five measures of burnout co-vary in regular and predictable ways with self-reports about physical symptoms. Four sections detail the findings which, in turn, focus on the three MBI subscale scores, the Total score, the phases of burnout, and a comparison with two national samples. Straightforward, direct associations are expected between burnout and all of the physical symptoms. Results will be reported for the individual symptoms, as well as for a purely additive Total Symptoms score.

Three Subscale Scores

The MBI items are most often utilized to develop subscale scores, as by their originators (Maslach and Jackson, 1981), and two observations about the first three columns of data in table 5.2 suggest the usefulness of these subscales. First, fifty-five of the fifty-seven correlation coefficients are in the expected direction, and 95 percent of them achieve statistical significance. The sample size helps account for this record, of course. Nonetheless, the nineteen physical symptoms and the three MBI subscale scores share approximately 4.2 percent variance in the statistically significant cases.

Second, the degree of association with the burnout measures varies for different physical symptoms, but the overall pattern in table 5.2 seems clear. Thus, Total Symptoms correlates significantly in all three cases with the subscales of burnout, and the average shared variance approximates 11.2 percent.

Total Burnout Scores

MBI items have been used infrequently to generate a Total Score, but that usage proved revealing in one study (Golembiewski and Munzenrider 1981), and the extreme right column of data in table 5.2 reinforces this conclusion. Thus, Total MBI Score correlates significantly with all nineteen physical symptoms and, moreover, almost 7 percent of the variance is common, on average.

Again, the degree of association of burnout with individual symptoms differs, but the overall pattern is quite robust. Witness the association of two scores in table 5.2—Total Symptoms and Total MBI—which share nearly 18.5 percent of their variance.

TABLE 5.2
Simple Correlations of MBI Scores and Symptoms of Physical Distress

Physical Symptom	Four Kinds of MBI Scores			
	Depersonalization	Personal Accomplishment (reversed)	Emotional Exhaustion	Total Score
Leg cramps	.09	.09	.16	.15
Heart pains	.15	.10	.20	.20
Tightness in chest	.20	.11	.29	.27
Trouble breathing	.15	.11	.23	.22
Swollen ankles	.04[a]	.06	.09	.08
Back pains	.13	.10	.21	.20
Stomach pains	.17	.15	.25	.25
Headaches	.17	.11	.27	.25
Coughing and colds	.12	.09	.15	.15
Stiffness	.09	.02[a]	.17	.13
Fatigued	.24	.18	.35	.34
Trouble getting to sleep	.18	.11	.26	.25
Trouble staying asleep	.20	.14	.26	.27
Trouble getting up	.19	.19	.39	.34
Heart pounding	.18	.10	.24	.23
Sweating hands	.20	.10	.23	.24
Nervous	.25	.18	.37	.36
Feel worn out	.27	.18	.58	.47
Poor appetite	.22	.10	.28	.26
Total symptoms score	.29	.20	.46	.43

Note: [a]*All but* these two coefficients achieve or surpass the .05 level.

Phases of Burnout

The phases also relate in regular ways with self-reports about the nineteen symptoms, but the magnitude of that patterning varies. This conclusion rests on two types of analysis: a one-way analysis of variance involving the eight phases and Total Symptoms scores, and a factor analysis of the nineteen symptoms which permits a one-way analysis of variance of factors versus phases of burnout.

One-way analysis of variance. The usefulness of the burnout phases also gets major support. Total Symptoms varies regularly as well as robustly by phases of burnout, as two points establish. Thus, over 96 percent of all paired comparisons vary progressively: that is, Total Symptoms for Phase I is less than for Phase II, which is less than for Phase III, etc. In addition, over 60 percent of the twenty-eight possible paired comparisons are statistically different at the .05 level, as judged by the LSD test, modified for unequal sample sizes. (For details consult table 5.6, first row, and table 5.7.)

Factor analysis of nineteen symptoms. Do specific clusters of the nineteen symptoms differentially co-vary with phases of burnout? Yes. Factor analysis implies that the nineteen symptoms do not simply elicit generalized feel-good/bad responses from respondents. As table 5.3 suggests, at least four separate dimensions or domains seem to exist, and they get labeled tentatively in table 5.3. Factor I accounts for over 33 percent of the variance, and the other three add about 20 percent in total.

To facilitate subsequent analysis, each physical symptom was assigned to a single cluster of symptoms, as table 5.4 details. The assignments took into account the original factorial loadings, as well as the effects of deleting a particular symptom from a cluster.

This analysis of the differential affinity of burnout measures for specific clusters of symptoms can be extended in two ways. First, table 5.5 displays the simple correlations of five aggregate symptoms scores with four MBI scores. Factor I and Total Symptoms share an average variance with the four aggregate burnout measures of nearly 16 and 13 percent, respectively. For the other three burnout measures, that average drops to 4.72 percent.

Second, this pattern of differential associations of burnout and specific clusters of symptoms is both reinforced and extended by a focus on the phases. The point is developed in three stages, beginning with table 5.6, which reports on the variation of the five aggregates of symptoms and the eight phases of burnout. Note that in all five cases, statistically significant overall variation exists, and especially so in the cases of two clusters of symptoms—Factor I and Total Symptoms, in that order. This establishes the differential but substantial robustness of this association: self-reports of physical symptoms increase as burnout phases progress from I to VIII.

TABLE 5.3
Factor Analysis of Nineteen Physical Symptoms, by Varimax Rotation

	Factors[a]				
	I General Enervation and Agitation	II Cardiovascular Complaints	III Noncardiac Pain	IV Sleep-lessness	
Variable					H^2
Leg cramps			.56		.37
Heart pain		.68			.52
Tightness in chest		.73			.64
Trouble breathing	.32	.56			.49
Swollen ankles			.41		.19
Back pain			.51		.35
Stomach pain	.36		.36		.33
Headaches	.42		.42		.27
Coughs and colds	.30				.16
Stiffness			.64		.47
Fatigued	.52		.36		.52
Getting to sleep	.31	.43		.76	.70
Staying asleep				.82	.78
Getting up	.56				.37
Heart pounding	.40	.53			.49
Sweating hands	.36	.32			.50
Nervous	.60				.50
Worn out	.67				.52
Poor appetite	.35				.52
Eigenvalue	6.4	1.5	1.1	1.0	
Percent variance accounted for	33.4	7.9	6.7	5.4	
Percent cumulative variance	33.4	41.4	48.1	53.5	

Notes: +N=1,512, with alpha for all items=0.89.
[a]Only loadings ⟩ .30 are listed.

A second perspective establishes that these differences are generally regular as well as robust, overall, with the most marked regularity again being associated with Factor I and Total Symptoms. The central point is established by the Least Significant Difference test. LSD determines the statistical significance of the differences between each of the 140 possible paired comparisons for all aggregates of symptoms of phases: that is, for any measure of symptoms, is the score for Phase I less than that for II; is the score for Phase II less than that for III; and so on through Phase VIII?

The data are not reproduced here but, overall, 43.6 percent of all 140 paired comparisons attain the .05 level of statistical significance. There are no ab-

TABLE 5.4
Modified Factors, Nineteen Physical Symptoms

	Corrected Item-to-Total Correlation	Alpha, Item Deleted
Factor I: General enervation and agitation (alpha = 0.81)		
Stomach pains	.49	.79
Headaches	.47	.79
Coughs and colds	.35	.81
Fatigued	.61	.78
Trouble getting up	.52	.79
Sweating hands	.45	.80
Nervous	.62	.78
Worn out	.61	.78
Poor appetite	.42	.80
Factor II: Cardiovascular complaints (alpha = 0.81)		
Heart pain	.62	.76
Tightness in chest	.69	.72
Trouble breathing	.61	.76
Heart pounding	.57	.78
Factor III: Noncardiac pains (alpha = 0.67)		
Leg cramps	.48	.58
Swollen ankles	.36	.66
Back pain	.44	.61
Stiffness	.53	.54
Factor IV: Sleeplessness (alpha = .085)		
Getting to sleep	.73	
Staying asleep	.73	

solutes in such matters, but anything greater than 20 percent statistically significant cases could be taken as indicating a noteworthy regularity of increases in scores, phase by phase.

However, this aggregate record obscures even as it supports the conclusion that phases of burnout and physical symptoms co-vary both regularly and robustly. Table 5.7 provides useful specificity. Two clusters of symptoms again stand out as having the most marked associations with the phases of burnout: Factor I and Total Symptoms. In sum, over 96 percent of the comparisons of pairs increase, phase by phase, for those two clusters of symptoms, over 62 percent of those expected differences in paired comparisons achieve statistical significance, and none of the 3.6 percent of contrary cases attain the .05 level.

The other three aggregates of symptoms also support the regular increase in reported symptoms, by progressive phases of burnout, but with variable

TABLE 5.5
Correlations of Five Symptom Scores and MBI Scores

Aggregates of Symptoms	Four Kinds of MBI Scores				Average Shared Variance
	Depersonalization	Personal Accomplishment	Emotional Exhaustion	Total Score	
Total symptoms	.29	.20	.46	.43	12.99
Factor I	.32	.22	.51	.47	15.79
Factor II	.22	.14	.31	.29	6.18
Factor III	.12	.10	.22	.20	2.82
Factor IV	.21	.13	.27	.27	5.17
Average shared variance, %	5.87	2.70	13.78	12.04	

TABLE 5.6
One-Way Analysis of Variance, Five Aggregates of Symptoms versus Phases of Burnout

Aggregate of Symptoms	Phases of Burnout I Lo Lo Lo (352)	II Hi Lo Lo (109)	III Lo Hi Lo (193)	IV Hi Hi Lo (124)	V Lo Lo Hi (107)	VI Hi Lo Hi (176)	VII Lo Hi Hi (109)	VIII Hi Hi Hi (367)	F-ratio (Df=7,153)
Total symptoms	33.5	34.2	33.9	35.5	38.7	40.1	40.5	42.6	39.625[a]
Factor I: General enervation and agitation	17.0	17.1	17.1	18.1	20.0	20.5	21.2	22.2	54.995[a]
Factor II: Cardiovascular complaints	5.9	6.2	5.9	6.3	7.0	7.1	7.4	7.5	17.134[a]
Factor III: Noncardiac pains	7.1	7.2	7.6	7.3	7.8	8.2	8.0	8.3	7.766[a]
Factor IV: Sleeplessness	3.6	3.5	3.5	4.0	3.9	4.3	4.0	4.6	15.421[a]

Note: [a]p ⟨ 0.001

TABLE 5.7
Summary of Associations of Five Aggregates of Symptoms with Burnout Phases, All Paired Comparisons

Aggregates of Symptoms	Summary of Paired Comparisons, (in percentages)			
	In Expected Direction	In Expected Direction and Stat. Signif.[a]	In Contrary Direction	In Contrary Direction and Stat. Signif.[a]
Total Symptoms	96.4%	60.7%	3.6%	0.0%
Factor I: General enervation and agitation	96.4	64.3	3.6	0.0
Factor II: Cardiovascular complaints	92.9	42.9	7.1	0.0
Factor III: Noncardiac pains	92.9	17.9	7.1	0.0
Factor IV: Sleeplessness	71.5	32.1	28.5	0.0

Note: [a]Refers to 0.5 level on Least Significant Difference test, as modified for unequal sample sizes.

force. Factors III and IV patently reflect the least-marked pattern of association of phases of burnout and reported symptoms.

So How Bad Is Bad?

These detailed data manipulations provide strong evidence that physical symptoms worsen as all measures of burnout increase, with the phases seeming to be particularly useful indicators of an individual's state. This analysis provides no direct sense of the magnitudes involved, but that is remediable here, and briefly. Comparisons with two national samples of respondents provide a real sense of the costs of advanced burnout.

Details are available elsewhere (Golembiewski and Munzenrider 1988), but some gross comparisons suggest the virulence of burnout's covariants. In sum, those in Phase VIII experience some multiple of the symptoms reported by two national samples—two, five, or even ten times *more* symptoms (e.g., Quinn and Shepard 1979). In contrast, those in Phase I experience a small fraction of the symptoms reported by all survey respondents.

Greater Success by Specifying Phases of Burnout

At a global level, these findings suggest that people will differ in their levels of burnout, and these differences should be associated directly with a person's willingness and ability to successfully undertake choice or change.

That establishes a direct connection with the probable success of OD applications. In this case, the physical symptoms associated with progressive burnout suggest a reduced willingness and ability to deal with daily living, let alone accelerated change. In preview, the results above suggest some guides for action, as well as some qualifications on assuming too much.

Clear Guides for Action

It seems reasonable to conclude that OD interventions will be more successful if they specify differences between targets, including (but not restricted to) their degree of burnout. Such specification is rare, although increasing, but even at this early point it seems obvious that individuals at advanced phases may be poor choices for some kinds of planned change—for example, job enrichment. Such designs require, or at least profit from, a sense of personal efficacy, a quantum of start-up energy, and self-esteem sufficient to buoy a person beyond toleration of unattractive conditions. Those in advanced phases seem to lack precisely such qualities (e.g., Golembiewski and Kim 1989). To simplify the results of a complex research design, self-esteem levels of one population covaried regularly with the phases. A few details provide context for this summary. In about 90 percent of the cases, Phase I assignees had lower self-esteem scores than those in Phase II, those in Phase II surpassed the levels associated with Phase III, and so on. In addition, over 30 percent of the paired-comparisons were statistically significant as well as in the expected direction. No cases falling in a contrary direction achieved significance, in contrast.

The results of tests of over 200 variables similarly imply that individuals in advanced phases will be preoccupied with personal issues. In sum, advanced burnout is associated with such factors, regularly and robustly:

- poorer profiles on self-reports that relate to the worksite; for example, lower satisfaction, higher job tension, lower participation and involvement, and so on (Burke, Shearer, and Deszca 1984; Burke and Deszca 1985; Deckard, Rountree, and Golembiewski 1986)
- greater physical symptoms (Burke, Shearer, and Deszca 1984)
- lower performance appraisals
- generally lower productivity
- higher levels of affective states associated with poor mental health (Deckard 1985)
- greater need for social support, but less of it (Burke and Deszca 1986)

Evidence supporting this full catalog of effects, and others, is available elsewhere (Golembiewski and Munzenrider 1988; Golembiewski, Munzenrider, and Stevenson 1986).

The dual elegance of the phases especially encourages their use. Not only do they relate regularly and robustly with many central covariants, but the phases also suggest useful interventions in ways beyond the other four measures of burnout used here.

Broadly, people in the several phases of burnout might be differentially responsive to the same intervention. Specifically, interaction-centered designs seem more appropriate for those in Phase II, who are having problems with depersonalization. These designs include short-cycle designs such as confrontations or the sharing of three-dimensional images (e.g., Golembiewski 1979, 1: 318–23), as well as more time-extended interventions such as interpersonally oriented team building (e.g., Dyer 1987). In contrast, interaction-centered designs seem less appropriate for those in Phases VI, VII, or VIII, at least initially. For them, low-stimulus designs to reduce the burnout may have a priority. These designs include flexible work hours (e.g., Golembiewski, Hilles, and Kagno 1974), role negotiation (e.g., Harrison 1972), and job rotation.

These suggestions seem quite robust, in fact. For supporting evidence, consult chapters 6 and, especially, chapter 7.

But it seems both possible and useful to be more elemental even here. Indeed, the focus on physical symptoms was deliberately chosen to suggest various practicalities—the likely association of burnout with sick days, insurance usage, and perhaps workmen's compensation. On the present showing, it seems advisable to use the phases of burnout to profile an organization. Such monitoring might well isolate trouble spots—both individual and organizational. In addition, periodic surveys might help anticipate evolving trouble spots by observing changes in the profile of the phases over time.

Such opportunities might lead to success in broader terms, both by allowing an organization to react to emergent situations as well as by allowing the organization to proactively anticipate them, for personal and organizational benefit. The required data base might be misused, of course, but appropriate models seem to be evolving that would provide safeguards against abuses. The Occupational Safety and Health (OSH) group of Shell Canada, for example, represents one effort to provide sophisticated intelligence about system health while retaining both executive support and employee trust that guarantee good-quality data. This is no place to detail the Shell OSH network but, illustratively, it has its own computer capabilities independent of those available to general management.

Some Tethers on Enthusiasm

One should be careful not to be overly exuberant, beyond these general expectations. Four points provide more detailed perspective on the present findings, and some of them urge "Whoa" as well as "Go."

First, although the results imply a substantial covariation of physical symptoms and psychological burnout, as variously measured, the present research does not specify the direction of the arrow of causality, so no firm conclusions are appropriate about what causes what. But the associations are marked and consistent, and results to date suggest this pattern of linkage:

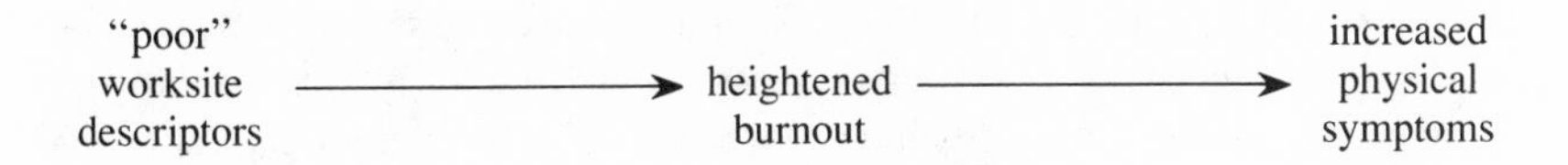

As in this chapter, a large majority of tests of various measures of this prototypic linkage attain statistical significance. No doubt feedback loops exist, but the case for the mainline effects sketched above seems quite strong (Golembiewski, Munzenrider, and Stevenson 1986). Thus, sixteen worksite descriptors and burnout phases share approximately 17 percent common variance; various measures of burnout and of physical symptoms share a range of 5–20 percent of their variance, with the highest proportions involving Total Score and Factor I derived from the sixteen symptoms; but worksite descriptors account for only about 5 percent of the variance in physical symptoms, on average.

However, research on the direction of causal arrows has only begun in burnout research (e.g., Deckard, Rountree, and Golembiewski 1989). Hence this first tether on enthusiasm.

Second, burnout (as variously measured) is not uniformly associated with all symptoms or clusters of symptoms. Medical authorities report no great surprise about the apparently great salience of Factor I, or General Enervation and Agitation, for example. Factor I also substantially contributes to Total Symptoms, which has the next most marked pattern of association with burnout as variously measured.

Third, the results provide variable support for using the MBI items to calculate three subscale scores. Tables 5.2 and 5.5 imply that—when separate MBI subscales are used, as is the conventional practice—Emotional Exhaustion reflects the most marked degree of association with both individual symptoms and aggregates of symptoms. For example, Emotional Exhaustion shares nearly 14 percent common variance with the five aggregates of symptoms, on average, or 2.5 to 5 times the magnitudes of the other two subscales.

The MBI Total Score also reflects quite marked associations with self-reports of symptoms. For example, Total Score shares somewhat over 12 percent variance with the five aggregates of symptoms.

For multiple practical and theoretical reasons, however, the associations of the phases of burnout with self-reported symptoms seem most compelling. Most prominently here, perhaps, Factor I and Total Symptoms share approximately 18 percent of their variance in common with the burnout phases. Reinforcing this working conclusion, the present analysis supports other work (e.g., Golembiewski and Munzenrider 1988) that establishes the regularity and robustness of the covariation of burnout and numerous worksite descriptors. In sum, as burnout phases progress, numerous indicators of the perceived quality of working life deteriorate.

The phase model has two other basic attractions. The use of MBI items to calculate a Total Score of subscale scores differs fundamentally from the use of items to develop the phase model. Phases I and VIII contain the lowest and highest Total Scores, respectively, but internal phases have a very mixed pattern on Total Scores and on subscale composition. Details are available elsewhere (Golembiewski, Munzenrider, and Carter 1983), but even brief reference to the phase model establishes the point.

Moreover, and of great potential significance, the phase model implies a variety of practical and theoretical opportunities not provided by Total Score and the three subscale scores. For example, targeted interventions—at least at first blush—should differ as Total Scores are differentially loaded by Depersonalization, Personal Accomplishment, or Emotional Exhaustion. The phase model provides one approach to responding to such differences in subscale components, while it also differs in major particulars from a Total Score approach. Less-obvious inferences drawn from the phase model have been developed elsewhere (Golembiewski, Munzenrider, and Stevenson 1986), and these deviations at times challenge or even contraindicate major features of the conventional wisdom concerning prominent managerial theories and practice.

The fourth point concerns the validity of self-reports as data. The conventional tendency will be resisted here to write: "Of course, the focus on *only* self-reports requires that results be confirmed with the use of objective and unobtrusive data." The self-reports here *should be* cross-checked by a variety of other kinds of data, but evidence indicates that self-reports can lay substantial claims to usefulness. Moreover, for many purposes, self-reports provide the data of choice (e.g., Howard et al. 1980). For confirming evidence of the usefulness of self-reports, see also French, Caplan, and Harrison 1980 (102–3). Hence, the sobriquet "*only* self-reports" will be avoided here.

Note

1. The bulk of this chapter is from Golembiewski, Munzenrider, and Stevenson 1984.

References

Burke, R., and Deszca, G. 1985. "Correlates of Psychological Burnout Phases among Police Officers." Unpublished ms. York, Canada: York University.

Burke, R.; Shearer, J.; and Deszca, G. 1984. "Burnout among Men and Women in Police Work." *Journal of Health and Human Resources Administration* 7:162–88.

Cherniss, C. 1980. *Staff Burnout: Job Stress in Human Services*. Beverly Hills, Calif.: Sage.

Deckard, G. J. 1985. *Work Stress, Mood, and Ecological Dysfunction in Health and Social Services Settings*. Ph.D. diss. University of Missouri. Columbia, Mo.

Deckard, G. J.; Rountree, B. H.; and Golembiewski, R. T. 1986. "Worksite Features and Progressive Burnout." *Journal of Health and Human Resources Administration*. 9:38–55.

______. 1989. "A Causal Path Analysis of Burnout and Agitation." *Journal of Health and Human Resources Administration* in press.

Dyer, W. 1987. *Team Building*. Reading, Mass: Addison-Wesley.

French, J. R. P., Jr.; Caplan, R. D.; and Harrison, R. V. 1980. *The Mechanisms of Job Stress and Strain*. New York: Wiley.

Freudenberger, H. J. 1980. *Burnout: The High Cost of High Achievement*. Garden City, N.Y.: Anchor Press.

Golembiewski, R. T. 1979. *Approaches to Planned Change*. New York: Marcel Dekker.

______. 1984. "Organizational and Policy Implications of a Phase Model of Burnout." In *Organizational Policy and Development,* edited by L. R. Maise, 135–47. Louisville, Ky.: Center for Continuing Studies, University of Louisville.

______. 1985. "Enriching the Theory and Practice of Team-Building." In *Contemporary Organization Development,* edited by D. D. Warrick, 98–113. Glenview, Ill.: Scott, Foresman, and Co.

Golembiewski, R. T., and Kim, B-S. 1989. "Self-Esteem and Phases of Burnout." *Organization Development Journal* 7:51–58.

Golembiewski, R. T., and Munzenrider, R. F. 1981. "Efficacy of Three Versions of One Burnout Measure." *Journal of Health and Human Resources Administration* 4:228–46.

______. 1984. "Phases of Psychological Burnout and Organizational Covariants: A Replication Using Norms from a Large Population." *Journal of Health and Human Resources Administration* 6:290–323.

______. 1988. *Phases of Burnout*. New York: Praeger.

Golembiewski, R. T.; Hilles, R.; and Kagno, M. 1974. "A Longitudinal Study of Flexi-Time Effects." *Journal of Applied Behavioral Science* 10:502–32.

Golembiewski, R. T.; Munzenrider, R. F.; and Carter, D. 1983. "Phases of Progressive Burnout and Their Worksite Covariants." *Journal of Applied Behavioral Science* 19:461–82.

Golembiewski, R. T.; Munzenrider, R. F.; and Stevenson, J. 1984. "Physical Symptoms and Burnout Phases." Paper presented at the Second Annual Conference on Organizational Policy and Development. University of Louisville, Louisville, Ky., 11–13 April.

______. 1986. *Stress in Organizations*. New York: Praeger.

Harrison, R. 1965. "Group Composition Models for Laboratory Design." *Journal of Applied Behavioral Science* 1:409–32.

______. 1972. "Role Negotiation." In *The Social Technology of Organization Development,* edited by W. W. Burke and H. Hornstein, 84–96. Washington, D.C.: NTL Learning Resources.

Howard, G. S.; Maxwell, S. E.; Wiener, R. L.; Boynton, K. S.; and Rooney, W. M. 1980. "Is a Behavioral Measure the Best Estimate of Behavioral Parameters? Perhaps Not." *Applied Psychological Measurement* 4:293–311.

Maslach, C., and Jackson, S. E. 1981. "The Measurement of Experienced Burnout." *Journal of Occupational Behavior* 2:99–113.

______. 1982, 1986. *Maslach Burnout Inventory*. La Jolla, Calif.: Consulting Psychologists Press.

Munzenrider, R. F., and Golembiewski, R. T. 1987. "Is Burnout Idiosyncratic or Generic?" Paper presented at the Annual Meeting, American Society for Public Administration. Boston, Mass.

Quinn, R. P., and Shepard, L. J. 1979. "The 1972–73 Quality of Employment Survey." Ann Arbor, Mich.: Survey Research Center, University of Michigan.

Yalom, I. D., and Lieberman, M. A. 1971. "A Study of Group Casualties." *Archives of General Psychiatry* 25:16–30.

Irony IV

Relative Success without Specifying Contexts

6

Team Building under Diverse Conditions: Kinds of Crises and Members

Team building constitutes a common family of OD designs, and for good reasons (e.g., Dyer 1987). Those designs have substantial success rates, as chapter 1 suggests is true of all OD designs at the level of the small group. This implies that intervenors are generally quite clever in fitting design variants to specific single settings, despite the general theoretical failure to explicitly provide for differences likely to be encountered in large collections of small-group settings involving a superior and his immediate cluster of first reports.

But ODers need to do better than to rely on their individual sensitivity to one or a few groups, if only because it is increasingly commonplace to hold team-building experiences for twenty or even a hundred or more teams exposed to the same learning design. Individual sensitivities are not sufficient for this scale of intervention. Moreover, as the technology for differentiating groups develops, so also will individual consultants dealing with single groups be more effective in fitting specific designs to different contexts.

This need to differentiate contexts to facilitate the fitting of tailored designs is both necessary and neglected. Not only does observation suggest a diversity of types of small groups, but both the general literature (e.g., Golembiewski 1962) and specific tests (e.g., Bowers and Hausser 1977) imply that a substantial number of small-group varieties need distinguishing. In turn, different designs seem appropriate for this gaggle of varieties (e.g., Bowers and Hausser 1977). Unfortunately, with all-too-rare exceptions (Dyer 1977, 1987), the tailoring of designs to contexts has not been an OD priority. Enhanced success rates require just such work on a broad front, which this chapter illustrates in two particulars.

A Conceptual Context for Irony IV

This chapter tries to do better in the critical regard of differentiating contexts so that appropriate designs can be fitted to them. The initial approach has three emphases: an anomaly in team-building success rates will provide a rationale for introducing two instrumented ways of distinguishing between small groups.[1] The first emphasis deals with two classic conditions in groups, and the second again directs attention to differences in psychological burnout among a group's members, following the approach introduced in chapter 5.

Toward Resolving an Anomaly

Some readers of the OD literature have recently directed attention to an apparent anomaly. On the one hand, individual applications of team-building designs seem to be increasingly popular and appear to have the expected effects, on balance (Dyer 1977, 1987; De Meuse and Liebowitz 1981; Golembiewski, Proehl, and Sink 1981). On the other hand, *simultaneous* applications of a common team-building design to large numbers of work units in the same organization have fared less well (Harris and Porras 1978; Porras and Wilkins 1980).

Hence, experience with team building can be fairly characterized as Janus-faced. Most observers reflect a sunny and optimistic visage. For example, De Meuse and Liebowitz (1981) review thirty-six applications usually involving single teams and, despite concern about the casual methodology of many of the studies, they see a robust and burgeoning theory-cum-technology. Other observers (e.g., Harris and Porras 1978; Porras and Wilkins 1980) are dour after surveying their attempts at mass team building. Things just did not turn out as predicted. Perhaps too much was expected of a brief design, goes the overall evaluation of one of the efforts (Harris and Porras 1978). The other effort motivates far greater concern: the authors interpret their result as possibly undercutting the basic role of effective socio-emotional processes, which in turn could undermine OD's credibility among potential users. Porras and Wilkins conclude:

> Several key measures of performance . . . [show] significant improvement. . . . Yet, measures of organizational processes indicated a deterioration of the internal dynamics of the system. This was clearly . . . unexpected. . . . Other alternatives must be sought or OD will be viewed as irrelevant to large-system change (1980, 531–32).

This chapter is not deterred by the apparent anomaly. Quite the opposite, in fact. This chapter seeks to encompass both anomalous positions in a direct way that will elaborate the theory underlying team building and that also may enrich its practice. Specifically, the two reactions sketched above may reflect the impact of two seldom-diagnosed conditions in team-building settings:

- the underlying character of the conflict or tension in the subsystem, which can be highlighted by distinguishing conditions of agreement versus disagreement in small groups

- the degree of psychological burnout experienced by members of the team

Generally, then, the present argument has a direct thrust. Individual team-building applications do not have to encompass the degree of variation in these two contextual features prominent in mass team-building ventures. Skillful intervenors working with single teams, goes this line of argument, can adjust to incongruencies between the design and the specific context for intervention. A design useful for some teams in a mass design, in contrast, is likely to be beside the point or even counterproductive for other teams in that batch. If the standard confrontational design is utilized (Dyer 1977, 1987; Golembiewski and Kiepper 1976; Boss 1979), for example, there is some probability that it will be inappropriate to some or even many units in the batch, while it well serves others.

Hence enhanced diagnostic power is the goal here. Available work provides instrumentation for such diagnosis, fortunately, and it also suggests the character of appropriate designs. That is an attractive combination.

Conditions of Disagreement versus Agreement

Attention to disagreement versus agreement as a central condition in a group has a substantial history, in various forms, from Janis (1972) to Harvey (1977) to Dyer (1977, 1987). Harvey's is perhaps the most arresting formulation, which he began expressing as "the Abilene Paradox" and subsequently refined into a comparison of a "crisis of agreement" with a "crisis of disagreement." Table 6.1 generates the fuller sense of the critical distinction (see also Golembiewski 1979, 2:151–58).

The thrust of the differences in table 6.1 seems direct: basically, concern about membership seems to dominate in the crisis of agreement—given that prestige of membership can derive from the "best and brightest" view characteristic of the Kennedy administration (Janis 1972), or from the desire for continued membership rooted in suspicion and fear, as seems to have been the case with Nixon appointees who reasonably seemed to believe there was no other way they could attract similar power or salary (Raven 1974). Testing for actual agreement would risk membership, in both cases, and hence the test tends not to be made. In disagreement, the primal concern is one of unsatisfactory inclusion, which typically is reflected in we/they modes. Here, there is less to lose and more to gain.

Appropriate interventions in the two systems will differ profoundly. In disagreement, only a legitimate process for exploring differences is needed, and that need can be easily satisfied by various confrontational and interaction-oriented designs (Golembiewski 1979, vol. 1, chap. 6). One key source of leverage inheres in the fact that actors risk only an unattractive relationship, which may encourage boldness and highlight any progress. In agreement,

TABLE 6.1
A Contrast of Underlying Behavioral Processes for Two Types of Crises

Crisis of Agreement	Crisis of Disagreement
1. Organization members experience pain from some specific collective problem(s), with feelings about impotence or incompetence deriving from the failure to resolve or manage the problem(s) somehow.	1. Organization members may or may not experience pain from some specific collective problem(s), but such problem(s) do exist although consciousness raising about them may be required.
2. Members share the same private concept of problem(s) facing their organization, and individually recognize the same or similar underlying explanations or causes of the problem(s).	2. Members do not share the same private concept of problem(s) facing their organization, and individually have very different underlying explanations of causes of the problem(s), if any are acknowledged.
3. As individuals, many or all organization members have similar and compatible preferences for coping with the problem(s).	3. As individuals, many or all organization members have different and incompatible preferences for coping with the problem(s).
4. As individuals, many or all organization members see the same or similar solution as appropriate for resolving or managing the problem(s).	4. As individuals, many or all organization members see different or incompatible solutions as appropriate for resolving or managing the problem(s).
5. In public settings, organization members consistently do not communicate accurately to one another—about their preferences, beliefs, knowledge of causes and consequences of organization problems—and hence mutually create a false or misleading collective reality. ● In the longer run, the probable result is a low-energy system—careful, perhaps polite, and very conscious of roles and jurisdictions. ● In some highly prestigious groups, the facade may emphasize potency and a high-energy level.	5. In public settings, therefore, organization members may deal with one another in two basic ways ● Probably in a minority of cases, members will risk open conflict, hostility, etc., attendant to the expression of disagreements. ● Probably in most cases, members will avoid the risk of acrimony (as by agreeing not to disagree openly on certain issues) but at the expense of suppressing real issues and conflict.

TABLE 6.1 continued

Crisis of Agreement	Crisis of Disagreement
6. Given a false or misleading collective reality, on definite balance, collective decisions get made that reflect neither member preferences nor their real views of reality, with the results more than likely being counterproductive both for individual and organization goals.	The openly conflictful organizations probably will be high-energy systems, with substantial but perhaps incompatible personal commitment and involvement, great but perhaps fruitless expenditures of effort, and so on.
	The suppressing organization probably will be characterized by low levels of energy, commitment, and involvement.
7. Greater member pain is likely, and a sense of both individual and collective incompetence and impotency probably will grow.	6. The probability seems high that both adaptations—if for different reasons—will lead to a false or misleading collective reality, over time. Openly conflictful organizations may develop polarizations that inhibit or preclude members from communicating accurately with one another. Suppressing organizations may create the same effect by defining certain subjects as off-limits.
8. The cycle is set to repeat itself, probably with greater speed and intensity as well as with a lessened probability of corrective action.	

TABLE 6.2
Some Questions for Diagnostic Interviews and Guidelines for Using Them to Differentiate Agreement from Disagreement

A. Diagnostic Questions

1. In general, how are things going in the organization?
2. What in particular is going well?
3. What are some specific organization problems which need to be solved?
4. What actions do you think need to be taken to solve them?
5. What problem-solving actions have you and others attempted, and what were the outcomes?
6. If you have not taken action, what prevents your taking action to solve them?

B. Diagnostic Guidelines

1. If answers to question 1 are consistently positive, the organization presumably experiences neither conflict of disagreement nor conflict of agreement. Only reporting back to confirm the health of the organization is necessary.
2. If answers to questions 1–4 consistently differ, the organization may be presumed to be in a conflict of disagreement. A design like the confrontation design would be appropriate.
3. A crisis of agreement may be presumed when:
   - Pain and conflict get emphasized in responses to questions 1–3.
   - Agreement about organization problems surfaces on question 3.
   - Agreement about probable solutions exists on question 4.
   - Much rationalization about why what should be done cannot be done gets expressed in responses to questions 5 and 6.
   - Evidence is presented about actions actually taken, especially in response to question 5, that are contrary to what respondents believe should be done.

valued membership must be safeguarded—first and foremost, whatever the process. This is a delicate and chancy matter.

Although the distinction has been in the common realm for a time, and in attractive formulations, the distinction gets reflected in diagnosis and design only in rare cases (e.g., Dyer 1977, 1987). And more's the pity, for solid guides for both diagnosis and design are available.

Table 6.2, following Harvey (1977, 169–71), provides a clear guide for diagnosis. It lists a set of questions for interviews with all members of a work unit before a specific team-building design is decided upon. The interview schema shown in table 6.2 is more demanding than (for example) a paper-and-pencil diagnostic instrument that might be applied to very large populations, later to be machine-scored. But the set of questions still provides considerable aid, even as it requires interviewing prior to diagnosis.

Prescription of a specific team-building design for disagreement seems to pose no great problem, at least as a first approximation. The usual confrontational designs should work well; and simple interview/feedback designs also could do the job (Fordyce and Weil 1971). My preference is for designs building around three-dimensional (3-D) images, which have been widely used and reported on (e.g.,Golembiewski and Blumberg 1967; Golembiewski and Kiepper 1976; and Boss, 1979). These designs share data in response to three questions:

- How do we see Other?
- How does Other see us?
- How do we see ourselves?

Two or more parties can then compare their answers to such questions, in what amounts to a design encouraging telling the less-varnished truth.

Three-dimensional designs tend to work for several reasons, with two being perhaps primary. Such designs inherently provide a procedure for gathering data, which rests on specific values and empirical theory fragments. This provides the "legitimate process" that table 6.1 sees as central in a condition of disagreement. In addition, 3-D designs seem to quickly liberate energies, which by hypothesis are used to repress conflict in disagreement. Such energy release can be exhilarating and, in combination with the newly legitimated process for problem analysis, can induce a very tangible sense of movement or progress in what was a blocked and frustrating situation. This release of energy often comes as a tangible whoosh, in fact, once the energy is no longer needed for suppressing conflict or avoiding unsatisfactory inclusion. Crudely, one guesses that the cost:benefit ratio is very favorable in conditions of disagreement. If the design works, new data and membership become available. If the design fails, one is not very much worse off.

As for prescribing a basic design for a condition or crisis of agreement, let us begin with exclusions. For openers, it seems clear that confrontational designs have significant drawbacks in such cases. Indeed, they may be generally counterproductive. Recall that continued membership is postulated as central in conditions of agreement. Hence a confrontational design might well fail basically even as it succeeds tactically in generating the public sharing of data. In short, confrontational designs raise very troubling questions for those preoccupied with membership:

- What is there about us as a group that led us to publicly suppress what we in fact largely agreed about?
- How can we be confident that we will not again fall into a condition or crisis of agreement?

We can be less certain about what designs will work for a diagnosed crisis of agreement, in addition, because little research or experience has been accumulated. However, Harvey (1977) seems to provide a useful way of

TABLE 6.3
Sketch of an Intervention for a Condition of Agreement

1. Sort the interview data into the basic themes of agreement.
2. Themes get reported back in a public session in ways that use respondents' own words as much as possible but that protect anonymity.
3. All those interviewed then write a collective summary of all of the data supporting each theme of agreement, decide on the action implications of the themes, and plan specific actions.
4. Summarize the theory of agreement sketched in table 6.1, to reinforce understanding of why and how members were inhibited from sharing agreements with each other.
5. Individual organization members are coached, in private, about actions they might take in light of the agreements with their colleagues.

approach in table 6.3. Read between the lines a little, and his basic thrusts seem clear. The design's multiple checks imply care to establish that only broadly held materials get admitted to analysis. Pretty clearly, this rechecking process no doubt seeks to reduce the probability that anyone's membership is threatened, even as it seeks to raise the likelihood that not just another crisis of agreement is being developed.

The careful character of table 6.3 contrasts markedly with the wham-bang quality of many confrontational designs. For example, Boss (1979) reports a threatened fistfight in one of the latter designs. There is too much to be lost in the ideal conflict of agreement for such precipitous acting out; and even an impactful learning design could generate very mixed results. Crudely, again, the cost:benefit ratio seems relatively balanced in a crisis of agreement. Hence the careful character of table 6.3.

Conclusions should not be rushed beyond the reasonable suggestions of Harvey, but the argument thus far does suggest a range of other designs that are indicated, as well as some designs that are contraindicated for the conditions of agreement and disagreement. The provisional assignments shown in table 6.4 seem reasonable for the two diagnoses of agreement or disagreement.

In a rough sense, the designs in the Condition of Disagreement column initially emphasize differentiation and, although this will often lead to integration, such a beginning could pose definite threats to membership in the group. This constitutes no basic problem for a condition of disagreement—where the key issue is unsatisfactory inclusion with which, obviously, even extended initial differentiation is consistent. The designs in the Condition of Agreement column in Table 6.4 focus ab initio on a common product, and hence will be less upsetting where the issue is continuing membership.

TABLE 6.4
Indicated Designs for Conditions of Disagreement and Agreement

Condition of Disagreement	Condition of Agreement
• Interaction-centered team building (Dyer 1977)	• Task-centered team building (Dyer 1977)
• T-groups with intact work groups	• Role negotiation (Harrison 1972)
• Specific goads to quick confrontation such as those used in some organizations: "Tell your boss what's wrong with him or her."	• Designs that focus on a task or product: e.g., skill building (Golembiewski and Kiepper 1976) or developing a management credo or statement of missions-and-roles
• Third-party interventions and other conflict-oriented designs (Filley 1974)	

In addition, some designs seem to be more or less equally applicable to the two conditions. Survey/feedback and interview/feedback designs permit such flexibility. Why? Possible reasons include a subtle relocation of responsibility for what gets said, and how it gets said, to the survey, and perhaps even the disavowal by members of any and all feedback by the external intervenor if membership seems threatened. In one such application, for example, an executive team was not willing to deal with a critical situation till they heard the results of interviews, which had this tenor: "Eleven of thirteen of you agreed about X, twelve of thirteen about Y, and all of you agreed about Z." Such a report could not threaten group membership very much, patently.

More broadly, this line of thought also supports a reasonable conclusion. Consider the work which supports the "greater effectiveness" of (for example) survey/feedback as compared to laboratory training or T-grouping (e.g., Bowers 1973). Common interpretations conclude that some designs are better than others. The present line of thought encourages a more restricted interpretation. When you cannot differentiate targets for interventions, some designs like survey/feedback may be safer in that they will not create problems in either a condition of disagreement or one of agreement. Other designs may be more target-specific, being good fits for some settings and poor fits for others. The moral of the research is *not* that some designs are better than others. In contrast, the highlighted need involves diagnosing the specific conditions to which various designs are more or less applicable.

Take care in boarding the bus to Abilene. The crisis of agreement appears in several forms (e.g., Janis 1972), but there is no question that its most popular representation derives from Jerry Harvey. That popularity came early in the delightful format of Jerry's family "going to Abilene" on a bus when all (or most) would have preferred sitting on the front porch with a fan and a glass of lemonade on a blazing-hot day (Harvey 1988a, 1977). Hence the common reference to "the Abilene paradox." (There was no air conditioning, one gathers, either at home or on the bus.) That popularity has persisted, with *Organizational Dynamics* recently having reprinted Harvey's Abilene story, (1988a), along with an extended personal commentary and update (Harvey 1988b) as well as with two notes that highlight the importance of the Abilene paradox (Kanter 1988; Carlisle 1988).

So popular has that Abilene bus become, as it were, that the crisis of agreement has been extended very far—probably too far. In being associated with so many situations, the formulation stands in danger of meaning less and less about more and more. Hence this commentary, which is intended to save the best far more than to criticize overexuberant extensions.

Let me back up a bit. Few (indeed, more likely, no) empirical tests exist of the ways suggested by Jerry and others for dealing with the condition. And the few case studies are not only sparse, but they also are unclear about the outcomes of specific designs for dealing constructively with a crisis of agreement.

This curious gap says something about the state of empirical research in human system development and change, to be sure.

But let me also suggest that this unsatisfactory state has something to say about the Abilene paradox itself: that Harvey's seminal concept has been stretched to cover situations that it fits only poorly, or even not at all. This boosterism can devalue the concept, and discourage empirical inquiry. A concept can be associated with everything only at the cost of failing to clarify anything. "One size fits all" applies even less to metaphors and situational descriptions than it does to socks, where it applies poorly enough.

Specifically, at least four types of situations normally remain undifferentiated in discussions of Abilene. They distort or camouflage useful distinctions, especially when it comes to prescribing what it will take to do the job of resolving a crisis of agreement. Consider these four types of crisis of agreement:

1. garden variety conflicts of agreement, as in the case of Jerry's family that made the famous trip to Abilene
2. the conflict of agreement among the "best and the brightest," like that which seems to have affected President Kennedy's associates in the apocalyptic decision making surrounding the Cuban missile crisis (e.g., Halberstam 1969).
3. the conflict of agreement like that apparently existing among President Nixon's confidants in the Watergate days, where a "war mentality" prevailed (e.g., Raven 1974) and where "real" self-esteem seems low.
4. the conflict of agreement among true believers—in an ideology, a mythology, or whatever—as they come to question their orthodoxy (e.g., Festinger, Riecken, and Schachter 1956).

My sense is that these are very different situations, and that they respond to different interventions, even diametrically opposed interventions. Significantly, also, the probable success rates are sometimes at a slam-dunk level. In other cases, intervening approximates a last-second, eighty-foot, behind-the-ear, game-winning fling, with defender Wilt Chamberlain standing underneath the basket, in the days when goaltending was legal.

Let me be brief in highlighting each type, and in sketching some implications of each for theory and practice.

The garden variety case, type 1, poses no great problems when I encounter it, which is far more often than types 2–4. I resist even referring to it as a crisis of agreement. That could result in some cases, of course. Far more likely, however, this type situation provides opportunities for poking fun, and soon after the fact, very much in the manner that Harvey attributes to his family. Typically, direct confrontations will suffice, and the probable success rate is very high. The common reaction on exposure of the agreement is spoken in a bemused tone: "Well, how about that?"

Why? Basically, powerful factors in such cases cushion the severity of the dour conditions Harvey rightly associates with a real crisis of agreement. These cushioning factors in type 1 include long-standing relationships, presumed continuation of affective bonds, the multiple opportunities for face-to-face dealing with the issues and their consequences, and the usefulness of such victories in building cohesiveness.

The second class, type 2 conflicts, seems to me to have major redemptive features that help leverage change, with the most prominent feature being the lofty self-esteem of the participants. Theoretical reasons and experience alike suggest that such individuals can hear surprising or even hurtful feedback better than most, and then get on with it. Direct confrontations should be able to do the job.

There are downsides to intervening in this second case, of course. The fear of exclusion exists, and that can be very real. Moreover, the feedback must come from someone most group members see as staunch as they see themselves. That someone can be an insider or an outsider, but that someone must have high standing with group members.

However, the general prognosis is good in type 2 situations. Perhaps basically, such people pride themselves on their coping skills, and have the reservoir of self-esteem to recover from situations that might herniate others. I recall one joyous post-insight whoop in such a group: "When we do it, we really do it. We set a record for going to Abilene. No doubt. Let's set some other records now."

Type 3 poses the most serious issues, since the potential loss of membership can be crippling, if self-esteem is low and selection processes have been sufficiently diabolic. "Where could I ever make as much money, and exercise as much power, at my age and experience," echoes a plaintive cry common to several Watergaters as they sought to explain why they did not do something that could have saved them and their country from a painful and dangerous experience.

Why the difference between 2 and 3? In contrast to 2, here the key descriptors are negative and even passive versus active and positive—a "connection" or serendipity versus achievement in gaining membership, dependence versus a certain rambunctiousness of spirit, a sensitivity to commands versus a questioning if not counterdependent spirit, lower versus often towering self-esteem, and a garrison mentality versus a perception of self as a competent in a hurry to get to Camelot, to enjoy.

In type 3, Harvey's conceptual elaborations seem to me to apply most directly—indeed, point by point; and his prescriptions about intervening via careful and slowly unfolding designs seem right-on. Such groups can't win for losing—usually sooner rather than later, and often with a precipitous fall from grace rather than a setback uncovered sufficiently early to contain losses, and perhaps to motivate learning. The probability of successful intervention in type 3 seems low to miniscule to me, but no definite study exists.

Type 4 seems most problematic to me, and the vital issue seems to me whether a high-enough proportion of members, appropriately located and wired-in, come to have similar reservations about the same leading ideas, at around the same time. If so, successful change has a real chance. Otherwise, I see the chances in the range of slim to none.

Type 4 is not strictly a conflict of agreement in Harvey's terms, in any case. Perhaps it is best described as a movement toward a possible crisis of agreement, but as having protean forms that feature aggressive denial at many stages, and with many branches in its developmental tree. An extreme case of type 4 involves a religious group, whose members have variously prepared for the end of the world, *on a specific date*, as by selling or giving away their possessions. Intervening here will be extraordinarily complex, because faith will sustain the true believers at least until the specific date, when deep despair or convoluted denial suddenly set in (e.g., Festinger, Riecken, and Schachter 1956).

Whatever one calls it, or them, I see a greater frequency of type 4 than 2 or 3. A recent case concerns the organizational belief about the alleged felicitous qualities of "natural fire" in the national forests, whose limits were dramatically revealed in Yellowstone Park during 1988.

I suspect Gorbachev today faces just such a situation, for example, as did the officials of the Forest Service in the late 1960s. In both cases, their respective orthodoxies portrayed them as being in great shape, just as their respective abysses loomed ahead of them. Growing numbers came to perceive the burgeoning distance between leading ideas and reality. The Forest Service saved the baby from the bathwater—as it added to its product line, added various new specialists, diversified the gender and race of its employees, encompassed people as well as trees as clients, and generally got in better shape to compete for budgetary support. We shall see about Comrade Gorbachev.

Differences in Psychological Burnout

New evidence also suggests that team-building diagnoses and designs, especially when masses of teams are involved, need to be sensitive to one major characteristic of participants as individuals and in the aggregate—their members' degrees of psychological burnout. This emphasis on individuals complements the preceding emphasis on the character of their relationships. Broadly, burnout has a central conceptual status as "a syndrome of inappropriate attitudes towards clients and towards self, often associated with uncomfortable physical and emotional symptoms" (Kahn 1978, 61). In addition to reduced productivity, burnout's dreary inventory of effects includes "job turnover, absenteeism, and low morale (as well as) various self-reported indices of personal distress, including mental exhaustion, insomnia, increased use of alcohol or drugs, and marital and family problems" (Maslach and Jackson 1981, 100).

This chapter can rely to a degree on chapter 5, and chapter 7 will provide detail about one worksite; but some overlap will be risked on the general premise that repetition is preferable to overlooking a significant point. To review a substantial body of research (Golembiewski, Munzenrider, and Stevenson 1985; Golembiewski and Munzenrider 1988), progress has been made toward the development of a paper-and-pencil measure of burnout (e.g., Maslach and Jackson 1981, 1986), but it is not yet clear how best to aggregate the items of the MBI. Several alternative ways have been tested, using as a basic referent twenty-two target variables thought to tap important aspects of the worksite. The variables and predictions about them can be introduced in three categories:

1. Job Descriptive Index (JDI), which measures satisfaction with five facets of work and also provides a total satisfaction score (Smith, Kendall, and Blood 1969). As burnout increases, one expects reduced satisfaction on all JDI measures with the possible exception of JDI-Pay. The host organization's pay policies are considered superior, generally, and satisfaction with them consequently might not differ among those experiencing various degrees of burnout.
2. Job Diagnostic Survey (JDS), which measures satisfaction with ten facets of the job (Hackman and Oldham 1981). As burnout increases, with the possible exception of JDS-Compensation, one expects reduced satisfaction on all JDS facets.

3. Assorted scales which, with one exception, should decrease as burnout increases. The Job Tension scale (Kahn, et al. 1964) should reflect a direct relationship with burnout. These other scales should decrease as burnout increases:

    - Trust in supervisors (Roberts and O'Reilly 1974)
    - Trust in fellow employees
    - Job involvement (White and Ruh 1973)
    - Willingness to disagree with supervisor (Patchen 1965)
    - Participation in decisions concerning work (White and Ruh 1973)

Tests of four ways of aggregating MBI items may be summarized briefly. First, as table 6.5 shows, the MBI Total Score correlates quite regularly with a number of variables describing important aspects of the worksite. That puts it mildly, in fact. All twenty-two of the correlations are in the expected directions; twenty-one of them attain the .05 level; and the significant correlations account for a substantial 13 percent of the total variance, with several cases accounting for as much as a quarter of the total variance.

Second, as table 6.5 also shows, the three MBI subscales have marked patterns of association with the twenty-two target variables. The level of association is lower, on average, for the three subscale scores than for the Total Score. Moreover, the subscales differ substantially in their association with the target variables. Specifically, on average, the subscales singly account for the following percentages of variance:

- Emotional Exhaustion accounts for 12 percent, with subscale items tapping the degrees to which respondents feel inadequate in coping with strain in their lives, to which they are "at the end of the rope" in psychological and emotional terms;
- Personal Accomplishment accounts for 8 percent, and subscale items here relate to feelings about the effectiveness of performance on a meaningful and worthwhile job;
- Depersonalization accounts for 4 percent of the variance, with its items referring to the degree to which humans and relationships with them are considered to be objects or things.

Third, the MBI items can also be used to generate a set of burnout phases. Since they have been introduced in chapter 5, only a brief introductory review will be made here. By dichotomizing one population of respondents at the median for each subscale, and by assuming that Depersonalization characterizes the least-virulent phases of burnout while Emotional Exhaustion impacts the latter phases, the eight phases or stages shown in table 5.1 are distinguished.

The complex tests of the burnout phases cannot be summarized here in any detail but, briefly, two kinds of evidence suggest solid support. Thus, the

TABLE 6.5
Correlations between Total and Subscale MBI scores and Twenty-two Scales

	Correlations with MBI Items, Aggregated as Total Score or Three Subscale Scores				
	Alpha	Total Score	Depersonalization	Personal Accomplishment (reversed)	Emotional Exhaustion
I **JDI Scales:** Satisfaction with					
• Work	.80	−.51[a]	−.26[a]	−.34[a]	−.49[a]
• Supervision	.83	−.37[a]	−.21[a]	−.20[a]	−.37[a]
• Coworkers	.86	−.24[a]	−.16[a]	−.25[a]	−.29[a]
• Promotion	.90	−.28[a]	−.12	−.16[a]	−.29[a]
• Pay	.92	−.15[a]	−.01	−.07	−.19[a]
• Total JDI	.73	−.49[a]	−.25[a]	−.33[a]	−.45[a]
II **JDI Scales:** Satisfaction with					
• Experienced meaningfulness of work	.78	−.39[a]	−.20[a]	−.30[a]	−.31[a]
• Experienced responsibility for work	.66	−.19[a]	−.12[a]	−.26[a]	−.05
• Knowledge of results	.71	−.26[a]	−.23[a]	−.12	−.20[a]
• Work in general	.75	−.51[a]	−.26[a]	−.33[a]	−.50[a]
• Work motivation	.58	−.26[a]	−.13[a]	−.32[a]	−.08
• Growth	.84	−.51[a]	−.17[a]	−.32[a]	−.32[a]
• Job security	.84	−.33[a]	−.19[a]	−.20[a]	−.26[a]
• Compensation	.86	−.13[a]	−.03	−.02	−.15[a]
• Coworkers	.67	−.36[a]	−.18[a]	−.33[a]	−.24[a]
• Supervision	.90	−.34[a]	−.18[a]	−.17[a]	−.33[a]
III **Selected Scales**					
• Trust in supervisors	.83	−.43[a]	−.23[a]	−.29[a]	−.39[a]
• Trust in fellow employees	.78	−.36[a]	−.27[a]	−.24[a]	−.26[a]
• Job involvement	.77	−.45[a]	−.25[a]	−.42[a]	−.33[a]
• Willingness to disagree with supervisor	.70	−.12	−.02	−.25[a]	−.02
• Job-related tension	.81	.40[a]	.23[a]	.13[a]	.42[a]
• Participation	.76	−.31[a]	−.08	−.34[a]	−.25[a]

Source: Robert T. Golembiewski and Robert F. Munzenrider. 1981. "Efficacy of Three Versions of One Burnout Measure: MBI as Total Score, Subscale Scores, or Phases?" *Journal of Health and Human Resources Administration* 4:231.

Note: [a]Indicates a correlation coefficient statistically significant at .05 level.

phases isolate nonrandom variation on almost all of the target variables described above, almost all of the time, in all of the several tests run thus far. On average, eighteen or nineteen of each twenty variables on which significant variation was expected generate F-ratios that surpass the .05 level. In addition, paired-comparisons establish the robustness as well as regularity of the differences in target variables isolated by the phases. Depending upon the specific site tested, as many as 60 percent of the paired-comparisons of differences on the target variables attain statistical significance. Details are available in several sources (e.g., Golembiewski, Munzenrider, and Stevenson 1985; Golembiewski and Munzenrider 1988).

Especially in its phase formulation, burnout seems to have significant implications for team-building designs, particularly in mass populations. For teams with all or many members in phases II and IV, for example, standard interaction-centered or confrontational designs should suffice. In those phases, individuals score High on Depersonalization, and interaction designs should be helpful in arresting or reversing such a trend. Here new stimulation would be effective, in general: individuals receive heightened feedback and disclosure concerning the effects of their viewing others as objects; and, ideally, individuals also come to feel the rewards of greater acceptance and liking that typically follow as a consequence of responding to individuals as persons.

For more advanced burnout phases, however—let us say, phases VI through VIII—interaction-oriented designs seem awkward, even counterproductive. Individuals already have a surfeit of negative stimuli, and may even possess a response-set that encourages them to perceive neutral or even positive stimuli in negative terms. Here, the additional stimulation characteristic of interaction-centered designs might result in overstimulation, even bombardment escalating to non-helpful or even hurtful proportions. Looked at from another perspective, cases of advanced burnout might be particularly responsive to policy and structural amelioration—as in reductions in role-overload, the greater clarification of roles, and so on. The evidence is far from conclusive on the point, but some experience in day-care centers supports the present position. There, staff with high burnout responded positively to various restructuring efforts—for example, job rotation and rescheduling the children's day so as to ease the demands on the adult staff (Pines and Maslach 1980).

Greater Success by Specifying Kinds of Crises and Memberships

Will the specification of kinds of conditions in groups, as well as the distributions of the burnout phases of their memberships, increase the success rates for OD intervenors? The implied support for an affirmative answer seems strong. The failure to make these two differentiations will likely lead to mischief.

In this spirit, let us bring these introductory considerations to three tentative conclusions. In turn, they sketch the basic orientation of this chapter, emphasize the possibility of the convenient instrumentation for the two kinds of differences emphasized here, and sketch some guidelines for designs sensitive to kinds of group conditions and differential burnout in groups.

Significance of Mass Team Building

There seem to be ample reasons for intervenors to broaden their conceptual perspectives to include two classes of differentia—agreement versus disagreement and degree of burnout—when considering a team-building design. This seems apt counsel even when an intervenor works with a single group or team. Mass team-building efforts *require* such specification. This bottom-line conclusion alone justifies the demonstration above.

Mass team-building efforts are no longer exotic, please note, and concerns about their efficacy constitute one of the major challenges to OD's credibility. For a time, very few examples of mass team building could be found in the literature (e.g., Golembiewski 1978, 2:131–38). But more recently, their incidence has increased substantially (Harris and Porras 1978; Porras and Wilkins 1980), as have reports about their mixed or unexpected results. By hypothesis, these surprises are provisionally attributed to the common imposition of a standard design on mass team-building populations, whose probable heterogeneity will have an uneven fit with the standard design. As the number of teams increases, roughly, so will variant conditions appear to which the usual confrontational designs adapt poorly. With single units or small numbers of units, in contrast, alert intervenors will be able to adapt standard designs to the specific texture and flow of individual teams. Here the success rates are substantial, even formidable (e.g., De Meuse and Liebowitz 1981).For example, I have reported success rates in changing group variables in individual teams via a standard design that approximate 80 percent (Golembiewski 1978, 2:338–44).

The basic notion about group heterogeneity underlying this chapter should not astound. Even brief consideration—which can be reinforced by sophisticated research (e.g., Bowers and Hausser 1977)—strongly suggests that work units are not essentially homogeneous. No one yet knows, but as many as a score of subtypes may be needed to encompass the diversity which exists in nature. Hence the lower success rates of applying standard team-building designs to large populations of formal work units.

Availability of Instrumentation

Fortunately, convenient approaches exist for testing for agreement versus disagreement, as well as for burnout. The paper-and-pencil instrument de-

FIGURE 6.1
A Provisional Grid for Team-Building Diagnoses

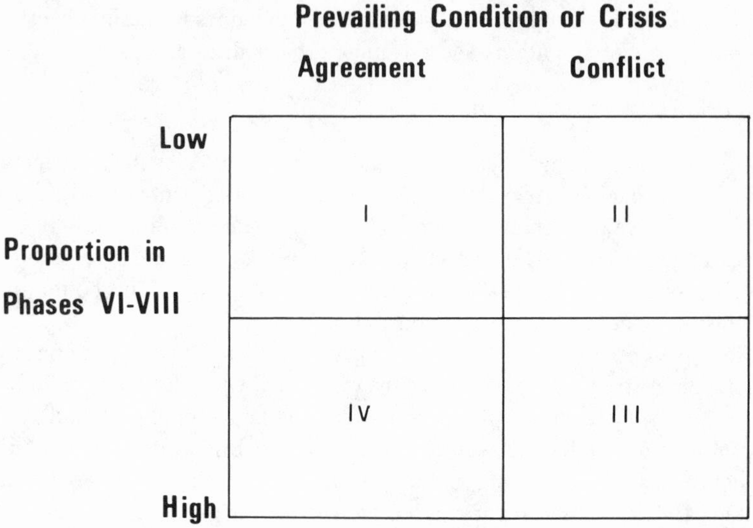

Proportion in Phases VI-VIII	Prevailing Condition or Crisis: Agreement	Prevailing Condition or Crisis: Conflict
Low	I	II
High	IV	III

veloped by Maslach—her Burnout Inventory, or MBI—is easily applied in large populations. Harvey's guidelines for interviews also can be applied to large batches of work units. Clearly, this requires some effort and skill. But even brief interviews with members of teams-to-be-built seem useful, on general principles. Moreover, OD's credibility depends on increasing effectiveness in making desired or predicted things happen. So convenience cannot be a determinative criterion, even though it remains a reductive one.

Different Designs for Different Teams

Provisionally, intervenors ought to keep a 2-by-2 grid in mind as they diagnose team-building populations. See figure 6.1, which supports a brief sketch of dominant properties of the four grid quadrants and also suggests implications for appropriate OD designs. Broadly, the point is that OD successes will increase, and failures become less common, as different designs are fitted to the context-sensitive quadrants of figure 6.1.

Quadrant I. This is likely to be a high-energy condition, at least initially. Thus, the condition of disagreement should induce some frustration, which can be energizing for at least a time, and may indeed erupt into open conflict. In addition, low levels of burnout imply few energies bound up in symptomology and its consequences.

Here the full battery of conventional high-stimulus designs seems applicable (e.g., Golembiewski 1982). They include interpersonal confrontations and team building.

Quadrant II. Quadrant II will probably be characterized by a reduced but still substantial energy level. The positive appeal of membership should generate substantial flows of energy, discounted to a meaningful degree by the prevailing condition of agreement. The low burnout implies no great drain on the basic energy level.

Designs like Harvey's may be appropriate here. Confrontational designs threaten membership, and thus might seriously reduce the energy available for isolating and solving problems. Harvey's design is slow moving and hence may conserve energy, but it lacks the potential for the quick great-leaps-forward characteristic of confrontational designs.

Quadrant III. Quadrant III seems a more difficult target for change than I or II. The energy level will probably be low, but the potential for substantial mischief increases.

A two-phase design may be appropriate here. Structure- or policy-oriented designs could be used to arrest or reverse burnout, to begin, and especially low-stimulus designs such as flexible work hours (see chapter 8), role negotiation (Harrison 1972), and job rotation. Standard confrontational designs then might be applied. Such efforts seem likely to reinforce one another. Any increases in energy due to amelioration of burnout could be applied to the condition of disagreement, and the possible bursts of energy from such progress could in turn reduce burnout.

Quadrant IV. Quadrant IV seems the chanciest condition, especially if feelings of low self-esteem or self-worth characterize team members. In such a case, their attachment to membership might be desperate, and hence their willingness to risk its loss might be exceedingly low. A two-stage design seems indicated, as in quadrant III, but the prognosis seems less favorable. The key question is whether prior amelioration of burnout can release sufficient energies to risk the threat to membership associated with any choice or change under the condition of agreement.

These general musings rest unevenly on theory and practice, especially in the case of the Abilene paradox. Chapter 8 provides some scarce support for the present position, for example, and in the process suggests the usefulness of an elaboration of quadrants III and IV in figure 6.1. Details will follow but, generally, it appears that there are two modes of response to each burnout phase. Advanced burnout, active mode, seems to permit greater leeway in the application of conventional OD designs, most of which are high stimulus and arousing. Advanced burnout, passive mode, encourages a more cautious approach, as the notes about quadrant III outline. It also appears that most of those in advanced phases—phases VI, VII, and VIII of table 5.1—are passive.

TABLE 6.6
Partial Products of A Three-Dimensional Image Design

How Team B Sees Team A	How Team A Believes Team B Sees Them
1. Not communicative enough	1. Divergent group
2. Floundering, indecisive	2. Lack of evidence of authority and decisiveness
3. Defensive, unreceptive	3. Spend much time on *non*-key issues
4. Too involved in day-to-day operations and decisions	4. Poor catalysts
5. Cautious	5. Lack of communicating a sense of direction and purpose
6. Under tight Corporation control (i.e., restricted and at a competitive disadvantage for corporate resources)	6. Nice Guys!!? (i.e., not competent)
	7. Too much resistance rather than encouragement

Nonetheless, the distinctions above should be confirmed by the experiences of many intervenors, and that is certainly true in my case. Consider one example from approximately 15 years ago, which came as something of a shock after a number of early successes with a three-dimensional image design (e.g., Golembiewski and Blumberg 1967). This design basically proposes that two or more participating work units develop three lists for sharing in response to three questions:

- How do we see our work team?
- How do we see the other work team?
- How do we believe the other work team sees us?

The design's intent is clearly confrontational, and seeks to orchestrate a mutually empathic escalation based upon (if for different reasons) both successes and failures in describing selves as others seem them. The "successes" of shared perceptions would enhance self-esteem and in effect build bridges between the two work units. The "failures" also would be there for both groups to see, with knowledge being gained and with reward and reinforcement consequently characterizing the learning environment.

Matters turned out differently in one case, radically. The two groups were right-on in their mutual perceptions, basically, as table 6.6 illustrates (using only one of the three cross-comparisons possible via the sharing of 3-D images). Team A was the top-level Operating Committee (OC), and the larger Team B was composed of the directors who were the first reports of OC members. After much prodding, the two groups separately developed images—which table 6.6 illustrates—that were more or less unanimous expressions of previously private materials. The result? General silence and apathy followed considerable effort at analysis of what happened and why. "It surprised me that pretty much everyone saw matters as I did," reported one participant. "It was not our style to talk about such things. My reaction was despair. All of us saw things as awful, I learned, and we all did nothing. I felt communally flaccid afterward; I always had felt individually impotent. We huddled together in our common nakedness, more fearful than ever of acting."

In retrospect, diagnosis was lacking in this case. I would now see the situation as a condition of agreement, type 3, as reinforced by advanced burnout, with most of the executives in the passive mode. In terms of figure 6.1, the mini-case falls in quadrant IV but we disingenuously applied a quadrant I design. The common and consensual disclosure did not release energies, but rather bound them more tightly to preserving the increasingly tenuous membership. Even that strained comfort was soon forfeited when the corporation made wholesale personnel changes.

Note

1. An earlier form of this argument appears as Golembiewski 1985.

References

Boss, W. 1979. "It Doesn't Matter If You Win or Lose, Unless You're Losing." *Journal of Applied Behavioral Science* 9:21–43.

Bowers, D. G. 1973. "OD Techniques and Their Results in 23 Organizations: The Michigan ICL Study." *Journal of Applied Behavioral Science* 9:21–43.

Bowers, D. G., and Hausser, D. L. 1977. "Work Group Types and Intervention Effects in Organizational Development." *Administrative Science Quarterly* 27:76–94.

Carlisle, A. E. 1988. "An Abilene Defense: Commentary Two." *Organizational Dynamics* 17:40–43.

De Meuse, K. P., and Liebowitz, S. J. 1981. "An Empirical Analysis of Team-Building Research." *Group and Organization Studies* 6:357–78.

Dyer, W. G. 1977, 1987. *Team Building*. Reading, Mass.: Addison-Wesley.

Festinger, L.; Riecken, H. W.: and Schachter, S. 1956. *When Prophecy Fails*. New York: Harper Torchbooks.

Fordyce, J. K., and Weil, R. 1971. *Managing with People*. Reading, Mass.: Addison-Wesley.

Golembiewski, R. T. 1962. *The Small Group*. Chicago: University of Chicago Press.

______. 1978. *Public Administration as A Developing Discipline*, 2 vols. New York: Marcel Dekker.

______. 1979. *Approaches to Planned Change*, vols. 1 and 2. New York: Marcel Dekker.

______. 1982. "Organization Development Interventions." In *Job Stress and Burnout*, edited by W. S. Paine, 229–53. Los Angeles: Sage Publications.

______. 1985. "Enriching the Theory and Practice of Team Building: Instrumentation for Diagnosis and Design Alternatives." In *Contemporary Organization Development*, edited by D. D. Warrick, 98–113. Glenview, Ill.: Scott, Foresman, and Co.

Golembiewski, R. T., and Blumberg, A. 1967. "Confrontation as Training Design in Complex Organizations: Attitudinal Changes in a Diversified Population of Managers." *Journal of Applied Behavioral Science* 3:524–47.

Golembiewski, R. T., and Kiepper, A. 1976. "MARTA: Toward an Effective, Open Giant." *Public Administration Review* 36:46–60.

Golembiewski, R. T., and Munzenrider, R. F. 1981. "Efficacy of Three Versions of One Burnout Measure: MBI as Total Score, Subscale Scores, or Phases?" *Journal of Health and Human Resource Administration* 4:228–46.

______. 1984. "Phases of Psychological Burnout and Organizational Covariants." *Journal of Health and Human Resources Administration* 6:290–323.

______. 1988. *Phases of Burnout*. New York: Praeger.

Golembiewski, R. T.; Munzenrider, R. F.; and Phelen-Carter, D. 1981. *Proceedings*. Organization Development Network, Semi-annual meeting, September, 163–70.

Golembiewski, R. T.; Munzenrider, R. F.; and Stevenson, J. G. 1985. *Stress in Organizations*. New York: Praeger.

Golembiewski, R. T.; Proehl, C. W. Jr., and Sink, D. 1981. "Success of OD Applications n the Public Sector: Toting-up the Score for a Decade, More or Less." *Public Administration Review* 41:679–82.

Hackman, J. R., and Oldham, G. R. 1981. *Work Redesign*. Reading, Mass.: Addison-Wesley.

Halberstam, D. 1969. *The Best and the Brightest*. New York: Random House.

Harris, R. T., and Porras, J. L. 1978. "The Consequences of Large System Change in Practice: An Empirical Assessment." In *Proceedings '78*, edited by J. C. Susbauer. Annual meeting, Academy of Management, August.

Harrison, R. 1972. "Role Negotiation." In *The Social Technology of Organization Development*, edited by W. W. Burke and H. Hornstein. Washington, D.C.: NTL Learning Resources.

Harvey, J. B. 1977. "Consulting During Crisis of Agreement." In *Current Issues and Strategies in Organization Development*, edited by W. W. Burke, 160–86. New York: Human Sciences Press.

______. 1988a. "Abilene Revisited." *Organizational Dynamics* 17:35–37.

______. 1988b. "The Abilene Paradox: The Management of Agreement." *Organizational Dynamics* 17:17–34.

Janis, I. 1972. *Groupthink*. Boston: Little, Brown.

Kahn, R. L. 1978. "Job Burnout: Prevention and Remedies." *Public Welfare* 16:61–63.

Kahn, R. L., *et al.* 1964. *Organizational Stress*, New York: Wiley.

Kanter, R. M. 1988. "An Abilene Defense: Commentary One." *Organizational Dynamics* 17:37–40.

Maslach, C., and Jackson, S. E. 1981. "The Measurement of Experienced Burnout." *Journal of Occupational Behaviour* 2:99–113.

______. 1986. *Maslach Burnout Inventory*. La Jolla, Cal.: Consulting Psychologists Press.

Patchen, M. 1965. *Some Questionnaire Measures of Employee Motivation and Morale*. Monograph no. 41, Ann Arbor, Mich.: Survey Research Center.

Pines, A., and Maslach, C. 1980. "Combatting Staff Burnout in a Day-care Center: A Case Study." *Child Care Quarterly* 9:5–16.

Porras, J., and Wilkins, A. 1980. "Organization Development in a Large System: An Empirical Assessment." *Journal of Applied Behavioral Science* 16:506–34.

Raven, B. 1974. "The Nixon Group." *Journal of Social Issues* 30:297–320.
Roberts, K., and O'Reilly, C. A. III. 1974. "Failures in Upward Communication in Organizations: Three Possible Culprits." *Academy of Management Journal* 17:205–15.
Smith, P. C.; Kendall, L. M.; and Blood, C. L. 1969. *The Measurement of Satisfaction in Work and Retirement*. Chicago: Rand McNally.
White, J. K., and Ruh, R. H. 1973. "Effects of Personal Values on the Relationships Between Participation and Job Attitudes." *Administrative Science Quarterly* 18:506–14.

7

Fine-Tuning OD Designs: Reducing Burnout and Improving Group Properties

This chapter preaches an old message, and adds technology to it. OD can profit from specifying differences between the targets of interventions. As chapter 5 details, people in advanced phases of burnout seem to be characterized by progressively greater physical symptoms. Given the implied different personal slack to adjust and respond to changes, different OD designs and expectations about their effects seem appropriate for persons in (let us say) phase I versus phase VIII.

Hence, OD can and should go beyond mere description, as important as that is. Initial profiling of a target population and its context should be extended to fine-tuning OD designs, as chapter 6 proposes. This chapter takes the next compound step: it not only illustrates up-front analysis, but it focuses on a specific design for context, tests for effects of the design, and details some conclusions about increasing OD success rates by taking into account the degrees of burnout of individuals within a specific group context. In contrast, chapter 6 deals with the same two features, but in general terms.

The specific focal points here are burnout and group properties, with the goal of responding to an initial diagnosis so as to increase the levels of personal slack available to individuals in a small system. This contrasts sharply with merely profiling what exists, as is done in chapter 5. The broader purpose here is to do something about what exists, so as to ameliorate burnout and its consequences as well as to change group properties.

Increasing rather than decreasing personal slack, as represented by the phases of burnout, will not come easily.[1] Despite the profusion of advice on how to deal with burnout, few direct interventions exist and almost none provide data sufficient to assess effects. Kilpatrick (1986) isolates 661 published items on burnout, of which 138 (or 40 percent) offer how-to prescriptions. However, only 132 of the 661 cases rest on data bases, and a meager 4 provide data from conscious interventions (Anderson 1982; Haack 1980; Pines and Aronson 1983; Slutsky 1981).

Of necessity, then, this chapter seeks to explore largely new territory. This research blends prescription and research in a Human Resources (HR) corporate group, which initially numbered thirty-one. Conventional OD designs reduce burnout, as well as improve group properties and turnover. All three effects should serve to reduce the stressors acting on people, and thus should increase their emotional and psychological margin of comfort in responding to life's exigencies.

Six major sections describe this action research. Thus, crucial associations of stress and burnout with OD will be drawn, a conceptual approach to burnout phases will be sketched, methods will be detailed, a mini-history will emphasize milestones in the HR unit's multiple transitions in response to its demanding work environment, active interventions will be reviewed, and results of the interventions at three points over nearly three years will be highlighted.

Conceptual Context for Irony IV, Revisited

Although OD often focuses on the "O," rather than on individual differences, encompassing burnout is not only attractive but seems necessary. Briefly, the world is full of "stressors," or stimuli that upset the "constancy of the [person's] internal environment" (Selye 1956, 27). Stressors can herniate or energize—with effects specific not only to different individuals but to different points in time. Stressors consequently can create strain and dis-stress, which induce deficits or deficiencies in people and their relationships; but stressors also can generate constructive energies, or "eu-stress."

We neither can nor should avoid stressors, but we can experience so many of the wrong kinds of stressors that strain develops. Hence comes burnout, which relates to the degree of strain that individuals experience, relative to their normal coping skills and attitudes; hence, also, burnout's relevance to OD, which is deeply concerned with creating favorable balances of eu-stress versus dis-stress for individuals and their employing organizations, as Warrick (1981) aptly demonstrates.

OD's interest in burnout is—or should be—*specific* and *practical*. Specifically, OD's basic orientation toward choice and change exposes individuals to potential strain. Moreover, practically, a large battery of OD designs and experience with them stand ready to guide data-based efforts to reduce burnout (e.g., Golembiewski 1982), and failure to tap this potential deprives OD of a major target for applications in moving toward the vision of the responsibly free workplace (e.g., Golembiewski 1979, 1:1–132).

But how to be specific and practical? Two earlier chapters introduce the reader to an ongoing program of research with an eight-phase model. For immediate purposes, attention gets directed at two features of that research:

the range and depth of the impact of burnout, and the apparent conceptual roadblock the phase model places in the path of OD applications.

Range and Depth of Impact

Several independent programs of research with the phase model show that people in advanced phases of burnout are characterized by low levels of energy, self-esteem, and efficacy, as well as by the dreary catalog of effects illustrated in chapter 5.[2] The mainline linkages seem direct, for physical symptoms as well as other human deficits or deficiencies. Worksite features can induce advanced phases of burnout which, in turn, are associated with such effects as a high incidence of reported physical symptoms. To suggest the flow, worksite features and burnout phases each share 15–20 percent of their variance with physical symptoms in one study, but worksite features explain only 2–5 percent of the variance in symptoms (Golembiewski, Munzenrider, and Stevenson 1986, 62–84). (See also chapter 5.)

Advanced phases of burnout also seem to have a startling incidence and persistence. Over 42 percent of thirteen thousand respondents in thirty-three organizations fall in the three most-advanced phases (Golembiewski and Munzenrider 1988, chap. 7). Moreover, advanced phase assignments seem quite stable over the period of a year in about 75 percent of the cases (Golembiewski, Munzenrider, and Stevenson 1986, 135–39).

Apparent Roadblock to OD

Such effects and attributes suggest a high-leverage target for OD, but the response has been underwhelming—*and for a very good reason*. In part, the virulence, pervasiveness, and persistence isolated by phase research constitute obviously formidable challenges. In far larger part, I believe, the apparent character of burnout encourages cautious approaches, if it does not intimidate OD applications. Because of the deficits or deficiencies associated with advanced burnout—as in research with the phase model—intervenors have been apprehensive that burned-out individuals lack the emotional slack to respond to ameliorative OD designs, which generally require what individuals in advanced phases seem to lack.

This apparent conceptual roadblock is easy to describe. Although authorities often recommend high-stimulus designs for advanced burnout—interpersonal encounters, confrontations, interpersonally-oriented team building, and so on—the condition does not suggest the coping slack which such designs require. Tersely, traditional interventions risk overstimulation. This seems to be a significant limitation on the use of OD because its theory and practice emphasize high-stimulus interventions (Golembiewski, Munzen-

TABLE 7.1
Two Classes of OD Designs

High-Stimulus Designs	Low-Stimulus Designs
• Interpersonal confrontations • Interpersonally oriented team building • T-groups for intact work groups • Basic policy or structural change • Confrontive "stress management workshops"	• Time off from work • Flexible work hours • The kinds of job rotation that require variable intensity and provide variety • Mild role negotiation

Source: Golembiewski, R. T., Munzenrider, R., and Stevenson, J. G. (1986). *Stress in Organizations*, New York: Praeger, pp. 193–94, 215–18.

rider, and Stevenson 1986, 191–94). The concern will be especially strong for those many ODers who remember the single major criticism of some forms of sensitivity training or encounter: that they are high-stimulus designs capable of propelling vulnerable persons into a "stimulus overload" condition, and that in turn might overwhelm fragile emotional defenses and even induce psychotic episodes (e.g., Lieberman, Yalom, and Miles 1973).

This conceptual impasse seems avoidable, in part, because two modes of individual response seem to exist to all phases of burnout—active, and passive or withdrawn modes. Directly, the distinction suggests two intervention strategies. When advanced burnout is associated with a passive mode, coping requires creating slack. Provisionally, then, intervenors might well distinguish the two classes of designs shown in table 7.1 Moreover, intervenors also might consider a two-stage strategy for ameliorating advanced burnout, passive mode: to begin to reduce burnout via low-stimulus designs; and then, beyond some as-yet-undetermined level, to intervene with a broad range of designs to further reduce burnout and to anchor it at lower levels. For example, this first case might begin with a week's vacation, patently a low-stimulus opener.

This research uses standard high-stimulus OD designs in focusing on a headquarters HR staff group—initially numbering thirty-one—all but two of whom had an active orientation to their work even though they were in advanced phases of burnout. The key assumption is that "actives" have the emotional slack to respond to high-stimulus interventions.

Methods for Assessing the Impacts of Action Planning

Archival data about turnover and three kinds of self-report data assess effects of this action research. One kind of self-report permits assigning individuals to eight phases of burnout; the second kind supports a characterization of the present HR population as "active"; and the final kind of self-report describes the immediate work setting. The three kinds of self-reports are introduced, in turn, and then turnover gets attention.

Phases of Burnout

Two earlier chapters provide detail on the phases, so two reminders here should suffice. The reader will remember that the phase model rests on the three subdomains isolated by Maslach (Maslach and Jackson 1982, 1986):

- *Depersonalization,* high scores on which indicate individuals who distance self from others and who view other humans as objects or things;
- *Personal accomplishment (reversed),* low scores on which characterize individuals who believe they are doing poorly on a task that is not particularly worth doing;
- *Emotional exhaustion,* high scores on which indicate persons who are near or beyond "the ends of their ropes" in psychological and emotional terms, who are beset by stressors beyond their comfortable coping limits.

In addition, the phase model builds on these three subdomains of burnout, and transcends them. Operationally, High and Low scores on each subdomain are distinguished, using norms from a large population (Golembiewski and Munzenrider 1984). Assuming the progressive virulence of the subdomains in the order given above, the High versus Low distinctions generate the eight-phase model shown below.

	Phases of Burnout							
	I	**II**	**III**	**IV**	**V**	**VI**	**VII**	**VIII**
Depersonalization	Lo	Hi	Lo	Hi	Lo	Hi	Lo	Hi
Personal accomplishment (reversed)	Lo	Lo	Hi	Hi	Lo	Lo	Hi	Hi
Emotional exhaustion	Lo	Lo	Lo	Lo	Hi	Hi	Hi	Hi

Mode of Adaptation

How to estimate active versus passive modes remains unsettled. The scale Job Involvement (JI) has been used, with High versus Low JI subgroups differing regularly and robustly on a large panel of indicators, phase by phase (Golembiewski and Munzenrider 1984). Active phase VIIIs all-but-unanimously report being better off than passive phase VIIIs, and so on.

Here, three Work Environment Scales (WES) are used to make the active versus passive judgment: Involvement, Autonomy, and Task Orientation (Insel and Moos 1974). Operationally, mean *standard* scores greater than 50 on each of the three scores define "active," based on national norms for "general work settings" (Moos 1981, 27–28). By this criterion, twenty-nine of the thirty-one initial HR members qualify as "active." Specifically, the two lowest-scoring persons average 90 when their three WES scores are combined. The twenty-nine other HR members average over 180, and over 93 percent of their seventy-seven individual WES scores are greater than 50.

This convention requires qualification. WES scales focus not on the respondent but on the respondent's *milieu*. Witness the orientation of a typical WES item: "Employees function fairly independently of supervisors." Interviews and observation confirm the assumption that perceived milieu requirements and personal responses are overwhelmingly congruent.

Work Environment Scales

Worksite features are measured by the sixty WES items, which track ten dimensions. Briefly (Moos 1981, 2):

- *Involvement:* the extent to which employees are concerned about and committed to their jobs
- *Peer cohesion:* the extent to which employees are friendly and supportive of one another
- *Supervisor support:* the extent to which management is supportive of employees and encourages employees to be supportive of one another
- *Autonomy:* the extent to which employees are encouraged to be self-sufficient and to make their own decisions
- *Task orientation:* the degree of emphasis on good planning, efficiency, and getting the job done
- *Work pressure:* the degree to which the processes of work and time urgency dominate the job milieu
- *Clarity:* the extent to which employees know what is expected of them in their daily routine, and the degree to which rules and policies are communicated explicitly
- *Control:* the extent to which management uses rules and pressures to keep employees under control
- *Innovation:* the degree of emphasis on variety, change, and new approaches
- *Physical comfort:* the extent to which the physical surroundings contribute to a pleasant work environment

WES measurement properties are conveniently available (Moos 1981).

Turnover Rates

The focus here is on a number of people leaving the firm divided by average HR headcount. Other measures—such as intent to leave—would provide less-conservative estimates of the commitment to continued employment.

Notes about Uses of Data

The four kinds of data are here used to estimate the impacts of interventions, basically, and were *not* used to provide grist for planning, as is common in action research. The intervention's public focus was on "a major morale problem," and on what the HR personnel could do collaboratively to alleviate this problem. The self-report data were gathered following this survey schedule (see also table 7.2 for a schedule of non-survey events):

- Day 45: Administration I
- Day 200: Administration II (phases only)
- Day 295: Administration III
- Day 425: Administration IV
- Day 575: Administration V

Since the major interventions occurred through day 265, administrations I and II may be considered as long and short pre-tests, respectively. Administrations III, IV, and V constitute post-tests, and are conveniently labeled short, long, and very long, respectively. Turnover data became available at approximately day 90 for 1984 and day 455 for 1985.

No doubt some sense of the data did percolate into the planned interventions, but incidentally. Three general and short briefings were held for the five person HR management team, shortly after administrations I, III, and IV. Participants were promised a full briefing on all aggregate measurements after implementing their action plans. This occurred at day 575, just after administration V.

Thumbnail History of HR Transitions

Both HR and its corporate home had grown sharply *and* raised their goals, 1981–83. To illustrate, mid-1981 saw a formal HR integration of two organizationally separate activities—dealing with operational matters like recruitment and employee relations versus training and development, basically—whose close collaboration was required to meet the firm's goals of major expansion while lowering turnover via better recruitment, training, and organization development. Corporate turnover in both 1979 and 1980 approximated 43–45 percent, while it fell in the next three years to 24, 18, and then 14 percent in 1983, even as total employment increased by more than 25 percent.

Still, in early 1984 the HR management team feared that such progress often came at the expense of neglecting important work within HR. Staff were strained, and the VP and his directors expected "high turnover." Expectations concerning HR's contributions escalated, and so did the workload.

TABLE 7.2
A Schedule of Non-Survey Events

	Day	
Problem sensing	1	• Human Resources (HR) managers express fears
Baseline data gathering	45–75	• Solicitation by memo of "concerns" from all employees
Begin data flow	115	• Share concerns with all HR staff to encourage reaction and confrontation • Four "interest groups" focus on special targets for improvement
Initial action planning	140–170	• Interest groups report recommendations to all HR staff • HR members each report back on "five recommendations you would most like to see implemented"
Continued action planning	200	• Begin planning to implement high-priority recommendations
Presentation to corporate HR oversight committee	230	• HR turnover rates for 1984 higher than expected • HR Career Progression Plan proposed
Major policy intervention	265	• HR Career Progression Plan announced
Review, extend, and recommit	295	• Ten-hour meeting of all HR staff to review progress, plan future initiatives, and celebrate achievements
Major reorganization	475	• "Chunking" occurs: several "strategic operating areas" replace a basically functional structure
Report on all changes	575	• Share all data on Administrations I–IV • Two-hour review and planning session for adapting to the newly decentralized HR activities

This concern birthed an OD effort whose major events are detailed in Table 7.2. (The table does not include the five survey administrations described immediately above.)

The earliest survey data confirmed the initiating concern. As rows A.I and B.I in table 7.3 indicate, administration I saw over 50 percent of the HR staff in burnout phases VI, VII, and VIII. The percentages are similar for all respondents as well as for that subset of fourteen who responded to the first four surveys. In addition, 75 percent of the total staff rate as phase V or greater; and only one person among the two top levels of management scores *less than phase V.* This not only seems high, it was the second-least desirable profile of phases observed at that time (Golembiewski, Munzenrider, and Stevenson 1986, 127–34).

TABLE 7.3
Phases of Burnout, Administrations I–V

Administration		Respondents by Phases (in Percentages)							
		I	II	III	IV	V	VI	VII	VIII
A. All Subjects, N Varies									
Administration	N							52%	
I	31	19%	0	3	3	23	23	10	19
			22%			26%			
								57%	
II	34	18%	6	6	3	11	21	9	27
			30%			14%			
								39%	
III	36	33%	6	11	0	11	22	6	11
			50%			11%			
								31%	
IV	35	29%	6	14	0	20	11	3	17
			49%			20%			
								38%	
V	37	35%	5	5	3	14	19	14	5
			46%			16%			
B. Matched Subjects[a]									
Administration								64%	
I		14%	0	0	7	14	43	7	14
			14%			21%			
								51%	
II		22%	7	7	0	14	22	7	22
			36%			14%			
								36%	
III		36%	14	7	0	7	22	0	14
			57%			7%			
								14%	
IV		21%	7	21	0	36	0	7	7
			50%			36%			
								46%	
V		15%	8	0	8	23	23	23	0
			23%			31%			

Note: [a]N = 14, except for N = 13 in Administration V.

The WES scores provide no more reason for cheering in a corporation proud of its first-class status. See table 7.4 columns 1 and 4. Recall that a standard score of 50 indicates a raw score at the mean of respondents from a large cohort in "general work settings" (Moos 1981, 27). HR Peer Cohesion was especially low, for example; and Work Pressure approximated the maximum possible score.

The 1984 HR turnover rate also proved to be high—37 percent, as table 7.5 shows. This is almost three times the 1984 corporate average, and over 80 percent of the HR separations are voluntary. HR turnover in 1982 and 1983 approximated the corporate average.

TABLE 7.4
Work Environment Scales, Standard Scores, on Three Administrations, N Varies

WES Dimensions	Mean WES Scores, All Respondents*			Mean WES Scores, Matched Respondents, (N=14)		
	1 Administration I (N=31)	2 Administration III (N=36)	3 Administration IV (N=35)	4 Administration I	5 Administration III	6 Administration IV
Involvement	56.3	59.2	58.8	55.5^{a}	60.4^{a}	59.1
TARGET Peer cohesion	33.6^{af}	46.6^{a}	44.5^{f}	$32.6^{b'e}$	$39.6^{b'}$	42.7^{e}
TARGET Supervisor support	42.4^{bg}	52.0^{b}	50.6^{g}	43.6	48.3	49.9
Autonomy	54.1	55.6	57.8	55.6^{f}	60.2	63.1^{f}
Task orientation	61.5	62.9	61.4	61.6	60.3	60.2
TARGET Work pressure	80.9^{ch}	75.6^{c}	73.0^{h}	$82.5^{g'}$	$82.0^{j'}$	$77.9^{g'j'}$
TARGET Clarity	50.1	48.9	52.5	$40.1^{c'}$	$41.5^{c'k}$	50.8^{k}
TARGET Control	$55.1^{d'}$	$49.9^{d'}$	51.4	52.1^{hl}	44.3^{h}	44.9^{hl}
Innovation	49.6^{ei}	58.9^{e}	60.7^{i}	54.7^{di}	61.6^{d}	62.6^{i}
Physical comfort	62.1	$64.5^{j'}$	$59.3^{j'}$	64.6	65.1^{m}	60.8^{m}

Notes:
N.B. Any shared plain superscript indicates $P \leq .05$ by t-test, one tailed.
Any shared superscript ′ indicates $P \leq .10$.
*All t-tests utilize pooled-variance estimates, except for Work Pressure, I versus III, whose F-ratio (4.52, P⟨.000) requires a separate variance estimate.

TABLE 7.5
Turnover Rates, 1984 and 1985

	1984 Corporate Rate	1984 HR Rate	1985 HR Rate
Management	7%	0%	12%
Professionals	9%	30%	22%
Technicians	8%	67%	31%
Clerical	15%	66%	19%
Overall	13%	37%	20%

Fitting Interventions to Transitions

The OD design sought to fit and direct transitional dynamics, as two emphases demonstrate. Consider first the variable pace of intervention, and then the consistent underlying OD strategy.

Variable Pace

Expedience as well as change goals influence the design. As table 7.2 shows, data gathering at start-up consumed the first 100 days; active interventions spanned days 115 through 295, more or less; an anticipated reorganization urged a pause between days 295 and 575; and the design concluded with a first common HR experience under the aegis of the new structure.

The reorganization confounds the intervention, but also provides a stiff test of the persistence of its effects. Briefly, a traditional line/staff structure was quickly divisionalized (e.g., Chandler 1962; Golembiewski 1979, 2:3–69) around separate product lines to facilitate identification with smaller and more-focused efforts. Several "strategic operating areas" (SOAs) are identified and, after day 475, nearly half of the previously centralized HR staff report directly to SOA heads. For many HR staff, this requires not only a new direct supervisor, but also a strong dotted-line relationship with the VP, Human Resources (VP, HR). In addition, both "movers" and "stayers" will maintain some common ties, as by periodic meetings for goal setting. The reorganization was a friendly one, with the VP, HR playing a major role in its design and implementation, but its significant effects had by no means played themselves out by day 575.

Overall Strategy

This action research rests on a rudimentary causal network. Briefly:

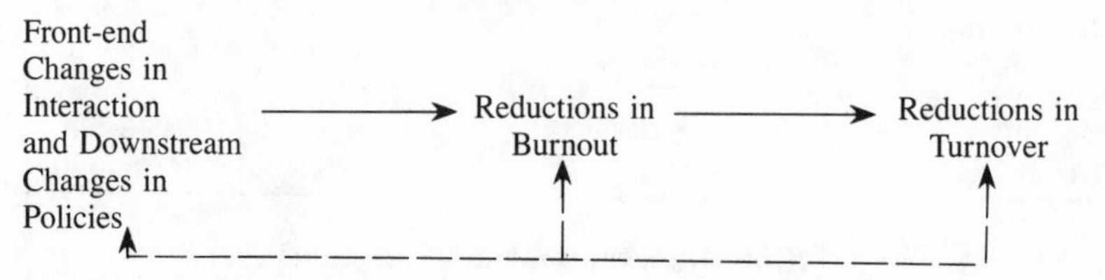

Main effects are indicated by the solid lines, with the broken lines indicating feedback or reinforcing linkages.

An environmental model dominates in management studies, and OD represents its most-focused contemporary expression. Briefly, OD provides—via values, theory, and learning designs—a coherent approach to meeting individual needs and to reducing stressors (Golembiewski 1982), which involves organization members in diagnosis and prescription. Conventional high-stimulus interventions based on OD theory and experience usually focus early on *interaction*—on the character and quality of relationships between people. Later attention may shift to *task*—to changes in *policies and procedures*. The basic intent is to induce an appropriate culture and process, and then to use that socio-emotional infrastructure to generate and support changes in policies, procedures, and structures.

Front-end interventions: a calculated risk. The intervention strategy was conventional—high stimulus and confrontational[3]—and may seem risky for advanced burnout. HR personnel maintained an active mode in all but two cases, however, and a high-stimulus design consequenlty had reasonable promise of reducing HR burnout by addressing worksite issues. The high-stimulus features include having HR staff confront superiors and peers about a range of concerns, and imposing energetic action planning on busy schedules.

The high-stimulus and confrontational character of the initial design elements essentially seeks to reverse tendencies toward degenerative interaction, and to develop or heighten tendencies toward regenerative interaction. In capsule, this involves increasing openness, owning, and trust, while decreasing risk (Golembiewski 1979, vol. 1).

Although details are beyond this chapter, the character of the initial design elements can be illustrated briefly. For openers, all HR staff were asked to list the three best things about their department, as well as the three "concerns" they would most like to change. In 50 percent of the responses, the best things involve the professionalism, skill, and dedication of their coworkers; and an additional 30 percent emphasize the proactive nature of their work and its rewarding character. These attractions constitute a base from which to deal with concerns, in effect. Nearly half of the respondents focus on the isolation and lack of cohesion within and between HR units; and 40 percent cite the pace of work—too many projects and too many hours of work. Sharing these data in a general session (day 115) involved developing examples and voicing reactions to them. In the process, employees and managers often had to confront the VP, HR. He was widely seen as demanding and unrelenting, and HR staff had to satisfy themselves that trust was sufficiently high, and risk sufficiently low, to warrant the expenditures of energy required to diagnose and remedy the unattractive aspects. As appropriate, the data also required confronting unit heads.

After extended feedback and disclosure focusing on the HR state of affairs, which sought to model the ideal of regenerative interaction, four "interest groups" of volunteers were formed to gather additional information as well as to make recommendations for improvement. In effect, these recommendations (days 140–170) deal with the five targets among WES scores highlighted in table 7.4. Specifically, Peer Cohesion, Supervisor Support, and Clarity rate too low; and scores on Control and Work Pressure are too high.

In sum, these front-end design features propose doing within HR what was more or less routinely done for clients. The goal involves building appropriate "processes"—a culture, values, and relationships—that will support changes in task features.

Major downstream response: policy intervention. Around day 200, the downstream search came to highlight the lack of HR promotion opportunities. A Career Progression Plan was developed and accepted by consensus, after being blessed by a corporate committee. The plan has these major objectives:

- to clarify career progression paths and opportunities
- to communicate information about such paths and opportunities
- to increase internal promotions, especially for the clerical and technical employees
- to hire individuals into jobs with a greater congruence between the person's abilities and aspirations and the job's realistic promotion opportunities

The Career Progression Plan tangibly reflects the improved HR infrastructure of processes and relationships, and also provides a clearer psychological contract with HR employees.

Results of Action Planning through Day 425

Three effects signal an effective intervention:

- the profile of phases of burnout will tend toward less-advanced phases;
- WES scores will vary in three specific ways: Involvement, Autonomy, Task

Orientation, Innovation, and Physical Comfort remain the same or increase; Control and, especially, Work Pressure decrease; Peer Cohesion, Supervisor Support, and Clarity increase;

- Turnover rates will fall in 1985 compared to 1984.

In capsule, the initial emphasis on interaction relates primarily to two WES targets—Peer Cohesion and Supervisor—but increases in Involvement, Autonomy, and even Innovation might well occur as barriers to regenerative interaction are removed. Changes in policies and procedures more directly impact the three other WES targets—Work Pressure, Control, and Clarity.

Administration III constitutes the first assessment of effects following major interventions. Since no interventions were made in the 130 days prior to administration IV, even maintenance of administration III levels implies a potent intervention. Two emphases suffice to summarize the data through day 425, and both imply that intended effects occur and are maintained.

Profile of Burnout Phases

Table 7.3 indicates that the proportion of those in phases I–III approximately doubles for All Subjects, and nearly quadruples for Matched Subjects, comparing administrations I and II with III. Chi-square analysis (3 x 2) shows that I versus III changes closely approach significance for All and Matched respondents ($P = .055$ and .06, respectively).

Without explicit reinforcement, the shift is not only maintained for All Subjects, but is extended for Matched Subjects. Chi-square analysis indicates only random differences in III versus IV profiles for both HR populations. In addition, the I versus IV difference achieves statistical significance for Matched respondents, and approaches it for All ($P = .088$).

Changes in WES Scores

The WES scores trend in expected ways, with All respondents providing the sharper pattern of differences. The data on Matched subjects are not reported here to conserve space.

All subjects. Considering administration III versus I in table 7.4, nine of ten cases are in the expected direction. Moreover, four of the eight cases on which major increases are expected achieve the .05 level of statistical significance, and an additional case approaches that level ($.05 < P > .10$). Moreover, for the five target variables, four trend as expected. Three achieve significance, and the fourth approaches significance. Clarity trends lower, albeit randomly.

For administration IV, all comparisons show random changes only. Physical Comfort drops, although not significantly, no doubt due to ongoing construction.

Turnover

Table 7.5 shows that turnover falls about 45 percent in HR, in 1985 compared to 1984. No change occurs in the corporate rates, in addition, which closely approximate 13 percent in both years.

No substantial reasons encourage attributing the sharp drop in HR turnover to factors other than the intervention. If anything, 1985 was a better time than the previous year for HR personnel to seek new jobs. Moreover, the years following 1985 suggest that the change had substantial staying power. In sum:

	1986	**1987**
Corporate turnover	15.0%	15.7%
HR turnover	13.0%	14.3%

Results of Action Planning through Day 575

Only very robust effects would survive in the face of the reorganization as well as the nine-month interval between administration V of the survey and the prior planned intervention. Three emphases provide summary perspective on what seems to be a substantial persistence between days 295 and 475.

Changes in Phases of Burnout

In table 7.3, the very long post-test at administration V shows two patterns of decay in the extreme phases of burnout. For All respondents, the decay is modest and not significant by chi-square test. For Matched Subjects who were with HR during the full observational period, the decay is substantial after administration IV. In both cases, however, 25 percent fewer individuals are classified in phases VI-VIII, comparing administration V to I. Moreover, the employees in phases I-III increase by 104 and 65 percent for All and Matched respondents, respectively.

Changes in WES Scores

Major and expected changes on the WES variables remain through administration V, and even increase, especially for All respondents. A detailed review of administration V appears elsewhere (Golembiewski, Hilles, and Kim 1986), and the data are not presented here to conserve space. However, a sense of the data trends can be suggested economically. For all variables, I versus IV and I versus V, thirty-six of forty comparisons show differences that remain in the expected direction. Moreover, 50 percent of the cases are statistically significant as well as in the expected direction, and an additional

17 percent of the cases closely approach statistical significance (P ⟨ .10). In sum, the very long post-test basically retains the post-intervention impact. This suggests a modest decay rate for the interventions which were deliberately not reinforced.

Trends in Turnover

The trend line for HR turnover in the first four months of 1986 continues downward from the very high levels of 1984. In sum, the rates are: 37 percent in 1984, 20.3 percent in 1985, and 16.8 percent in 1986, annualized.

In all three years, corporate turnover closely approximates 13 percent per annum.

Seven Findings for Guiding Action

This theory-based effort to ameliorate burnout had substantial and persisting effects, and seven points provide highlights.

First, overall, the results imply the sources of orthodox high-stimulus OD designs in ameliorating burnout, active mode, as well as in affecting the character of the worksite. This constitutes new news and confirmation of old news.

The finding concerning burnout and its association with group properties is unique, and constitutes very good news for conventional OD designs, if only for active cases of advanced burnout. A near-comparison group of other professionals implies that HR changes in phases are not attributable to factors other than the interventions. Compare the first two administrations in table 7.3 with this record for the near comparisons near the time of administration III:

I	II	III	IV	V	VI	VII	VIII
16.7%	5.6	5.6	13.9	8.3	8.3	11.1	30.6

Near-comparisons provide post-only data to avoid sensitization to the MBI items.

To complete this first point, the usefulness of conventional OD designs for advanced phases complements the strong case for maintaining low burnout via those designs (e.g., Warrick 1981; Golembiewski 1982). Chapters 1 and 2 report no aggregate of OD applications with less than a 50 percent success rate, with most estimates ranging between 60–80 percent.

Second, the results recommend distinguishing modes of adaptation to advanced burnout and, on the present showing, the combination of high burnout and active mode constitutes a reasonable target for conventional OD interventions. Passive cases of advanced burnout constitute a challenge for future work.

However, this research requires exploration of three related points of theoretical and practical significance. Thus, no one knows the overall proportion of actives and passives in the universe of those in advanced phases of burnout, but it seems 25 percent or fewer are actives (Golembiewski and Munzenrider 1984).

In addition, this study does not tell us whether active status is a prelude to the passive mode. If so, not only would this signal the criticality of timely identification,but it provides a conceptual explanation of what seems an anomaly—the existence of two passive employees in an active culture. If active mode derives from personality features—for example, from high self-esteem or a low propensity to helplessness—promptness is less critical. This alternative also may explain the two passive cases in an active culture.

Finally, we know a bit about the relative significance of the major conceptual actors in such planned change, but we need to know much more. For example, do the phases play the central role in explaining effects like those above, or do they constitute more of a reflection of the basic distinction between active and passive persons, as defined operationally here? In addition, acute observers might propose that the interaction-centered components of the learning design sketched above encourage the exchange of "social support," which can be defined briefly as the significant sense that HR members are valued and sustained by their colleagues. In general, early explorations of such critical assignments of theoretical and practical potency reinforce the conceptual network sketched in this and preceding chapters. Consider an analysis of covariance procedure that assesses the relative significance in explaining differences in physical symptoms assignable to the phases, social support, and the active/passive distinction (Golembiewski and Munzenrider 1989). Details cannot be developed here, but approximate orders of magnitude suggest major differences in the relative potencies: on average, the phases explain about twice as much of the variance in physical symptoms as does social support, and this support in turn explains two or more times as much variance in symptoms as the active/passive distinction.

Third, experimental mortality was high, but personnel changes do not explain the changes in phases. Most important, the Matched respondents improve their phase distribution substantially more than All respondents, through administration IV. Moreover, of those leaving, about 48 percent are in phases VI-VIII and 28 percent are in phases I-III, on the last recorded observation. These are roughly the same as the weighted proportions in the Total population at the approximate times of departure—43.2 and 30.6 percent, respectively.

Fourth, reasonable ways exist to enhance the present change process. For example, a planned reinforcement experience was to follow administration IV by three months. Uncertainty about the date of the reorganization discouraged this intervention, which the press of events delayed until administration V. Such periodic reinforcement experiences seem useful (e.g., Boss 1983), and that design loop has long been featured in our OD work (e.g., Golembiewski and Carrigan 1970).

Fifth, the research design probably generates a conservative estimate of effects. Deliberately, administration III was held *before* a ten-hour design concluding the active interventions in the action research. Moreover, administration IV followed that intervention by four months. So administration III picked up only expectation effects about day 295's major integrating experience; and fade-out had ample time to occur before administration IV. Administration V came long after the prior planned intervention, and before a two-hour general session.

Sixth, theoretical reasons suggest that the two passives are not likely to respond positively to high-stimulus designs, but they do not seem to have been adversely affected. Those two persons improved their WES scores substantially, and had these sets of five phase assignments:

WES Outlier 1: VII, VIII, VIII, VIII, IV
WES Outlier 2: VI, VII, VI, III, VI

The Employee Assistance Program officer was alerted concerning possible difficulties, but none surfaced.

Seventh, the data through administration IV suggest that WES scores seem more amenable to change, and hence may be "leading" indicators. Patently, a leading/lagging distinction has both theoretical and practical value. If WES scores are leading indicators in a simple and direct way, their monitoring could anticipate later changes in distributions of burnout phases. Alternatively, a two-stage process is possible. Thus, when WES scores improve from a low base, they might presage improvements in burnout phases. Beyond some point, however, a positive WES profile might constitute a kind of psychological floor, cushioning any regression to advanced phases of burnout and providing a base for recovery when stressors abate.

Greater Success by Specifying Differences between Contexts, Revisited

Despite some major open ends and blank spots, then, this analysis and the two previous chapters should establish the attractiveness of seeking to improve success rates of OD applications, by taking differential burnout into account, and by taking group differences into account. This chapter outlines a major way to do something about acting on this knowledge of burnout's strategic character, and thereby influencing the group context.

This cohort of three chapters implies a very real potential for improving the success rates of OD applications. Consider one direct and two reinforcing contributors to this conclusion.

Directly, the less-advanced phases of burnout are associated with group properties congenial to OD, and especially to the regenerative model of interaction. Put the other way, the most-advanced phases of burnout are uncongenial to OD processes and values, and arguably constitute a barrier to them.

This significant point can be supported by considering regenerative interaction which, the reader may recall, involves low levels of risk as well as high levels of openness, owning, and trust. There is no need to consider each of the Work Environment Scales to document the point, but to consider a few will illustrate the full range. For example, high Clarity—that is, the extent to which employees know what is expected of them—suggests high openness and owning. On the other hand, high degrees of Work Pressure imply low openness and owning, or at least an unwillingness by management to consider human responses to having the heat kept on, or to generate alternative ways of mobilizing effort—as by higher Involvement or Task Orientation that imply a willingness to risk and trust, as well as high openness and owning. From another perspective, high levels of Peer Cohesion, Supervisor Support, and Autonomy all suggest substantial degrees of trust as well as a moderated degree of personal risk. Individuals are encouraged to make their own decisions, but in the context of peer and supervisory support. Individuals are not left hanging, to twist in the wind, whenever their reach exceeds their grasp.

Readers with even a general grasp of OD will recognize other ways of establishing that the group properties associated with the less-advanced phases also serve OD processes and values. For example, high Involvement is a prime feature of OD efforts, and group processes—and hence Peer Cohesion and Supervisory Support—also are central in OD. Recall also that OD can be defined as increasing responsible freedom in organizations. Translated quite literally, greater freedom implies Autonomy as well as a moderated Control—or the use of rules and pressures to keep employees under control—that is ideally reinforced by diminished Work Pressure. Relatedly, *responsible* freedom requires high degrees of Involvement, Task Orientation, and Peer Cohesion.

In sum, and quite directly, reducing burnout has the effect of improving group properties in ways that move toward OD values and processes. This implies a powerful reinforcement of OD effects.

Among many others, two reinforcing points also suggest how this chapter and the two previous can help improve OD success rates. First, one can profile the distribution of burnout phases for some target unit, and that information could well contraindicate some design or suggest special targets-of-opportunity. For example, a job enrichment program would not obviously apply to a work unit with a high proportion of members classified in phases VI through VIII. Instead, a job enrichment intervention for (say) ten work units might be begun in the unit with the most favorable distribution of phases. This might not only improve the success rate of the initial application, but it could ease the way even for units with less-favorable distributions. Both favorable early experience with selective groups and assessing management's trustworthiness in these selective applications, for example, could ease applications in work units with high proportions of members in phases VI through VIII. Or direct efforts to reduce advanced burnout phases might be attempted.

Second, recognizing phases might increase success rates of OD applications in a long-run sense. That is, chapters 10 and 11 associate the burnout phases with the key measurement problem in OD: What is change? If changes in the profile of burnout phases prove serviceable as surrogates for gamma change, that would usher in an era of growing sophistication in measurement of which designs have which consequences under what specific conditions. That sophistication would provide a quantum boost for success rates in OD applications, patently.

But this possibility has to be delayed, to permit consideration of how some "easy pieces" can contribute to enriching OD praxis and success. The term "easy pieces" comes from an old Jack Nicholson film, and is used here in the sense of convenient and close-at-hand. Gamma change is neither. So we move on to illustrating two easy pieces in OD, saving the difficult piece for later attention.

Notes

1. An earlier version of this chapter appears as Golembiewski, Hilles, and Daly 1987.
2. Supporting evidence for a substantial catalog of effects can be found in Golembiewski, Munzenrider, and Stevenson 1986, 2–120.
3. For details of the confrontational design, consult Golembiewski 1979, 297–348. The intervenors consider this a basic design when a "crisis of agreement" does *not* exist.

References

Anderson, C. M. 1982. *Effects of Peer Support Groups on Levels of Burnout among Mental Health Professionals*. Ph.D. diss. University of Washington, Seattle, Wash.

Boss, R. W. 1983. "Team Building and the Problem of Regression." *Journal of Applied Behavioral Science* 19:67–83.

Chandler, A. D., Jr. 1962. *Strategy and Structure*. Cambridge, Mass.: MIT Press.

Golembiewski, R. T. 1979. *Approaches to Planned Change*. vols. 1 and 2. New York: Marcel Dekker.

______. 1982. "Organization Development Interventions." In *Job Stress and Burnout*. Edited by W. S. Paine, 229–53. Los Angeles: Sage Publications.

Golembiewski, R. T., et al., 1986. "The Epidemiology of Progressive Burnout: A Primer." *Journal of Health and Human Resources Administration* 9:16–37.

Golembiewski, R. T., and Carrigan, S. B. 1970. "The Persistence of Laboratory-Induced Changes in Organization Styles." *Administrative Science Quarterly* 15:330–40.

Golembiewski, R. T., and Munzenrider, R. 1984. "Phases of Psychological Burnout and Organizational Covariants." *Journal of Health and Human Resources Administration* 7:264–89.

______. 1988. *Phases of Burnout*. New York: Praeger.

______. 1989. "Phases of Burnout, Modes, and Social Support." Working paper.

Golembiewski, R. T.; Hilles, R.; and Daly, R. 1987. "Some Effects of Multiple OD Interventions on Burnout and Worksite Features." *Journal of Applied Behavioral Science* 23:295–314.

Golembiewski, R. T.; Hilles, R.; and Kim, B-S. 1986. "Longitudinal Effects of Interventions Targeted at Advance Burnout, Active Mode." Paper presented at Fourth Annual Conference on Organization Policy and Development, University of Louisville. Louisville, Ky. 23–24 May.

Golembiewski, R. T.; Munzenrider, R.; and Carter, D. 1983. "Phases of Progressive Burnout and Their Worksite Covariants." *Journal of Applied Behavioral Science* 19:461–82.

Golembiewski, R. T.; Munzenrider, R.; and Stevenson, J. G. 1986. *Stress in Organizations*. New York: Praeger.

Haack, M. R. 1980. *Burnout Intervention With Nurses*. Ph.D. diss. University of Illinois Medical Center.

Insel, P. M., and Moos, R. H. 1974. *Work Environment Scale, Form R*. Palo Alto, Calif.: Consulting Psychologists Press, Inc.

Kilpatrick, A. O. 1986. *Burnout: An Empirical Assessment*. Ph.D. diss. University of Georgia, Athens, Ga.

Lieberman, M. A., Yalom, I. D., and Miles, M. B. 1973. *Encounter Groups: First Facts*. New York: Basic Books.

Maslach, C., and Jackson, S. E. 1982, 1986. *Maslach Behavior Inventory*. Palo Alto, Calif.: Consulting Psychologists Press, Inc.

Moos, R. H. 1981. *Manual: Work Environment Scale*. Palo Alto, Calif.: Consulting Psychologists Press, Inc.

Munzenrider, R. 1986. "Is Burnout Idiosyncratic or Generic?" Paper presented at Fourth Annual Conference on Organization Policy and Development, University of Louisville. Louisville, Ky. 23–24 May.

Pines, A., and Aronson, E. 1983. "Combatting Burnout." *Children and Youth Services Review* 5:263–75.

Selye, H. 1956. *The Stress of Life*. New York: McGraw-Hill.

Slutsky, B. W. 1981. *Two Approaches to Treating Burnout*. Dissertation Abstracts International, 42 (5): 2086B.

Warrick, D. D. 1981. "Managing the Stress of Organization Development." *Training and Development Journal* 35:36–41.

Irony V

Relative Success while Neglecting Easy Pieces

8

Limited-Purpose Designs: Flexible Work Hours as Exemplar

Basic OD prescriptions often reflect paradoxes, or at least the general inability to say when some degree of allegiance to one prescription runs afoul of another, and perhaps equally prominent, prescription. For example, OD is often tied firmly to basic social transformation, as in the goal of creating appropriate cultures at work. That sounds well and good. But OD also typically prescribes: Start from where the client is. In this sense, OD is like Panasonic: ahead of its time, but self-consciously so.

The hitch is obvious. Many clients start from a point that makes the leap to an "appropriate culture" a fantasy, or at least a highly improbable aspiration. For those clients, starting from "where they are" implies baby steps toward OD values, not a giant step. The danger for the OD intervenor is that these baby steps may constitute a cop-out rather than reasonable initial steps toward an expanding approach to the full range of OD values.

So which prescription is correct? Is it the prescription that counsels the lofty objective, but really implies pie-in-the-sky, by-and-by? It lets our aspirations soar, but risks being impractical and setting objectives so high as to assure disappointment. Or do we accord priority to the "next reasonable bite" prescription? It proposes that we start from the client's present state—dismal and primitive though that may be, and even though that risks a fixation with Band-Aids if one is careless.

Typically, of course, OD literati answer "Yes" to the prescription for basic cultural change, dangers and pie-in-the-sky notwithstanding. And that is a reasonable response, even generally commendable.

My heart is with those who counsel, "Yes, go for it"; but my experience urges stout tethers on exuberance.

The position here is that both prescriptions are appropriate, but in a complex way. That is, both prescriptions probably will be appropriate in the life of any organization, but *not at the same time*. Moreover, neither one of the prescriptions is likely to be useful at the same time for all parts of any organization. Further, I suspect that most organizations are relatively poor targets for the comprehensive social contract implied by pervasive cultural change. For most organizations, that is, limited-purpose designs will have a greater applicability initially. In sum, they will facilitate incrementally-expansive movement toward OD ideals; this progress at some future date may provide a foundation for more pervasive interventions.

A Conceptual Context for Irony V

Irony V deals with two easy pieces that illustrate limited-purpose contracts. The initial focus is on flexible work hours,[1] and a following chapter will focus on a "demotion experience." The intent? These easy pieces have success rates that seem very high, even formidable, and they will help lead organizations incrementally down the road to the hard piece—basic cultural change.

This chapter will deal with an easy piece—"easy" in the sense of convenient, simple, and with very high success rates—but it deliberately chooses to focus on the worst case of the flexible work hours genre. The focus will not only be on the public sector, which is widely said to be recalcitrant in the extreme to efforts at planned change via OD, although readers of chapter 1 will know better. In addition, the focus will be on productivity effects where, again, the public sector is widely viewed as being generally deficient, if not broadly unconcerned.

Programs of flexible work hours—henceforth, Flexi-Time or F-T—have proliferated around the world, and most observers generally associate them with a broad range of positive effects for organizations as well as for their members, in personal life as well as at work (e.g., Nollen 1982). F-T may rightly be said to be a major managerial innovation, simple though it seems.

The innovation initially permeated business organizations, and lately is getting much more public-sector notice. Paradoxically, the diffusion of this innovation early proceeded apace, in both arenas, without two crucial kinds of knowledge: a comprehensive review of the available F-T literature, and a sophisticated understanding of why, when, and how F-T works.

More recent years have seen a decided improvement in the first particular, especially around the turn of the decade. Specifically, several comprehensive summary studies (Golembiewski and Proehl 1978, 1980; Nollen 1979; Ronen 1981; Ronen, Primps, and Cloonan 1978) indicate that F-T applications have been associated with a variety of favorable effects in public as well as in business organizations. These summary studies deal with hundreds of separate applications, excluding duplicates. So any conclusions suggested can lay substantial claim to relevance and generality.

The second crucial gap in our knowledge—a sophisticated understanding of why, when, and how F-T works—has proved far more resistant, and reducing

FIGURE 8.1
Schema of Workday with Flexible and Core Hours

Flexible Hours e.g., 7-10 AM	Core Hours including lunch, e.g., 10 AM - 3 PM	Flexible Hours, e.g., 3-6 PM

that gap a bit preoccupies this chapter. It considers sixteen public-sector F-T applications, with the specific goal of illustrating how three general concerns about public-sector OD applications are substantially met by one intervention. Specifically, OD applications in the public sector often have been seen as constrained by three factors:

- Confusion has been expressed concerning how the behavioral theories underlying OD apply in government, given that their development has been rooted largely in business or industrial contexts;
- Unique, or at least especially intense, institutional and historical constraints are said by many to make OD interventions more difficult in the public sector, if not impossible;
- The effects of public-sector interventions are more difficult to judge, since "hard data" are seldom available and because "soft data" relating to attitudes and opinions are said by some to pose problems of reliability and validity.

The discussion below will show how these three factors apply only in diminished senses, if at all, to the OD intervention called F-T. Of course, chapters 1 and 2 have already illustrated the limits of these three aspects of the common wisdom when applied to a large panel of OD interventions.

Basic F-T Format

Although it has appeared in diverse forms, the F-T model is quite simple. Schematically, the F-T day takes a form such as the one shown in figure 8.1. Every employee works the "core hours" each day of the normal five-day workweek. Both arrival and departure times can vary according to employee need or even whim, during the several flexible hours at the beginning and end of each day. Some plans permit banking of hours over some accounting period—say, two weeks. If applicable legislation permits, for example, an individual on a thirty-five-hour workweek might accumulate thirty-nine hours in the first week and bank the surplus for the second week. The next week that individual would work thirty hours, as by taking off early on Thursday and Friday afternoons—working, let us say, five hours on Thursday and Friday rather than seven hours each day.

So F-T is definitely not like the 4-by-10 plan, or a "compressed work-week," which requires ten hours a day for four days, with one normal workday off. Hence, not every alternative work hours plan is F-T, but many variations exist in specific plans concerning the length of core hours, how many hours can be banked to reduce work hours, what conditions constrain employee choice, and so on. Time-recording devices are also often used, but not always. For some purposes, these differences can be critical (e.g., Harvey and Luthans 1979). But they get no further attention here.

F-T and "Growth Psychology"

Modest original ambitions have big implications in this case. F-T had a very specific initial goal: to reduce traffic congestion at a German plant at which everyone stopped work at 5 P.M. and then spent long periods in ill-tempered queues of traffic, crawling homeward on expressways turned into large parking lots. But the simple innovation has a lot more going for it, both practically and theoretically. Basically, F-T may be viewed as a way of increasing responsible employee freedom and discretion at work, and also has the advantages of being inexpensive and requiring little in the way of skills or training.

Why focus on increasing responsible freedom and discretion at work? Basically, since work nowadays commonly demands more of growing proportions of people, work must increasingly give them more. Years ago, I wrote about people "going to work with one buttock," which nowadays is decreasingly possible and increasingly dangerous for all of us. Put another way, F-T is clearly consistent with the "growth psychology" which underlies OD. The reader can easily develop the numerous senses in which F-T fits with various prominent behavioral models: Maslow's pyramid of needs, McGregor's Theory Y versus X, Argyris's dimensions for self-actualization, and Herzberg's distinction between motivators and hygiene factors, among many other possible and variously precise variations on substantially common conceptual themes. For example, F-T permits movement from dependence to growing independence, in Argyrian terms. And F-T similarly enhances the work itself as well as the employee's sense of personal responsibility, which the reader will recognize as Herzbergian motivators.

From a related perspective, F-T also can be viewed in frustration/aggression terms (Golembiewski 1962b, 127–48). F-T increases an employee's control over the environment—as by allowing the employee to sleep late on some days, responding to individual diurnal rhythms (Patkai, Petterson, and Akerstedt 1973), by allowing the employee to be more able to make arrangements for a suddenly sick child unable to attend school, and so on. Hence, F-T can be said to decrease frustration, with possible positive effects on work. Let us develop the point somewhat. In the general case, for example, a frustrating stimulus probably will not increase productivity. In fact, at least five outcomes can occur and (as Coach Bear Bryant used to say about passing in American football) four of them are bad:

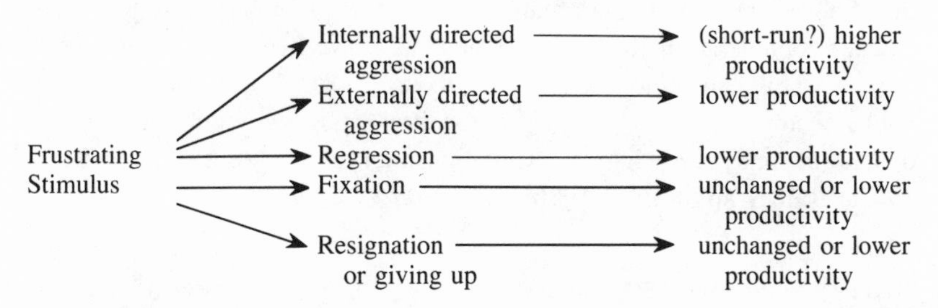

The odds on frustration leading to increased productivity are not great, then. And even internally directed aggression—as when one is aggressive against oneself by "working harder"—can have a range of consequences, not all of them favorable to the person or to the organization. We all know about the workaholic, or the person who works him or her self "to death."

Constraints on OD Applications

There has been an appreciable time lag in public-sector applications of F-T, to be sure, and this suggests some general public-sector constraints against change. This lag could be established in many ways. But here consider only that F-T applications spread quite widely in Europe by the early 1960s, and the first major longitudinal research study in American business appeared in the early 1970s (Golembiewski, Hilles, and Kagno 1974), but it was not until the later 1970s that the major public-administration journal carried any extensive mention (Rubin 1979; Golembiewski and Proehl 1980) of what many consider a major managerial innovation. F-T is even now spotty in government, even after a multiyear study at the federal level induced more heat than light.

Beyond this general time lag, however, F-T appears not to have encountered any special difficulties in public-sector applications. The results in business (Golembiewski and Proehl 1978; Glueck 1979; Nollen 1979) seem quite comparable to the public-sector experience (Golembiewski and Proehl 1980). Moreover, applications in both sectors have similar failure rates—very, very low. Finally, prevailing institutions and practices in public personnel administration do not present anywhere near the obstacles to F-T that they pose for other kinds of OD designs. Interaction-centered OD has experienced some resistance, sometimes of a political character (e.g., Warwick 1975, 59–83), and sometimes because of concerns that democratic administration may undercut popular control over administration (Mosher 1968, 374). OD focusing on structure presents a mixed picture. On one hand, autocratic bureaucracy is deeply entrenched in the ideation and practice of public personnel administration (Golembiewski 1984, 1985)—in structure, position classification, job design, and related manifestations that were originally intended to isolate administration from politics and that have been in place for over a century. This can inhibit structurally focused OD. On the other hand, the public-sector arena is pervasively procedural, and *that* implies a recognition of (and at times receptivity to) structural interventions (e.g., Golembiewski 1962a; Rainey and Rainey 1986).

Panel of Public-Sector Applications

Despite such constraints, a number of public-sector applications were available through 1980, and they constitute our analytical target here. Table 8.1 introduces our panel of sixteen applications which also had the feature of presenting hard data about changes in productivity associated with a F-T application.

Before testing our panel for hard productivity effects, six caveats about the sixteen studies help frame later analysis. This early and up-front catalog follows.

First, despite major efforts, the original reports of seven of the studies are not available for present review. These studies are available in summarized form only in one of two sources (Ronan, Primps, and Cloonan 1978; Nollen 1979).

Second, most F-T applications involve units of small size doing clerical or professional work. So questions about the generalizability of results to larger contexts are appropriate.

Third, individual studies measure one or a few aspects of the quantity or quality of production. This suggests the possibility that data reflect "balloon squeezing"—looking good on some measures of the job by neglecting others.

Fourth, the studies typically use only pre- versus post-comparisons, often with short observational intervals of less than six months, without comparison groups. Longitudinal studies covering a year or longer—referred to as "long-post" in table 8.1—would be more helpful in eliminating alternative explanations of observed effects. Use of comparison groups would serve a similar purpose, but only one of the sixteen present cases does so. For example, an apparent change on a short-post observation might constitute only a temporary outlier in a data set covering a broader span of time. Without comparison groups, similarly, one might miss the fact that an apparent increase might only

TABLE 8.1
Public-Sector F-T Studies Presenting Hard Productivity Data

Setting	N	Union Involved	Study Design	Comparison Group(s)?
Air University, Maxwell Air Force Base (Ronan, Primps, and Cloonan 1978)	N = 100	?	Post only	No
Bureau of Policy Standards (Ronan, Primps, and Cloonan 1978)	N = 200	?	Pre/Post	No
Bureau of Recruiting and Examining (Ronan, Primps, and Cloonan 1978)	N = 240	?	Pre/Post	No
Civil Service Commission, Seattle Region (Ronan, Primps, and Cloonan 1978)	N = 129	?	Pre/Post	No
Department of Labor (1977)	All 112 employees in three units of Office of Accounting	Yes	Pre/Post/ Long-Post	No
Library of Congress (Ronan, Primps, and Cloonan 1978)	N = 150	?	Pre/Post	No
Social Security Administration (1974)	N = 120 in Bureau of Data Processing	Yes	Pre/Post	No
Social Security Administration (Nollen 1979)	?	Yes	Pre/Post	No
Social Security Administration (Nollen 1979)	N = 353 in three work units	Yes	Pre/Post	No
Social Security Administration, Bureau of Disability Insurance (Swart 1978)	100 benefit organizers	Yes	Pre/Post	Yes
U.S. Army (1977)	Detroit Engineer District	?	Pre/Post	No

TABLE 8.1 continued

Setting	N	Union Involved	Study Design	Comparison Group(s)?
U.S. Army (1977)	Regional Dental Activity, Alameda, Calif.	?	Pre/Post	No
U.S. Army, Tank Automotive Command (1974)	400 production employees	?	Pre/Post	No
U.S. Geological Survey (1977)	2,700 employees in Washington, D.C. headquarters	Yes	Pre/Post	No
U.S. Information Agency (1975)	33 employees	?	Pre/Post	No
U.S. Navy Finance Office (Lampman 1975, 1975a; U.S. Navy Sea Support Center 1976)	Long Beach, Calif., "small office" of 100+	?	Pre/Post/ Long-Post	Yes

reflect a general trend rather than the effect of the F-T application. Experience also implies that some F-T difficulties take several months to develop, especially with respect to supervisory behaviors and attitudes (Golembiewski, Fox, and Proehl 1979, 248–50).

Fifth, only one of the sixteen studies in table 8.1 uses any statistical treatment beyond simply arrays of data. Patently, this implies questions as to whether observed changes are only random variations in data rather than noteworthy shifts due to F-T applications. One cannot answer this key question by eyeball examination: When is a change big enough to be considered nonrandom?

Sixth, despite a few exceptions that seek to get at underlying processes (e.g., Golembiewski, Billingsley, and Yeager 1976; Graf 1976), almost all F-T studies have an outcome bias. Informed speculation abounds as to the specific processes energized by F-T applications, but data concerning them are in short supply.

Flexible Work Hours Applications and Hard Outcomes

Despite these six caveats, the data strongly encourage the view that F-T applications have a substantial usefulness. Other studies (e.g., Golembiewski and Proehl 1978, 1980) make it clear that F-T applications have positive "soft" effects on attitudes about work and satisfaction with worksites. For example, over 95 percent of both employees and managers want to retain F-T programs, it appears, a figure relatively constant in hundreds of applications.

Table 8.2 provides hard data counterpoint to this positive pattern of attitudinal effects, and from the public sector where productivity improvements are both needed and widely thought to be difficult or impossible to achieve. Three emphases provide useful detail on this basic conclusion.

A Surprising Attentiveness

To begin, public-sector studies of F-T are (if anything) more concerned about measured productivity than studies in the private sector. Most private-sector studies of F-T report few hard data (Golembiewski and Proehl 1978, 845–47), although the prevailing opinion there sees F-T as a low-cost program that has overwhelmingly positive reflections in soft data—as in satisfaction, self-reports about productivity, cooperation; an enhanced worksite; greater control over one's work; and so on.

A Robust Usefulness

Despite the earlier cautions about our sixteen studies, four major factors encourage a definite conclusion about the hard productivity effects of F-T applications summarized in table 8.2. First, the sixteen studies encompass a broad range of relevant conditions that imply some generalizability. For example, at least six of the sixteen applications—and no doubt several others—occur in union settings. Some of the literature (e.g., Goodman, 1979) suggests that unions generally complicate OD efforts. Hence, F-T's successful application in union contexts encourages some optimism about the usefulness of the intervention and its attractions to diverse publics.

Second, the thrust of table 8.2 suggests a definite balance of positive effects on measured productivity. Specifically, eighteen of the total of twenty-three reported measures imply increased productivity, and markedly so in a number of cases. Only two of the twenty-three measures reflect any drop in productivity.

Third, this overall thrust of the data is quite powerful when coupled with other observations of effects associated with F-T applications. Specifically, extensive cross-comparisons clearly reinforce the overall thrust of table 8.2. Thus, attitudinal data very affirmatively attribute a broad range of favorable effects of F-T on aspects of productivity (Golembiewski and Proehl 1980; Nollen 1979; Ronen, Primps, and Cloonan 1978; Swart 1978). Moreover, a range of hard data—on absenteeism, overtime, various costs, and so on—provide similar reinforcement for the positive effects implied in table 8.2 (Golembiewski and Proehl 1978, 1980; Ronen, Primps, and Cloonan 1978).

TABLE 8.2
Changes in Hard Productivity Measures Associated with F-T Applications

Setting	Statistical Treatment?	Hard/Soft Data?	Effects on Hard Productivity Indicators
Air University, Maxwell Air Force Base (Ronan, Primps, and Cloonan 1978)	None	H/S	Increase of 10% in "successful contacts made on first call from outside"
Bureau of Policy Standards (Ronan, Primps, and Cloonan 1978)	?	H/S	"Inconclusive results"
Bureau of Recruiting and Examining (Ronan, Primps, and Cloonan 1978)	?	H/S	Measured (but unspecified) increase "in hours of morning service"
Civil Service Commission, Seattle Region (Ronan, Primps, and Cloonan 1978)	None	H/S	Increase in indicator of "communication with other offices in Washington and Alaska"
Department of Labor (1977)	None	H/S	Increase of 3% "per net staff hour"
Library of Congress (Ronan, Primps, and Cloonan 1978)	?	H/S	Increase of 6.9% "over first quarter"; increase of 14.0% "over second quarter"
Social Security Administration (1974)	?	H/S	Increase of 11.6% in "office productivity" measured in terms of "median productivity per hour per clerk"
Social Security Administration (Nollen 1979)	?	H/?	Increase of 40% in "work units per hour"
Social Security Administration (Nollen 1979)	?	H/?	Increase of 21% in "work units per hour" comparing "three-month post-test average versus same period prior year"
Social Security Administration, Bureau of Disability Insurance (Swart 1978)	None	H/S	No difference in quantity in experimental versus comparison unit, although productivity increased in both

TABLE 8.2 continued

Setting	Statistical Treatment?	Hard/Soft Data?	Effects on Hard Productivity Indicators
U.S. Army (1977)	None	H/S	Increase of 5%; hours per standard work unit decreased from 2.93 to 2.79 hours
U.S. Army (1977)	None	H/S	Increase of 10.7% for technicians; average monthly weighted work units per hour increased from 7.82 to 8.66
U.S. Army, Tank Automotive Command (1974)	None	H/S	Increase of 2%
U.S. Geological Survey (1977)	None	H/S	Decrease of 3.6% in Map Production in one area; and increase of 14.3% in another area Decrease of 11.5% in Map Distribution Increase of 13.5% in vouchers processed in Finance Increase of 6.3% in Technical Reports processed
U.S. Information Agency (1975)	None	H/S	Increase of 4.5% of vouchers processed in Accounts Payable and Claims Section; and reduction of 16% in backlog
U.S. Navy Finance Office (Lampman 1975, 1975a; U.S. Navy Sea Support Center 1976)	Wilcoxon test	H/S	No change in quantity of work of experimental group as compared to control group; although the "expected increase" did not occur, reports note a significant decrease in error rate in experimental versus control group

Fourth, the trend in table 8.2 gains added attractiveness in the light of the low cost of F-T applications. Available data indicate that F-T requires changes only in the behaviors of supervisors. But these changes come in an attractive package: they involve competencies that almost all supervisors have or can come to develop in brief time frames, they involve little training and other overhead support, and those new supervisory behaviors or attitudes tend to be ones that employees prefer and respond positively to (Graf 1976; Golembiewski, Fox, and Proehl 1979).

The low costs of F-T applications and related training contrast sharply with the high costs often associated with other OD interventions, especially interaction-centered designs. These often imply costly training in attitudes and behavioral skills, as in having intact work units undergo T-group or team-building experience. On the general point, see Golembiewski (1979, 1, esp. 85–132).

Toward "Limited-Purpose" Designs

The results are interesting enough in themselves, but the present intent is to encourage generalization from F-T rather than fixation on it. How many other "limited-purpose" designs await discovery or invention? That is the single central question, and answers to it will help in the diffusion of OD values and practices, especially in organizations beginning from a basically autocratic foundation.

The following chapter details another example of a limited-purpose design, albeit one of greater difficulty and sensitivity. Together, this chapter and the one following suggest that many other limited-purpose designs await discovery or invention. That is, in retrospect, both examples seem obvious.

Greater Success via Easy Pieces

This survey of F-T experience deliberately deals with what most would consider a tough case. The public sector is not renowned for its innovation, although that is often an undeserved reputation. Nor is the public-sector agency typically seen as very much interested in hard measures of performance, although that also often is a bad rap.

Stacking the deck against a favorable outcome does not seem to have mattered in this case. Just as in business organizations—no more so, but no less—F-T applications seem to have had the range of consequences that suggest favorable outcomes for employees and their organizations. Those are the dual goals of OD applications, needless to say.

While this demonstration was deliberately made tough, the typical F-T application causes no hernias—either in concept or in application. Only a few failures have been reported, to suggest the point. The intervention seems to provide what most individuals seem to want—a greater potential to control aspects of their worksite, even though the actual exercise of that potential may be infrequent (e.g., Golembiewski, Hilles, and Kagno 1974). In exchange, the overwhelming experience is that this freedom is used responsibly. That is, employees not only report almost-unanimous satisfaction with F-T, but most indicators of performance reflect either an enhancement, or at least no diminution, of performance (e.g., Golembiewski and Proehl 1978).

So it appears safe to say that F-T applications—wherever—seem to be relatively easy pieces that can sustain lofty success rates. That bottom line is made even more attractive by several features of the intervention. Thus, the design is a broadly applicable one, perhaps especially for initial OD interventions in organizations with little experience in participative management. Moreover, modest skills are required to make a go of it, and training costs are minimal. In addition, both management and labor unions (where they exist) may find grounds for common cause in F-T applications, with possible benefits that generalize far beyond the immediate intervention.

The case for F-T enhancing OD success rates also can be made in terms of the preceding analysis, if but briefly and selectively. For example, F-T seems a reasonable low-stimulus design, with attractive uses in general but especially when individuals report advanced degrees of burnout. F-T can be part of a first-stage effort to reduce strain on employees, in short, with the second stage being devoted to later systemic change when individuals develop greater emotional slack. Relatedly, F-T at once rests on and contributes to the kind of group properties that chapter 7 associates with low burnout—Supervisory Support, Peer Support, and Task Orientation. Typically, to illustrate, work units have to develop suddenly-shifting ways of covering for an employee who is flexing, and that happens most fluidly when Peer Support is high.

More generally, F-T fits best with the regenerative interaction systems at the heart of OD—high openness, owning, and trust, as well as low risk. Indeed, one of the leading F-T applications was presented in terms of not only resting on trust, but also as contributing to it as well as to developing the OD program (Golembiewski, Hilles, and Kagno 1974). In the absence of effective and nondefensive communication, in general, F-T applications could more easily degenerate into misuses of the new discretion. It seems to be a measure of the attractiveness of F-T as an intervention that such outcomes are infrequent, if not rare.

To be sure, the intervention does not come scot-free, but the costs seem generally bearable and might even be attractive to assume. On general grounds, consider only two of these costs—the first relating to a practical issue, and the other involving methodology.

Practical problems can exist in F-T applications. For example, in one F-T installation, a small percentage of supervisors still had a problem with the program after four years. These few supervisors—because they were deeply distrustful, or could not bring themselves to delegate, or could not monitor performance by developing shared objectives—*worked the entire F-T day*, which in their case was 10.5 hours. That surprising finding in an evaluative review of F-T experience inspired some training costs, but costs attractive both to most supervisors involved and to their organization (Golembiewski, Fox, and Proehl 1979).

The methodological issues are more intractable, and hence (if anything) in greater need of attention. As the summary above indicates, F-T studies are relatively numerous but will win no prizes for rigor of design or method. It will require a real avalanche of sophisticated studies with zero or negative effects to counterbalance the positive tenor of the F-T literature and, although that avalanche may come, it seems unlikely. We also lack an appreciation of the specific dynamics involved in F-T applications, and that needs early remedying. Models for the required work are available (e.g., Orpen 1981; Ralston, Anthony, and Gustafson 1985), but the general attractiveness of F-T applications has yet to be sufficiently complemented by detailed study.

Note

1. An earlier version of the following report appears as Golembiewski 1980.

References

Department of Labor, Office of Accounting. 1977. "Pilot Flexitime Project in the Office of Accounting." Internal memo. October.

Glueck, W. F. 1979. "Changing Hours of Work." *The Personal Administrator* 57:44–47, 62–67.

Golembiewski, R. T. 1962a. "Civil Service and Managing Work." *American Political Science Review* 56:961–73.

______. 1962b. *Behavior and Organization*. Chicago: Rand McNally.

______. 1979. *Approaches to Planned Change*. vol. 1. New York: Marcel Dekker.

______. 1980. "Public-Sector Productivity and Flexible Work Hours." *Southern Review of Public Administration* 4:324–39.

______. 1984. "Organizing Public Work, Round Three." In *The Costs of Federalism*, edited by R. T. Golembiewski and A. Wildavsky, 237–69. New Brunswick, N.J.: Transaction.

______. 1985. *Humanizing Public Organizations*. Mt. Airy, Md.: Lomond.

Golembiewski, R. T., and Proehl, C. W. Jr. 1978. "A Survey of the Empirical Literature on Flexible Workhours." *Academy of Management Review* 3:837–53.

______. 1980. "Public-Sector Applications of Flexible Workhours." *Public Administration Review* 40:72–85.

Golembiewski, R. T.; Billingsley, K.; and Yeager, S. 1976. "Measuring Change and Persistence in Human Affairs." *Journal of Applied Behavioral Science* 12:133–37.

Golembiewski, R. T.; Fox, F.; and Proehl, C. W. Jr. 1979. "Is Flexi-Time 'Hard Time' for Supervisors? Two Sources of Data Rejecting the Proposition." *Journal of Management* 5:215–22.

Golembiewski, R. T.; Hilles, R.; and Kagno, M. S. 1974. "A Longitudinal Study of Flexi-Time Effects." *Journal of Applied Behavioral Science*, 10:502–32.

Goodman, P. S. 1979. *Assessing Organizational Change*. New York: Wiley-Interscience.

Graf, L. A. 1976. "An Analysis of the Effect of Flexible Working Hours on the Management Functions of the First-Line Supervisor." Ph.D. diss. Mississippi State University.

Harvey, B. H., and Luthans, F. 1979. "Flexi-Time: An Empirical Analysis of Its Real Meaning and Impact." *Business Topics* 27:31–36.

Lampman, C. M. 1975a. "Flexi-Time, Organizational Change, and the Traditional Hierarchical Organization: An Action Research." Master's thesis. Pepperdine University.

______. 1975b. "Flexi-Time, Organizational Change, and the Traditional Hierarchical Organization: A Follow-up Report." Unpublished report. San Diego: Navy Finance Office.

Mosher, F. 1968. *Democracy and Public Service*. New York: Oxford University Press.

Nollen, S. D. 1979. "Does Flexi-Time Improve Productivity?" *Harvard Business Review* 57:16–18, 76, 80.

______. 1982. *New Work Schedules in Practice*. New York: McGraw-Hill.

Orpen, C. 1981. "Effects of Flexible Working Hours on Employee Satisfaction and Performance." *Journal of Applied Psychology* 66:113–15.

Patkai, P.; Petterson, K.; and Akerstedt, T. 1973. "Flexible Working Hours and Individual Diurnal Rhythms." *Reports From the Psychological Laboratories*, 406. Stockholm: University of Stockholm.

Rainey, G. W., and Rainey, H. G. 1986. "Structural Overhaul in a Government Agency." *Public Administration Quarterly* 10:206–23.

Ralston, D. A.; Anthony, W. P.; and Gustafson, D. J. 1985. "Employees May Love Flextime, but What Does It Do to the Organization's Productivity?" *Journal of Applied Psychology* 70:272–79.

Ronen, S. 1981. *Alternative Work Schedules*. New York: McGraw-Hill.

Ronen, S.; Primps, S.; and Cloonan, J. 1978. Testimony before Senate Committee on Governmental Affairs on S 517, Flexitime and Part-Time Legislation, 29 June.

Rubin, R. S. 1979. "Flexi-Time: Its Implications in the Public Sector." *Public Administration Review* 39:277–82.

Swart, J. C. 1978. *A Flexible Approach to Working Hours*. New York: AMACOM.

U.S. Army. 1977. "Flexi-Time Experience in the Department of the Army." Internal memo. September.

U.S. Army Tank Automotive Command. 1974. "Summary Report of Flexi-Time Program in the Federal Government." Working memo, U.S. Civil Service Commission, Bureau of Policies and Standards. October.

U.S. Information Agency. 1975. "Summary of Flexi-Time Program in the Federal Government." Washington, D.C.: U.S. Civil Service Commission, Bureau of Policies and Standards.

U.S. Navy Sea Support Center. 1976. "Continuation of Flexi-Time." Internal memo. San Diego, Calif. December.

Warwick, D. P. 1975. *A Theory of Public Bureaucracy*. Cambridge, Mass.: Harvard University Press.

9

"Rain" in Development: Demotion as Exemplar

Goodwin Watson was a wizened and wise facilitator of developmental experiences for individuals, and he was fond of noting: "It takes the rain as well as the sun to make flowers grow."

OD devotes far more attention to the sun—developing and trusting interpersonal relations, and building regenerative interaction, among other efforts. Thus OD evolved in basic response to the challenges of organizational growth—quite attractive challenges, as that genre goes. Despite the real risks, these challenges have definite practical and conceptual up-sides. They focus on expanding competencies and opportunities, and so on.

In general, organizational studies have not strayed far or often from the sunny side of the street. Although it is doing better, OD has given little attention to the organizational rain—to downsizing rather than growing, to contracting rather than expanding opportunities. (For some early exceptions, see Golembiewski 1979, 2: 201–11.) The Organization Behavior literature has a similar aversion, although that is changing in recent years (e.g., Sutton, Bruce, and Harris 1983).

This chapter proposes that this bias toward the sun is awkward, and that a greater balance is needed. Essentially, rain there will be, and neglecting it is Pollyannish. Moreover, despite the dangers, organizational rain provides real opportunities for moving toward the same OD values that can be more pleasantly approached via sun. This chapter continues on the theme of easy pieces—relatively convenient designs, which require only journeyman intervening skills, and which seem to have a high probability of inducing intended outcomes.

A Conceptual Context for Irony V, Revisited

The focus here is on the demotion design, whose initial application (Golembiewski et al. 1972) came before its time.[1] Nowadays, such an initiative could occur in many loci. Then, the locus was a corporate division in difficult economic straits, even as the national economy moved along at a good clip. The demotion design was developed nearly two decades ago for the express purpose of gaining experience with an adverse personnel action alternative to termination, with a second major goal of extending the values of an ongoing OD program. The challenges involved enlarging the repertoires of employee and managerial responses applicable at a difficult time in order to retain experienced personnel who could provide a valuable boost for organizational effectiveness when the economy revived.

The basic idea did not find an initially receptive local management, troubled as it was with making a too-long-delayed decision. Most experienced observers did not believe the demotion design would work. They doubted that demoted workers could be effectively integrated into the work force, which was the key to retaining their experience and productivity until the economy revived. They saw the exercise more in terms of encouraging later guerrilla warfare by those seeking to even the score.

The results prove otherwise, not only in the initial application but in several replications. The design generates attractive results—indeed, highly favorable ones. The beneficiaries are individuals who served their organization satisfactorily in the past, as well as the management that acknowledges its obligation but sees no alternative other than generous separation packages.

Bad times came upon us again in the late 1970s and early 1980s, and this time the repertoire of responses was broader than in 1972. Short weeks for all in work-sharing programs have replaced termination for some employees, union contracts have been renegotiated to support teetering firms, various job-sharing and part-time arrangements have been utilized to fine-tune the balance between employee needs and economic exigencies, and multiple if variously-useful efforts have been made to help employees constructively face loss of jobs from cutbacks, plant closings, and the like. In the case of a Canadian oil and gas firm, all of the employees were brought together in an auditorium, and emerged having met cutback requirements by a variety of self-choices: work sharing, permanent or temporary reductions in workweeks, and so on. For an overview, see Golembiewski 1979, 2: 185–214.

All in all, demotion can be said to constitute a growing future emphasis in OD's arsenal, and for at least four reasons. First, national economic recessions or depressions no doubt will always be with us—although perhaps with reduced dislocation, if we are skillful and lucky. Of course, some dour observers see such dark clouds just over the economic horizon. And virtually all observers see a future of persisting and increasing turbulence in which many job changes will be necessary.

Second, the value of demotion as a tactic will continue after national economic recovery occurs. For even then, demotion can be part of an organization's options because, among other reasons:

- Some firms or public agencies always will be experiencing bad times;
- Any recovery might be shallow and shortlived, and demotion may enable organizations to retain experienced employees for a quick push when the economic climate really improves;
- Even in very good times, skills will be obsolescing, employee needs and ambitions may be lowered, and products and missions will change.

Each of these possibilities, as well as others, implies room for demotion among the options available to forward-looking organizations.

Third, contrary to the common wisdom, at least some organizations already make substantial use of demotion. In one industrial organization with over 50,000 employees, for example, about half of the managers and executives surveyed saw "at least a pretty good chance for their own demotion" some time during their careers (Goldner 1965, 718). The author saw that bare fact as one of the most important findings in his study, given its discrepancy from general opinion about this personnel action. Relatedly, demotions show up clearly in statistical analyses of career progression (e.g., Rosenbaum 1979). This incidence motivates trying to do better with demotion, obviously.

Fourth, substantial evidence implies that major improvements in demotion practices and policies are possible—indeed, are probably necessary (e.g., Hall and Isabella 1985). In part, this potential derives from the multiple uses of the term "demotion." Thus, More isolates 11 meanings of the term (1962, 215–16). This does not reflect conceptual carelessness, however, but rather more a general embarrassment, lack of skill in doing a necessary thing, or native cunning motivated by a fear of diluting or destroying motivation in the demotion process. Thus, Goldner dwells on "the ways in which organizations make demotion socially acceptable" (1965, 715), while Veiga concludes of his review of five demotions that "top management had so sweetened the moves and given such misleading (though well-intentioned) counseling that only one of the five was perceptive enough, or perhaps secure enough, to recognize what had really happened" (Veiga 1981, 21).

These four perspectives, then, contribute motivation to this study's consideration of a pure-vanilla case of demotion—an open situation in which all in the organization were aware of the action, in which all demotees would experience loss of both status and compensation, and in which a deliberate effort was made to aid the coping of both management and demotees.

The following narrative sketches a simple design, first applied in 1972 for aiding in the adjustment of a national salesforce to a severe cutback, and since then applied on several occasions. This narrative illustrates the useful effects of such a design, and it encourages raising a number of ethical issues associated with similar interventions in organizations. More broadly, it demonstrates that adverse personnel actions arouse powerful emotions[2] that can and should be dealt with, directly and as they occur, for the sake of both management and employees. In the context of this book, the demotion design demonstrates another approach to increasing OD success rates in two senses—by enlarging the arena in which OD values can be applied, and by a design that seems to have intended effects in a high proportion of cases.

Purposes of the Design

This chapter focuses on an organization in which thirteen regional marketing managers were, as part of a major reduction in force, given a choice—demotion to senior salesperson, or termination. The managers ranged in age from thirty-three to fifty-five, they had been with the company for from nine to twenty-four years, and they had served as managers for periods ranging from six months to seventeen years. All had received satisfactory performance appraisals. Most of the demotees would suffer a major reduction in salary, in some cases as much as $4,000 a year, plus the loss of other perquisites, if they chose to "pick up the bag."

Several forces influenced the decisions of the thirteen managers. The generous separation allowances available to those with seniority encouraged choosing termination. On the other hand, the job market was chancy and the company was considered a fine employer. So real counterforces discouraged leaving the firm, even for those angry because of the adverse decision about them.

All but two of the managers accepted the demotion and, as table 9.1 shows, they were given an early assignment intended to facilitate their making the required adaptations as effectively and quickly as possible. It was referred to as an "integrative experience," and sought to counteract the apprehensions induced by the demotions, with emphasis on the sharing of resources in a community setting. The hope was that this would increase a demotee's sense of mastery over the consequences of his demotion and hence reduce the initial anxiety, depression, and hostility likely to be induced by the personnel action.

The approach sought to reinforce previous human resource developmental efforts. The firm had invested in a major way in an OD program in which an off-site sensitivity training experience was a major learning vehicle. The thrust of the initial sensitivity training was to help organization members in two ways: in developing attitudes and behavioral skills appropriate to OD norms, and in building those norms or values into their relationships at work. Eighteen of the twenty-two participants in the demotion design—the eleven demotees and their immediate supervisors—had such a learning experience, in fact. For them, that integrative experience was one more extension into work of their off-site sensitivity training sessions.

The demotion design was in effect an effort at the worksite to act on the values emphasized in the off-site training sessions. Briefly, those core values include:

TABLE 9.1
Timing of the Action Design and Major Activities

Day 1	Day 2	Day 6	Day 7	Day 45
Thirteen managers informed of choices: demotion to salespersons or termination	Decision required	Three major activities:	Two major activities:	Test of persistence of changes: long post-test
Employees understand that choice of demotion will require reporting to a Midwestern city for an "integrative experience" along with new supervisors	Eleven managers accept demotion	1. demotees and supervisors respond to MAACL[a] pre-test 2. demotees spend balance of day in discussion 3. supervisors have briefing meeting	1. demotees meet individually with their new supervisors 2. demotees and supervisors respond to MAACL[a] short post-test	Demotees and supervisors respond to MAACL[a]

Note: [a]Multiple Affect Adjective Check List (Zuckerman and Lubin 1965)

- full and free communication
- expression of emotional as well as task-oriented behavior
- acceptance of conflict between the individual and the organization, and coping with the conflict willingly, openly, and rationally

The demotion design is an "integrative experience" in several senses. Obviously, it brought new supervisor-salesperson pairs together. Moreover, it sought to relate feelings and action: feelings would be expressed *and* worked through, if possible. The working symbolism was the cauterization of a wound, and the design sought to avoid obsessiveness and the postponement of facing new work demands, which over time would probably have added to the negative emotional impact of demotion. In the absence of such emotional support—coming from demoted peers, superiors, and the employing organization—negative effects were probable, especially for the more senior men. Were depression to occur, the best-available information warned intervenors and management, its effects might "include insomnia, loss of appetite, excessive worrying, indigestion and decline in energy" (Kiev 1969, 2).

The integrative experience also provided an opportunity for all involved to obtain early data about possible adaptive difficulties—managers, demotees, and the consultants who included outsiders as well as in-house representatives from a human resources unit. The latter were essential since they could provide help if either supervisors or demotees later experienced difficulties.

Characteristics of Action Design

The design had two learning phases. For roughly 50 percent of the time, demotees worked together. Later, individual demotees attempted to work through issues of concern with their new supervisors.

First design component. All demotees spent about four hours together discussing mutual concerns and needs, with two consultants available. The intent was to harness emotional energies to organization purposes rather than to merely diffuse them through sheer ventilation. Several important themes were dealt with, beginning with personal reactions and moving toward work-related issues. The process included the following:

- Comparing experiences, especially about the diverse ways in which various relevant organizational policies were applied in their individual cases
- Encouraging expression of anxiety or hostility about the demotions themselves or about associated processes—for example, their style or timing
- Surfacing and testing suspicions regarding management, such as the concern that another personnel purge was imminent
- Isolating and, as much as possible, working through demotees' concerns about authority and dependence, as in their complaints that they were not

being treated as adults, or that they were "strong enough" to take the demotions without the integrative experience

- Dealing with a variety of issues in work relations—for example, how to explain the demotions to clients or other salespeople—in order to develop strategies and norms that would reduce the probability of avoiding issues or handling them awkwardly in the field
- Identifying specific relevant others with whom interaction had been stressful or with whom it might prove to be so, for the purpose of developing strategies for handling such interaction

Consultants intended to facilitate expression of feelings and reactions, to help reveal the diversity of the demotees' experiences and coping strategies, and to work toward a successful adaptation to the demands of the new job. In short, the consultants directed attention to both process *and* content, to use a convenient distinction. In their attitudes, the consultants were neither advocates of management actions nor emotionally neutral in response to the dynamics of the demotions. By conscious decision, they sought to remain in-between.

The consultants believed some demotees might decide to accept termination after the integrative experience, and that option was emphasized early and late. But none of the eleven participating demotees took advantage of the offer, which is consistent with the view that OD should increase responsible freedom. In this case, that meant multiple opportunities to choose, as an in vivo exercise of the power that demotees did have in a situation in which they might otherwise feel powerless. Virtually all of the managers-becoming-salespersons emphasized the positive meaning of the integrative experience, but one participant derided it as "hand holding" and "coddling."

The first component of the learning design emphasized some common elements among the demotees, as well as some differentiating factors between them. The former included the impact of demotion on self-image; experiences with important referents, such as spouses, colleagues, or salespersons from other firms; and concerns about taking on the salesperson's job—"picking up the bag again" to cover a sales territory, participating in sales meetings with peers they have previously managed, and so on. These elements contributed to a sense of shared concerns, as well as to building a learning community.

The design's strong emphasis on reality-testing required a basic challenge to this sense of shared interests. Prominent among the differentiating elements was the fact that the demotees included both long-service employees and recent managerial appointees. On balance, the future for the longer-service men was far less bright. Some men professed shock at being confronted with the choice of demotion and termination, in addition, while others maintained they had more or less expected some action, especially because of falling demand in the industry. A few even expressed pleasure that the adverse action did not hit them as hard as it had many others affected by the major reduction in force.

Second design component. The second major design feature involved the reintegration of the demotee into the work force. Hence it has strong implications for productivity and organizational effectiveness.

Two approaches were taken to building on the first phase, which sought to help demotees reduce their general anxiety as well as to sharpen their more specific concerns about developing new working relationships. First, the demotees' new managers met for two hours to discuss their role in the design for the next day—which they learned was to feature individual meetings with the demotees. The basic thrust was to sensitize managers about how the demotees felt, so as to help by suggesting ways of channeling those feelings toward making the most successful adaption possible.

Second, the demotees spent approximately three hours with their new managers in one-to-one situations. The consultants sat in on these several meetings, as time permitted. The major concerns in these one-to-one situations included:

- Building early supervisory relations, as in mutual pledges to work harmoniously together, which was easiest in those several cases where demotees were able to choose their new manager
- Discussing technical problems, such as going over sales territories
- Developing strategies by which the manager and salesperson could be mutually helpful, as in discussing ways to moderate the formation of cliques, which the demotions might encourage
- Isolating likely problems and cementing a contract to agree to meet any problems rapidly and mutually

Some one-to-one meetings concentrated on one of these concerns; other meetings dealt with several.

Measuring the design's consequences. The effects of the action design are judged by changes in the Multiple Affect Adjective Check List (MAACL), developed by Marvin Zuckerman and Bernard Lubin. The MAACL is an instrument for tapping the psychological aspects of emotion, and conceives of affect as a state, not as a trait. That is, a time referent is specified for respondents, who react as they feel "today" or "now" rather than "generally" or "occasionally." Zuckerman and Lubin describe the MAACL in these terms:

> [It] was designed to fill the need for a self-administered test which would provide valued measures of three of the clinically relevant negative affects:

> anxiety, depression, and hostility. No attempt was made to measure positive affects, but some of the evidence indicates that the scales are bipolar, and that low scores on the full scales will indicate states of positive affect. (1965, 3)

The intervenors had direct expectations about MAACL scores. The demotees were expected to have high initial scores on anxiety, depression, and hostility; and a successful intervention would reduce them significantly. The managers were expected to have lower initial scores on anxiety, depression, and hostility, and the post-treatment administration of the MAACL was not expected to reveal any major shifts, except perhaps on anxiety. This anxiety about role was expected to diminish for the supervisors as the design unfolded.

The MAACL was administered three times. One administration occurred just before the integrative experience, and a second immediately after. The third administration was by mail approximately a month after the intervention, so as to test the persistence of any changes. One of the twenty-two participants did not respond to the third administration.

Consequences of a Critical Intervention

The effects of the intervention are summarized in two ways. A first section provides a brief review of the measured consequences. A second section urges caution about assuming too much.

Five perspectives on what happened. What effects did the intervention have? They were almost entirely in the expected directions, as table 9.2 suggests. For the sake of simplicity, only gross trends are reported, but the discussion will emphasize all statistically significant changes.

Five points detail the major results. First, the demotees reacted strongly to demotion. Without going into technical details (e.g., Lubin and Zuckerman 1969), each of the three psychological states referred to in table 9.2 has a different maximum. How high were those scores? About one-third of the scores for demotees on the initial MAACL administration surpassed or closely approached the 98th percentile of scores of a large number of past respondents. So the initial MAACL scores for demotees in table 9.2 are very high, but not off-the-scale. The scores for managers approximate normal levels, with a marked elevation only for anxiety.

Since the demotions were announced about six days before the first administration of the MAACL (see table 9.2), the initial scores suggest that the demotions had a great and persisting impact that was unlikely simply to wither away. No data exist on this important point, but most scores were near the maxima. So the six intervening days did not do much to dampen reactions to the personnel action.

Second, as expected, the initial scores of the managers are significantly lower than the demotees' initial scores in all cases. Managers' scores for

TABLE 9.2
Overall Effects of Intervention on
Three MAACL Administrations

	Mean Scale Scores (by Days after Demotion)[a]		
	Day 6	Day 7	Day 45
Demotees			
Anxiety	9.8	7.5	6.5
Depression	17.8	14.9	13.6
Hostility	9.5	7.2	7.2
Managers			
Anxiety	6.3	5.3	4.6
Depression	9.8	9.5	9.5
Hostility	5.1	5.3	5.7

Note: [a]Since each scale has a different maximum score, interscale comparisons should not be made. A lower score reflects less of the emotion in all cases.

anxiety also decreased significantly twice—at day 7, the last day of the learning design, and again at day 45—and this implies that the managers were not upset by the integrative experience. Hostility scores rose, but not significantly.

Third, the effects of the design are consistent. The effects vary only randomly for employees who differ in age, years with company, years as regional manager, and loss of salary involved in the demotion. Details are available elsewhere (Golembiewski et al. 1972).

Fourth, the effects on individuals also establish the efficacy of the design. Overall, about 80 percent of all MAACL scores for demotees are reduced, and an additional 10 percent are unchanged, when the initial scores are compared with second and third scores for each individual. In addition, no demotee has an increased score on more than one scale. Overall, all average scores for demotees decrease significantly between days 6 and 7, which were the days of the learning design intervention, and the reductions are maintained through day 45. In fact, anxiety scores on the average are significantly lower, comparing days 6 and 7 as well as days 7 and 45.

Fifth, subsequent history suggests the value of the design. All but one of the demotees were on the job three years later and when interviewed, they reported vividly and positively on the integrative experience. Moreover, five had been re-promoted when the firm's markets improved. No strict efforts were made to track the demotees beyond the three-year mark but, essentially, the positive record continued.

Avoiding foolish claims. The results abstracted here could be elaborated, but they come to the same point. The design seems to work, and has done so several times. The initial success of the learning design undoubtedly profited from earlier attempts of the host organization to develop supporting attitudes and behavior. Hence, this design may not be applicable in organizations as a first-generation effort. This was a serious consideration when the design was first applied, but the seriousness diminished with the success of other applications that did not have the benefit of such advance work.

Nonetheless, intervenors should not be incautious. Methodological inelegances prohibit attributing the effects uniquely to the learning design, even though the presumptive evidence is strong, and especially so after several replications generate similar results. For example, some may attribute the initial reductions in anxiety, depression, and hostility to the passage of time. But the interval between the first and second MAACL administrations was a brief one, and the demotees had patently developed and sustained high scores on the three target variables over the six days between the demotion notices and the learning-design intervention. So no easy belittling of the results seems appropriate.

Greater Success by Utilizing Demotion Design

So what can we reasonably conclude about the demotion design or its variants relevant to applications of OD? Two separate points will be emphasized—one dwells on the empirical consequences, and the second focuses more on the moral or ethical considerations. The latter need to undergird applications of the demotion design if they are to rise above merely serving some establishment wishing to rid itself of a ticklish problem.

Probable Empirical Effects

As the findings above suggest, the demotion design seems to have benign or positive effects, on balance. A number of replications of the design, using *different* resource persons in *various* settings, have had similar effects. This reduces the credibility of two major alternative explanations of effects.

So the demotion design may not be an ideal one, but it seems useful for moving toward OD values. These OD values emphasize human responses to human problems—creating reasonable choices for people that permit them to exercise greater responsible freedom at the worksite. The design had those effects for both employees and management, who in their different ways saw no attractive choices and yet who were uncomfortable about the firings. These uncomfortable feelings tend to be turned around by the several choices permitted by the demotion design. In effect, the choices give participants the opportunity to commit themselves to the design, and hence to develop a real sense of the ownership of results.

Moral and Practical Concerns about Cooling Out

The demotion design does not generate effects in the abstract, but in the context of distinct moral and ethical biases, which deserve extended attention.

These moral and ethical issues have more to do with effectiveness than efficiency, of course. But an OD that fails to be alive to its value-filled character cannot remain successful for very long. The demotion design thus serves a useful purpose in providing a context for raising these moral and ethical issues.

Efforts like the demotion design raise tangled ethical and practical issues about which OD consultants clearly need to be concerned. Moreover, these issues also need attention from that broad range of decision makers who might consider or authorize interventions like the demotion option—executives and managers in all functional areas, personnel directors, and so on. Four points relevant to these broad-impact ethical issues deserve highlighting.

Value issues should be up-front. If organizational interventions are seen as a Band-Aid, as an after-the-fact ameliorative effort to salve the wounds of any actions management decides to take, then the organizational intervenor faces a range of serious ethical and professional issues. He becomes a "cooling-out" functionary, a person who merely dissipates the hostility that might otherwise possibly serve as a force for constructive change. In the long run, the intervenor's boss in this way can despoil a useful resource.

The best way of avoiding the Band-Aid role is to establish when interventions can make a difference, and to restrict applications to those situations. Facilitative situations include those where

- management has a real stake;
- management perceives that only traditional options exist;
- employees have real choices and can exercise them;
- an alternative has a real probability of working in an exchange sense: that is, the intervention helps management achieve its needs, on balance, while it also serves employee needs, within a normative context defined by the values underlying OD.

The consulting team saw all those conditions in the integrative experience described above.

Some authorities in organizations may desire only a reduction in conflict, of course, not an increase in employee options. The point here is that, as the intervenor's ability to generate real options is limited, so also will his or her usefulness decrease in helping deal with conflict. Many managements seem to be clearer on this point nowadays (e.g., Golembiewski and Kiepper 1988, 216–26), but war stories to the contrary exist, and OD as a profession has only begun to take the first steps in protecting practitioners from undue influence by management (Golembiewski 1986; Golembiewski 1988, esp. part 3).

Cooling out, or increasing options? The context of the present intervention created real confidence that this consulting team was not merely stabilizing the system, and thus subordinating the interests of the demotees to those of the organization. Specifically,

- The demotions were part of a broader reduction in force delayed by a management that for several years had vainly sought new products to occupy the full salesforce;
- Overstaffing, due to rapidly changing market conditions, was an objective dilemma that required confronting;
- Three consultants served various levels of management over the extended period during which policies and procedures for the reduction in force were developed;
- The demotion experience was suggested by the consultants in response to the expressed managerial concern that, unfortunately, there was no alternative to firing thirteen managers.

The consultants basically saw themselves as enlarging the options open to both managers and demotees, both in substantive and, especially, in process terms. Substantively, at a number of points the design provided several opportunities for specific choices by both management and demotees about whether or not to continue. Two of the thirteen men immediately chose termination in preference to demotion at the first of these decision points, which suggests the choices were real. Process enhancement was considered more significant by consultants, however. The purpose was to induce regenerative interaction between demotees, and then between the members of each demotee-supervisor pair. Such enhanced interaction intended to raise the probability that demotees could really handle choice and change—that they had valid and reliable data, and that they got appropriate help in group settings to make decisions that dealt with central issues. This contrasts with decisions that came unwound or, worse yet, generated worse problems than those they attempted to solve.

In process terms, the basic decision was to build the design in a conservative way—from lesser discrepancies to probably greater discrepancies. Hence, the integrative experience began with the demotee meetings, where some differences between individuals were expected but greater commonalities of experience were anticipated. Then the design escalated to encompass supervisor-demotee pairs, where complex discrepancies were expected—between individuals as well as between various areas of an individual's sense of the situation. See also chapter 3.

Real exchange or tenuous illusion? One might argue that the demotees were in no position to engage in meaningful exchange with management and, consequently, that the demotees were powerless pawns. In this view, the demotees could hardly do other than to feign a positive response to an integrative experience that was in reality forced on them.

The consulting team had no doubt, now or earlier, that meaningful choices did exist for the demotees, and their thought processes are revealing. Four factors are most prominent in the case for the position that meaningful choices did exist.

- All demotees had been rated satisfactory performers, and all or most saw the action against them as due to market conditions rather than poor performance.
- Management valued the managers' past contributions and did not relish the negative impact on morale that was expected to follow the outright termination of managers with substantial seniority. But management could initially see no way to retain the eventual demotees without creating managerial situations that they unanimously saw as both unattractive and unavoidable.
- Most of the demotees, given a choice, preferred staying with the firm despite real losses in money and status.
- The managers' work experience might later be valuable when market conditions became more favorable.

In the present case, the re-promotions mentioned above represent perhaps the best indicator that more than a tenuous illusion of exchange existed. A real basis for exchange might not have existed if, for example, the demotees had been marginal performers. But they all had been satisfactory performers.

Multiple and shifting clients. Multiple and shifting clients clearly existed in the case under discussion. The initial client was marketing management. The consulting team served it as process consultants, and also recommended the demotion design to them. The OD team also was in the long run held responsible by management for the effects of the intervention. Management's expectation was that most of the demotees (and perhaps all of them) would experience major coping problems, but past successful experiences with the OD team—coupled with a deep, visceral distaste for the cutback and its human consequences—motivated accepting the consultants' recommendation for demotion. But the consultants' reputation clearly was at stake.

The OD team's client was neither singular nor stable. Once the eleven men accepted demotion, for example, *they* became the focal clients. Later, when the immediate supervisors of the demotees were present, they also became part of the client population. The data suggest that the OD team served the immediate interests of the supervisors least effectively, inadequately helping them to deal with their anxiety in a situation that was novel and initially somewhat threatening to them.

Two points summarize the consulting team's biases in dealing with multiple and shifting clients. First, management was encouraged to apply control through results rather than through knowledge of specific details. Such specification of behavioral or attitudinal objectives may seem to put the proverbial noose around the intervenor's neck, but it has major redeeming virtues. Without such measurement of outcomes, management might be tempted to seek detailed information about "what went on," with serious implications for trust and learning.

Moreover, whether or not clients might be multiple and shifting, and whether or not client interests are starkly opposed, the intervenor's basic allegiance is to a relatively clear set of values and orienting perspectives. The allegiance should be articulated early and should be preserved even if all else is subject to compromise, blurring, or selective application. To do otherwise is to risk being considered a cooling-out functionary, and deservedly so.

From management's point of view, of course, this flexibility for intervenors did not, and will not, come scot-free. Only success in producing desired effects did, and should, motivate the necessary managerial adjustments. Hence the criticality of substantial OD success rates, and especially of efforts like the present one to heighten those success rates.

Greater Success via Easy Pieces, Revisited

In sum, the demotion design illustrates the usefulness of an applied behavioral science approach to a grave organizational issue. Acting on explicit values, it proves possible to help meet the needs of employees. Simultaneously, management husbands experienced resources for better economic times, while adding substance to the bold organizational proclamation: "People count." In addition, essentially similar replications have had similar effects. The focus below is on several senses in which the demotion design can contribute to greater success in OD. The discussion above details several significant caveats, and these should tether any overexuberance in what follows.

Paramountly, perhaps, the leverage for cost-effective outcomes seems high, though appropriate calculations pose formidable challenges. Of course, the narrow, intended effects do occur—levels of anxiety, depression, and hostility are not only reduced, but the reductions persist after what seems a precipitous jump. But such effects are certainly too selective, even if representative. In the present case, not only were the past contributions of employees acknowledged in a very direct way, which the grapevine saw in ways suggestive of future commitment and trust. Moreover, valuable experience was retained for possible use when the economic times improved, a possibility that was realized for almost every ex-manager in the present population. Economic times did improve, sooner rather than later, and five of the voluntary demotees were subsequently re-promoted and all but one continued working.

The demotion design also seems capable of contributing to greater OD success in several broader senses, only four of which get attention here. First, the design adds to the humanistic repertoire of responses relevant to an important type of situation, for organizations as well as for OD. That is, the demotion design vivifies regenerative interaction at a time of mutual need: the design rests upon high openness, owning, and trust, as well as low risk, and the design also seems likely to enhance any existing tendencies toward regenerative interaction. In contrast, under threat, people and organizations tend to resort to closedness and coercion. In this sense, the demotion design illustrates OD values in a situation in which it is common to act in opposite ways (Sutton, Bruce, and Harris 1983).

Second, the demotion design offers both individuals and organization authorities an opportunity to make real and responsible choices. Although extensions of freedom may seldom accompany crisis situations, the demotion design proposes just such an extension. For employees, to illustrate, the design calls for several explicit choices: a choice between the learning experience or termination, a choice between trying to deal constructively with a negative personnel action in community and with organization support, or alone with personal resources, and so on.

Third, the demotion design empowers OD professionals to "be there" at a critical time. This raises their organizational credibility, with management as well as with employees. But the capability also no doubt contributes to the self-esteem of OD practitioners and to their personal growth, as well as to OD's development as a corpus of values with a technology.

Fourth, the demotion design tests the values and core technology of OD in a crisis situation. There is no alternative to such risk taking, at least beyond stultification and stuckness.

The failure to employ designs like this demotion effort, then, is multiply lamentable. Even though this OD application fits a narrow niche, it relates to a critical time—for employees, their managers, and their employing organizations. And it offers the potential for doing something of value, when that is much needed.

Notes

1. An earlier version of this material appears in Golembiewski 1982–83. See also Golembiewski 1977, 2:99–122; and Golembiewski et al. 1972.
2. The point has been neglected, perhaps because it is so painful. For chilling details, see Slote 1977.

References

Goldner, F. H. 1965. "Demotion in Industrial Management." *American Sociological Review* 30:714–24.

Golembiewski, R. T. 1977. *Public Administration as a Developing Discipline*. New York: Marcel Dekker.

______. 1979. *Approaches to Planned Change*. New York: Marcel Dekker.

______. 1982–83. "The Demotion Design." *National Productivity Review* 2:63–70.

______. 1986. "The Fund for Displaced ODers." *Organization Development Journal* 4:12–13.

______. 1988. *Organization Development: Ideas and Issues*. New Brunswick, N.J.: Transaction.

Golembiewski, R. T., and Kiepper, A. 1988. *High Performance and Human Costs*. New York: Praeger.

Golembiewski, R. T.; Carrigan, S. B.; Mead, W. R.; Munzenrider, R.; and Blumberg, A. 1972. "Toward Building New Work Relationships." *Journal of Applied Behavioral Science* 8:135–48.

Hall, D. T., and Isabella, L. A. 1985. "Downward Movement and Career Development." *Organizational Dynamics* 14:5–23.

Kiev, A. 1969. "Crisis Intervention in Industry." Paper delivered at Annual Meeting, New York State Society of Industrial Medicine, Occupational Psychiatry Group. 10 December.

Lubin, B. and Zuckerman, M. 1969. "Level of Emotional Arousal in Laboratory Training." *Journal of Applied Behavioral Science* 5:483–90.

More, D. M. 1962. "Demotion." *Social Problems* 9:213–21.

Rosenbaum, J. E. 1979. "Tournament Mobility." *Administrative Science Quarterly* 24:220–41.

Slote, A. 1977. *Termination*. Indianapolis: Bobbs-Merrill.

Sutton, R. I.; Bruce, R. A.; and Harris, S. G. 1983. *Human Resource Management* 22: full issue.

Veiga, J. F. 1981. "Do Managers on the Move Get Anywhere?" *Harvard Business Review* 19:20–38.

Zuckerman, M., and Lubin, B. 1965. *Manual for the Multiple Adjective Affect Check List*. San Diego: Educational and Industrial Testing Service.

Irony VI

Relative Success without Differentiating Change

10

Multiple Models of Change: Judging How Much Change Requires Specifying What Kind of Change

A truism underlies this chapter. That is, you have to define "change" not only before you can estimate whether or not it occurs in a specific case, but also before you can estimate how much of it occurs. In this strict sense, then, the preceding chapters should be viewed tentatively, for neither the several researches nor this treatment yet have been specific about kinds of change. The time has come to begin to rectify that shortcoming.

If this reasoning is correct, applied research has a serious inadequacy. For change typically gets very general treatment, which is bad enough. Moreover, there may well be several kinds of change. So the definitional problems may be quite heavy, as can be their implications for anyone concerned with change in human affairs. ODers need to pay close attention, in short.

This chapter urges distinguishing kinds of change, distinctions which are suggested by experience and which also are supported by evidence generated with exotic statistical and computational techniques (Golembiewski, Billingsley, and Yeager 1976a; Golembiewski 1986). An immediate payoff of making such distinctions is more definite reliance on existing research findings, whose interpretation is necessarily related to an underlying concept of change. Indeed, as will become plain, *no* interpretation of much behavioral research is possible without a determination of what kind of change—if any—has occurred. More central still, the goal is to facilitate the design of and evaluate efforts to improve the human condition and the quality of life, especially in organizations.

Specifically, conceptual clarification of change will distinguish three kinds. Later, data from a study of a successful Flexi-Time intervention will be used to test these conceptual elaborations. Detailed statistical analysis will support the broad position that a unitary concept of change is not only inappropriate but may be seriously misleading.

The goal here is direct. By extending the boundaries of the known, applied research can contribute to the further development of scientific knowledge, as well as to the fulfillment of its stated goal of bettering the human condition. But applied research contributes in both senses only to the degree that one can ascertain whether a particular intervention succeeded or failed. That knowledge requires not only measuring the quantity of change, but it especially demands confidence in the concept of change that underlies the measurement.

Our focus here is on what is measured in experimental designs, such as those in OD, especially in those designs placing heavy reliance on self-reports.[1] More specifically, this paper deals with the paradox underlying a dilemma emphasized by Bereiter, who asks:

> When scores on a test are observed to change, how can one tell whether it is the persons who have changed or the tests? If the correlation between pre-test and post-test is reasonably high, we are inclined to ascribe change scores to changes in the individuals. But if the correlation is low, or if the pattern of correlations with other variables is different on two occasions, we may suspect that the test does not measure the same thing on the two occasions. Once it is allowed that the pre-test and post-test measure different things, it becomes embarrassing to talk about change. There seems no longer any answer to the question, change *on what?* [emphasis in original] (1963, 11).

By discussing change in OD contexts—via the application of modern technologies for data processing and analysis—this chapter accepts the challenge of Bereiter's central question. This chapter provides perspective on persistence and change in human affairs.

Change on what? Change for what? Our focus has serious implications for the OD practitioner, who cannot avoid these questions. Sometimes such value-laden questions get short shrift in technically-oriented treatments, or as a result of self-interest, as Ross (1971) reminds us forcefully. Yet OD ideologues early emphasized that OD interventions are value loaded (Tannenbaum and Davis 1970; Golembiewski 1972, esp. 59–110). The consciousness grows that OD interventions should be less involved with raising the level of indicators of some relatively stable system, and focused on the basic change of the quality of organizational life that should and can exist (e.g., Golembiewski 1988, part 1).

A Conceptual Context for Irony VI

Our point of entry to confronting the central, indeed crucial, complexities of change will be conceptual. After defining the three types of change in summary fashion, we further distinguish them by examples. The basic conceptual distinctions follow.

- *Alpha Change* involves a variation in the level of some existential state, given a constantly calibrated measuring instrument related to a constant conceptual domain.
- *Beta Change* involves a variation in the level of an existential state, complicated by the fact that some intervals of the measurement continuum associated with a constant conceptual domain have been recalibrated.
- *Gamma Change* involves a redefinition or reconceptualization of some domain—a major change in the perspective or frame of reference within which phenomena are perceived and classified, in what is taken to be relevant in some slice of reality.

Alpha Change

Most OD designs seem to recognize only alpha changes, measured by self-reports using pre-test/post-test designs, with or without comparison groups. Symbolically, such designs may be described as $O_1 - X - O_2$, where "O" stands for observation and "X" stands for OD intervention. That is, the typical design selects some frame of reference or criterion, with change being estimated by fluctuations in the levels of self-reports assumed to be triggered by the intervention.

Alpha changes, then, are conceived as occurring along *relatively stable dimensions of reality* that are defined in terms of discrete and constant intervals. Note that alpha changes can be nonrandom, as established by some test of statistical significance, or they can be random only. And alpha changes may be very large or very small, or anywhere in between. The only requirement is that alpha change occur *within a relatively fixed system or state*, defined in terms of stable dimensions of reality as estimated by a measurement continuum whose intervals are relatively constant. For example, a parent taking a baby to a shoe store is interested in alpha change. The parent's frame of reference is growth in the baby's feet between this visit and the preceding one. The crucial measurement of change occurs within a relatively fixed system of dimensions of reality (our conventional concepts of length and width), as defined by indicators whose intervals are more-or-less constant (the calibrated marks on the measuring rod against which the baby's foot is compared). Measuring T_2 minus T_1 change, where "T" stands for the time of observation, is simple in this case.

Beta Change

These changes involve the recalibration of some part of the intervals used to measure some stable dimension of psychological space, as in pre-intervention versus post-intervention responses. This contrasts with alpha changes, which are measured along more-or-less invariant intervals tapping a stable dimension of reality.

Take a baby's feet. If in a post-test those feet fall in that range within which a beta change had occurred, the parent could not know how much the baby's feet had grown between visits to the shoe store. It would not be meaningful to compare the two measurements because some intervals on the measuring rod had somehow changed. Of course, beta change could occur for intervals at a far extreme of the measuring scale, and that would not be relevant to the practical issue of growth in the baby's feet even though that beta change could be crucial for other people.

Beta change is a problem in the social and behavioral sciences, although analogues in the physical sciences have existed. A beta change on a rod for measuring feet is not very likely, for example, although such rods do expand and contract some. Social measuring rods can "expand" and "contract" significantly, however, even as their conceptual definition remains the same. Note that the reference here is to a phenomenon beyond test-retest reliability. For change in the measuring intervals is often *an intended effect of an OD intervention*, as contrasted with some defect of the measuring instrument. That is to say, OD efforts indeed can change the very measuring instrument being used to estimate the change. This complicates interpreting T_2 and T_1 findings, of course.

Put too simply, perhaps, instruments soliciting self-reports are more like rubber yardsticks than they are like the "standard foot" in the Bureau of Standards. That is, self-reports are rooted in socio-emotional or cultural definitions, or in an individual's knowledge and experiences, which provide variably changeable anchoring points to rate "the degree of participation in decision making," for example. OD efforts typically impact on such cultural definitions, and also significantly modify or enlarge an individual's knowledge or experiences. In this sense, applying the same instrument before and after a successful OD intervention—while assuming that the intervals along which self-reports are made are the same or very similar—may be rather like applying a given survey research instrument to several different cultures, as conventionally understood. Any resulting data must be compared and analyzed very carefully (Ward 1974, esp. 199).

To some, it may seem like splitting hairs to distinguish beta change from alpha, because both deal only with changes in condition within a relatively stable state. But beta change does point up a significant and generic problem in interpreting behavioral research, as an extended illustration will establish. Consider the two sets of descriptions of an organization unit in figure 10.1, before (designated "Now I") and after ("Now II") an OD intervention.[2] In a first hypothetical case, assume that only alpha change has occurred. Even here, figure 10.1 does not support a single or simple conclusion. The Now II score is consistent with an OD failure in one sense, as well as with a success

FIGURE 10.1
Pre- and Post-Test Means on a Representative Item from Likert's Profile of Organizational Characteristics

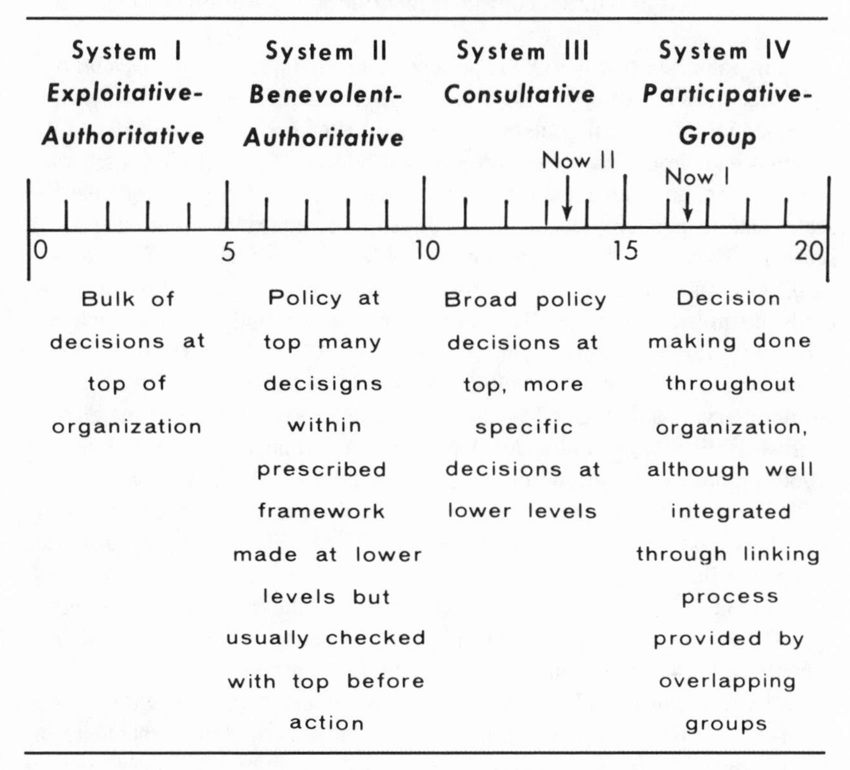

in another. The OD intervention may be said to be a *failure* because Now II is lower than Now I, and OD interventions should induce changes toward system IV. Or, the OD intervention can be taken to be *successful* because the respondents at Now II have a more realistic view of how things really are, a firmer descriptive base for subsequent ameliorative action.

Matters get more complicated if the possibility of beta change is acknowledged. Consider employees whose average pattern of responses following an OD intervention was like that in figure 10.1 (Golembiewski and Carrigan 1973). Yet things in their organization units were *not* worse than before the intervention, respondents reported in interviews supplementing their questionnaire responses. In fact, they say things had substantially improved. In effect, the OD experience may have encouraged respondents to recalibrate Likert's intervals after the intervention in at least two ways: respondents made different estimates of reality, given a clearer perception of what exists; and respondents changed their intervals for measuring value-loaded terms in the instrument, such as "throughout the organization," "well-integrated," and "overlapping."

We hypothecate that the OD experience had "lengthened" the psychological space between some intervals of the Likert instrument, while preserving the essential conceptual content of Likert's "managerial systems." The OD program had, in effect, shown respondents how much integration there was and could be, and they recalibrated the system III and IV portions of Likert's scale. One respondent added: "I don't need to be educated about what a '3' score is! I've seen that often enough." Likert's intervals are like rubber yardsticks, subject to expansion and contraction as personal and group standards are impacted by the OD intervention. Consequently, even though respondents verbally report "more participation" at Now II, their post-intervention scores are lower than for Now I. The content of the Participative Group interval had stretched further than actual participation had increased, as it were. For the technical development of a similar notion, see McGee's (1966) emphasis on "elastic distances" in multidimensional scaling.

Presumably, if the OD intervention had involved a month in an equivalent of Auschwitz, respondents would have recalibrated the system I portion of the Likert Profile.

Numerous other issues relate to, and exacerbate, the interval problem highlighted by beta change. For example, the "response instability" that has sometimes been taken to signal a "non-attitude" in political research (Converse 1970; Iyengar 1973) could in fact reflect a beta change. The difference is critical: non-attitudes can be treated cavalierly as opinional ephemera; a beta change, in contrast, signals differences in the intervals a rater uses to differentiate a given psychological domain. Other significant issues (Pepper and Prytulak 1974) also seem relatable to beta effects.

Gamma Change

This kind of change is conceived as a quantum shift in ways of conceptualizing salient dimensions of reality. This totally differentiates it from beta change, which refers only to variation in some of the intervals measuring a relatively stable dimension of reality.

This third kind of change involves the basic *redefinition of the relevant psychological space* as a consequence of an OD intervention. In sum, gamma is "big bang" change. It refers to a change from one state to another, as contrasted with a change of degree or condition within a given state. Thus, "freedom" for blacks in 1960 may have been defined, in part, as not having to ride in the back of the bus. By 1970, such freedom seems to have expanded to include success at lowering bus fares, increasing the number of black drivers, and impacting on the design of urban mass-transit systems. Measuring gamma change is extraordinarily difficult since the pre-intervention instrument is no longer appropriate. The post-intervention response is not off the scale; it is *on a different scale*.

Thus, if gamma change occurs as the result of an OD program, interpretations of results are chancy in the extreme, and research takes on an Alice-in-Wonderland quality. For example, issues of instrument validity become enormously complicated when phrased in these terms: valid for measuring which kind of change?

Bowers's study of fourteen thousand respondents in twenty-three organizations helps illustrate the importance of distinguishing gamma from beta and alpha change. Among other tendencies, Bowers reports that survey feedback interventions are associated with "statistically significant improvement on a majority of measures" based on The Survey of Organizations Questionnaire (TSOQ), while laboratory training interventions are "associated with declines" on similar measure (1973, 21). In the absence of knowledge about the distribution of types of change, however, it is *not* possible to conclude that Bowers's results demonstrate the greater potency of survey feedback.

Alternatively, survey feedback may have triggered alpha changes, which TSOQ picked up, while lab training induced gamma *in* TSOQ. This interpretation is consistent with the different "depths of intervention" associated with survey feedback and laboratory training, respectively. Moreover, Bowers's instrument does seem more sensitive to alpha changes, as all such instruments must be. Furthermore, TSOQ is based on factorial studies of organizational samples (Taylor and Bowers 1967) other than those in the 1973 study, but we do not know to what degree the 1973 factorial solutions from this sample are congruent with the 1967 baseline solutions. Nor is it known what degree of congruence exists between factorial solutions of pre-test versus post-test responses to TSOQ in the 1973 sample, which could provide a clue about the incidence of beta or gamma change.

Along with other concerns (Torbert 1973), then, interpretation of Bowers's results is made problematic by his failure to specify kind of change. In the case of both survey research and laboratory training interventions, that knowledge is profoundly significant in interpreting Bowers's results.

Typical descriptions of OD that seek to induce a new social order or culture into an organization reflect the fact that gamma changes are the prime intended consequences of OD interventions. They imply not only recalibration of intervals but also new content for concepts describing the quality of organization life. Hence, gamma change can be distorted or disguised by common measuring instruments whose conceptualization and operationalization are typically rooted in concepts of alpha change.

Since gamma change may be thought of as reflecting fundamental changes in conceptualizations or expectations, or as a basic redefinition of the content of the referents tapped by measures of organization and individual processes, it severely complicates the interpretation of the results of OD efforts. Most probably, the general failure to identify gamma change—and beta, as well—results in conservative estimates of OD outcomes. These estimates get distorted or camouflaged by beta and, especially, gamma change. If this is so, chapters 1 and 2 need to have their success rates adjusted upward.

A Cousinly Concept from Counseling

An added perspective on the usefulness of distinguishing kinds of change is provided by a recent distillation of the literature on counseling. When Watzlawick, Weakland, and Fisch (1974, esp. 10–11) distinguish "first-order" change from "second-order" change, they explain that the former "occurs within a given system which itself remains unchanged," while the latter "changes the system itself." A nightmare illustrates their distinction:

> A person having a nightmare can do many things *in* his dream—run, hide, fight, scream, jump off a cliff, etc.—but no change from any one of these behaviors to another would ever terminate the nightmare.

These many changes within the system seem comparable to alpha. The authors continue: "The only way *out of* a dream involves a change from dreaming to waking . . . a change to an altogether different state." This seems much like gamma change. The authors could easily have defined a third type, an analogue of beta change. Via dream analysis, a person might learn that recurring dreams are more revealing than scaring. Having thus expanded the non-scary or less-scary intervals of a personal rating scale, an individual might stay in the dream state yet change his reaction to it. This is the sense of beta change.

The distinction made by Watzlawick, Weakland, and Fisch between two orders of change is significant, perhaps even momentous. They note (1974, 27–28) that failure to distinguish between the two types of change can cause the "most perplexing, paradoxical consequences," as in "some of the tragicomic controversies between experimental psychologists and psychiatrists." Many of these controversies could be avoided by active recognition that when experimental psychologists "talk about change, they usually mean [alpha] change . . . while psychiatrists, though not often aware of this, are predominantly concerned with [gamma]." The difference is great. The former deals with a change in condition; the latter deals with a change in state or, perhaps, with a "change of change."

Analogies from the Several Sciences

Other considerations also encourage the search for beta and, especially, gamma effects. First, and very briefly, a substantial feature of recent advances in the physical sciences has involved a basic conceptual distinction between changes in condition and changes in state, between what are here called alpha change and gamma change. Consider complex homeostatic systems, for example. They may experience a bewildering variety of changes in their conditions, in highly variable order, and yet preserve their essentially steady state (Ashby 1954, 1956). On the other hand, common wisdom acknowledges that systems can sometimes be at such a developmental point that even minor changes in condition induce a profound change in state: hence the expressions "the straw that broke the camel's back," "the critical incident that induced a psychotic reaction," or "the push we needed to get over the hump." Failure to distinguish the two kinds of change implies inadequate description and, possibly, encourages dangerous prescriptions for action.

Convenient analogies also imply the ubiquitous character of the distinction between change in condition *within* a state and change *in* state. Consider the four known states of H_2O, simplified to consider differences in temperature only—solid, liquid, gas, and (perhaps) plasma. H_2O will remain in one of the states over a considerable temperature range induced by a substantial gain (or loss) of calories. Water in its known forms, in sum, can experience *major changes in condition without a change in state*. At critical temperatures, the addition or subtraction of a specific number of calories can induce a *change in the state* of H_2O with little or no effect on its condition as measured by temperature. In sum, a stepwise model applies. The condition (temperature) is linear. Each of the states of H_2O persists over a substantial range of conditions, but jumps to different states at certain critical points.

Consider the general case sketched in figure 10.2 for alpha change and gamma change. That is, the larger vector AB in the figure is associated with a major change in condition but no change in state. This vector may reflect either alpha or beta change; it is clearly not gamma change. In contrast, the smaller vector CD represents a minor change in condition but induces a major change in state. Here, a small change induces a gamma change, on the order of the prototypic effect associated with today's popular approach to analysis called chaos theory. A straw can break a camel's back under the appropriate condition. A very large change also might be necessary to induce a gamma effect, depending upon the initial condition of the system. In this sense, the approach via gamma has a conceptual advantage over chaos theory.

Much common wisdom in OD and experiential education also suggests the value of distinguishing changes in condition-within-a-state from changes in state. Thus, considerable time and effort may be expended in team develop-

FIGURE 10.2
An Illustration of Alpha Change in Condition and Gamma Change in State

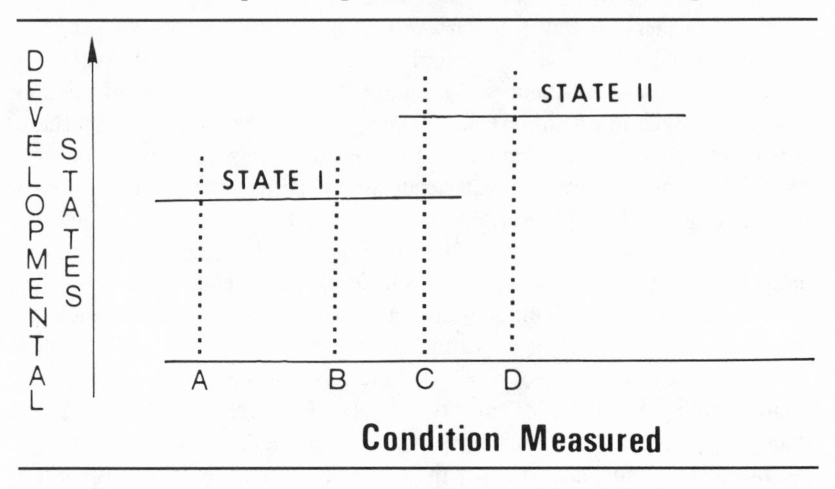

ment before "anything happens," and then quickly a team will "take off" and "go into orbit." Similar notions inhere in common concepts of developmental phases in laboratory education, as in Hampden-Turner's (1966) cyclical model of individual change, in all phase models such as that of Bennis and Shepard (1956), or in Lewin's venerable notions of unfreezing leading to choice, or change leading to refreezing (Zand and Sorensen 1975). To illustrate, Lewin's model clearly implies several different states, and it is important to distinguish which one exists at any point. Specific behaviors or interventions appropriate in the unfrozen state of consciousness or development might be impactless or even seriously counterproductive in the frozen state.

The graphics in figure 10.2 assume too much, of course. Analysis of social phenomena would be simple if we really could define and distinguish state I from state II. But all we have are vectors with known magnitudes. As noted, similar vectors might generate any of the three kinds of change, depending upon the initial state of the system.

Evidence of Gamma Effects in OD Efforts

Today, we simply do not know how to distinguish the three types of change in any reasonably rigorous and consistent way. Too much is left to the imagination. Our purpose here is to take a small step toward what we need to know, and the motivation is clear and direct. OD interventions are centrally involved with seeking change in the concepts of the quality of organizational life that should and can exist, and far less concerned with raising the level of relatively stable parameters or dimensions. Thus, gamma changes—not alpha—are the prime intended effects of such interventions.

We draw attention to the need to distinguish gamma, in effect, by establishing the inadequacy of alpha or beta in accounting for the variation in one specific set of data. The data come from an OD structural intervention—the installation of a Flexi-Time system of work hours (Golembiewski, Hilles, and Kagno 1974). Table 10.1 schematizes the research design. Self-reports on eighteen attitudinal items are reported along Likert-like continua of seven equal-appearing intervals, with the extreme positions being anchored by brief verbal descriptions.

Factor Analysis—Search for Degrees of Congruence

Overall, the search for gamma effects will employ factor-analytical techniques, whose resulting matrices will be tested for congruence. The reliance on factor analysis can be explained nontechnically. Factor analysis essentially seeks to isolate the major dimensions of reality necessary to economically account for the variance in scores on some large set of variables.

These properties of factor analysis encourage our reliance on it. That is, any major incongruence between the factorial structures representing each wave of Flexi-Time questionnaire data gathered at several points in time is interpreted as a change in the dimensions of reality necessary to account for the variance in the sets of responses. And, of course, gamma is defined as basic change in those dimensions of psychological space.

Specifically, six matrices are involved: one for each of the three administrations of the standard questionnaire for Experimentals only, and one for each of three administrations including all Experimentals and Comparisons taken together.[3] Responses from Comparisons only are not factor-analyzed, since there were only eighteen, which is not sufficiently greater than the number of questionnaire items to encourage confidence in any resulting factorial solutions. The six factorial structures will be compared both "within" and "between": within each of the three observations for Experimentals as well as for Experimentals plus Comparisons, and between the three individual observations for Experimentals. Two specific statements may be made.

- The essential congruence of factorial structures for Experimentals over the three administrations will imply that gamma effects did not occur.
- The essential congruence of factorial structures for Experimentals plus Comparisons for each of the three questionnaire administrations will imply that gamma effects did not occur.

As noted, it was not possible to compare directly the factorial structures of Experimentals versus those of Comparisons.

TABLE 10.1
Research Design of the Installation of a Flexi-Time System of Work Hours

	Schedule			
	Day 1	Day 15	Short-Post Test Day 195	Long-Post Test Day 375
Experimentals	O_1	X	O_2	O_3
Comparisons	O_1		O_2	O_3

Notes: O = Observations via self-reports on a standard questionnaire.
X = Flexi-Time installation.

Five major points require emphasis before introducing data. First, factor analysis will be used to help isolate gamma change, *defined as the substantial incongruence of pairs of between-wave factorial structures* as determined by Ahmavaara's (1954) technique. Put otherwise, no major changes in factorial structures are expected when only alpha changes occur. Even large changes from the pre-intervention mean may reflect only changes in the condition of a stable state, as contrasted with changes in state. Only changes in state, or gamma, are expected to generate major incongruence between pairs of factorial structures. Beta changes are essentially like alpha changes in this regard.

Second, this chapter reports on only one factor-analytical variant, PFA-2.[4] Any evidence here of gamma effects is almost certainly not an artifact of a specific factorial procedure, however. That three other factorial variants generate essentially the same structures as PFA-2 is established elsewhere (Golembiewski, Billingsley, and Yeager 1976b).

Third, the OD intervention studied was clearly impactful. That is, substantial patterns of intended effects were observed in comparisons of pre-test, short-post, and long-post scores, when the base of comparison was

- an item-by-item analysis of a standard questionnaire soliciting eighteen separate responses at three points in time;
- an analysis of changes along six dimensions apparently tapped by the eighteen items, as determined by factor analysis of responses to Wave 1 of the standard questionnaire, which structure was then used to score responses at all three points in time;
- an analysis of changes along six dimensions apparently tapped by the eighteen items as determined by factor analysis[5] of responses to Wave 2 of the standard questionnaire, which structure was then used to score responses at all three points in time;
- an analysis of changes along five dimensions apparently tapped by the eighteen items, as determined by factor analysis of responses to Wave 3 of the standard questionnaire, which structure was then used to score responses at all three points in time.

This may seem to be analytical overkill, but this early stage of analysis needs to be scrupulous in eliminating alternative explanations of results. Better to do too much, at this stage of the game, than too little.

Fourth, estimating the congruence between factorial solutions involved one strategic choice, since the several factorial procedures did not generate an equal number of factors in all cases. PFA-1—using Kaiser's (1960) criterion of an eigenvalue greater than 1.0 to govern the extraction of factors—generated seven factors for O_1, six for O_2, and five for O_3. In all three cases, the factors with eigenvalues ⟩ 1.0 accounted for some 70 percent of the variance.

The convention was adopted to use seven factors, even where this meant disregarding Kaiser's rule. Several attractions motivated this choice.[6]

Fifth, the procedure for comparing factorial structures is straightforward, if complex. For details, see the Appendix.

Statistical Procedures

Six tests are made of the notion that variation in the Flexi-Time data set can be explained only by gamma effects. Better said, perhaps, it will be shown that alpha or beta effects are not sufficient to explain that variation.

First, the within-wave congruence of the structures isolated by the four factor-analytic procedures is compared. A substantial congruence will make it difficult to argue that any relationships below are artifacts of any specific factorial procedure.

Second, between-wave congruence is determined, using the total batch of Experimentals plus Comparisons. Estimates of the variance in common between pairs of factorial structures will be used to estimate their congruence. Major reductions of common variance are consistent with the interpretation that gamma changes occurred in Waves 2 and 3 as a result of experimental intervention.

Third, a similar analysis is conducted for Experimentals only. Crudely, lower between-wave congruence of factorial structures for Experimentals (N = 32) is expected. Such an effect is consistent with the interpretation that gamma occurred. That is, the exclusion of Comparisons subjects—who experience only random changes over the observational period from Wave 1 to Wave 3—will remove a portion of the common variance that probably served to somewhat inflate the estimates of congruence of factorial structures for Experimentals plus Comparisons (N = 50).

Fourth, the congruence of factorial structures is tested for a randomly distributed N. This permits an estimate of the stability of factorial structures, as well as of their dependence on the size of N. The substantial congruence of within-wave structures will imply that any patterns isolated in the first three analytical approaches are not simply artifacts of N.

Fifth, a test will be conducted concerning the impact on between-wave comparisons of the present convention of setting at seven the number of factors to be extracted. The congruence of structures with five, six, and seven factors is tested. If allowing the number of factors to vary does not much affect the congruence of between-wave factorial structures, the implied conclusion is that gamma accounts for any substantial incongruence isolated by the second and third research emphases above. Note that analysis revealed that within-wave comparisons are affected only slightly by the convention of considering seven factors, but no data on the point are reported in this chapter.

Sixth, an estimate is made of the effects of limiting to five the number of iterations of the structures derived from PFA-2. The congruence of a random sample of structures will be ascertained when iterations are set at five versus ninety-nine. High congruence of pairs of factorial structures will imply that the major convenience of limiting iterations to five did not stop data manipulation when further substantial convergence of individual structures was possible. Hence, any major incongruence isolated in the second and third emphases will be credibly assignable to systemic effects such as gamma changes.

Congruence of within-wave structures ($N = 50$ and $N = 32$). To summarize briefly, it is easy to establish that the four factor-analytical procedures described above essentially isolate the same structures within each of the three questionnaire waves (Golembiewski, Billingsley, and Yeager 1976a). Conveniently, the summary below of r^2 implies a very substantial intrawave congruence of structures extracted by the four factorial procedures, given that the square of the product-moment correlation coefficient provides an estimate of the common variance between the structures of any two procedures. In sum:

- Wave 1: product-moment r^2, $\bar{X} = .9524$
- Wave 2: product-moment r^2, $\bar{X} = .9850$
- Wave 3: product-moment r^2, $\bar{X} = .9929$

The average r^2 permits the estimate that the eighteen within-wave comparisons of pairs of structures generated by the four factorial procedures share over 97 percent of their variance in common, on the average.

This pattern holds for an N of 50; the pattern for $N = 32$ is similar. For details, again consult Golembiewski, Billingsley, and Yeager 1975.

This is impressive congruence, and implies that any results below are almost certainly *not* artifacts of the single factorial strategy focused on below.

Congruence between waves, all subjects. The factorial structures change enough between waves to suggest that alpha or beta changes are not adequate to account for the low congruence between the pre-test factorial structure and the two post-intervention structures. For PFA-2 only, the product-moment correlation coefficients in table 10.2 imply that about 67 percent of the between-wave variance can be thought of as common. The pattern is similar for the other three factorial procedures, although they account for somewhat less of the variance (around 64 percent).

Table 10.2 suggests a qualified but stout conclusion. The interwave differences might be accounted for in several ways—and not only as signs of the fundamental variation in conceptual space here designated as gamma change. To be sure, no absolute criteria establish the point at which interwave changes become great enough to signal gamma changes. Yet the loss of some 30 percent of variance in comparisons of the congruence of factorial structures for the three waves of questionnaires has a compelling quality to us and, if nothing else, implies the inadequacy of at least alpha change as an explanation.

Several reasons reinforce this conclusion. First, it is difficult to credit most of the interwave variations to measurement error. Second, the reduction in variance seems large enough to imply major changes in the dimensions of the relevant psychological space, as contrasted with variations in the level of relatively stable dimensions or with variations in the measurement intervals associated with some stable dimensions of reality. The latter are beta changes, and the former are alpha changes. We presume they would not show up in the major incongruencies in factor-analytical structures reflected in table 10.2. Third, the N = 50 batch of subjects represented in table 10.2 contains both Experimentals and Comparisons. Other data convincingly demonstrate that Comparisons reflected only random variation in their three waves of self-reports. In a major sense, then, the 67 percent estimate of common variance between factorial structures no doubt understates the impact of the experimental intervention in changing the relevant psychological space as measured by comparisons of factor-analytical structures at three points in time.

Congruence between waves, experimentals only. Fortunately, it is possible to test this last surmise. Table 10.3 presents some relevant data using only the Experimental subjects. As expected, the estimate of common variance falls, to an average of 51 percent from 67 percent.

Table 10.3 supports two conclusions. Its pattern is consistent with the conclusion that gamma changes did occur in the data batch. Moreover, the reduced estimate of common variance when N is only thirty-two is both expected and large enough to further undercut the credibility of the proposition that alpha or beta effects alone are capable of accounting for the diminished congruence of factorial structures. If a 30 percent loss in interwave common variance is not sufficient to establish the likelihood of gamma effects, that is to say, a 50 percent loss provides very much more formidable support for that conclusion.

Congruence of within-wave structures for variable N. It may be the case, of course, that the lower percentage of common variance in the case of N =

TABLE 10.2
Congruence of Between-Wave Factorial Structures for Experimentals plus Comparisons (N = 50, Paired Comparisons of Three Waves, PFA-2)

	Interclass Correlation	Product-Moment Correlation	Estimated Common Variance
Wave 1 vs. 2	.7903	.8055	64.9%
Wave 1 vs. 3	.8054	.8186	67.0%
Wave 2 vs. 3	.8255	.8356	68.7%

32 versus N = 50 is an artifact of the variation in N itself, rather than an effect of excluding the Comparisons. This dependence of within-wave factorial structures on the size of N was tested in a very demanding way.[7]

The test reveals common and stable factorial structures that are substantially independent even of major changes in N. This finding does double duty. It prohibits gaining a cheap victory over table 10.2 by doubting or denying the stability of the underlying factorial structures. Moreover, the summary data above clearly imply that a reduction in N by itself cannot account for the pattern in table 10.3.

Congruence of between-wave structures for variable number of factors. As noted, the convention above was to compare the first seven factors in all structures, even in the case of an eigenvalue less than 1.0. This convenient convention does not seem to do violence to the data, as a test case implies. To illustrate for the PFA-1 only, for Experimentals plus Comparisons, the congruence of factorial structures was established when the number of factors for Wave 1 was seven, for Wave 2 was six, and for Wave 3 was five. Table 10.4 summarizes the analysis.

The estimated common variances are somewhat higher in table 10.4 than in table 10.2, but the average common variance increases only from 67 to 74 percent when the number of factors is varied to include only those with

TABLE 10.3
Congruence of Between-Wave Factorial Structures for Experimentals Only (N = 32, Paired Comparisons of Three Waves, PFA-2)

	Interclass Correlation	Product-Moment Correlation	Estimated Common Variance
Wave 1 vs. 2	.6121	.6533	42.7%
Wave 1 vs. 3	.7581	.7768	60.3%
Wave 2 vs. 3	.6711	.7023	49.3%

TABLE 10.4
Congruence of Structures with Different Number of Factors, All Cases

	Interclass Correlation	Product-Moment Correlation	Estimated Common Variance
Wave 1 vs. 2	.8218	.8326	69.3%
Wave 1 vs. 3	.7996	.8139	66.2%
Wave 2 vs. 3	.8544	.8612	74.2%

eigenvalues greater than 1.0. The effect is small, and in the expected direction. Consequently, the convention of setting the factors to be compared at seven had the effect of lowering the variance in common between pairs of structures, but not much.

The test case suggests that very little of the incongruence between structures reflected in table 10.2 can be attributed to its convention of setting at seven the number of factors to be compared. Moreover, the incongruence is great enough to suggest that alpha or beta changes alone cannot reasonably account for it.

A similar analysis for Experimentals only (N = 32) leads to a similar conclusion about table 10.3. In this case, the number of factors with eigenvalues greater than 1.0 for Wave 1 was seven, for Wave 2 was five, and for Wave 3 was six. The results indicate that it is possible to account for only a small part of the incongruence between factorial structures in table 10.3 as a consequence of setting the number of factors considered at seven. Table 10.5 summarizes the results for Experimentals.

Recall that table 10.3 indicates that only about 51 percent of the variance, on average, is shared in common among the several paired comparisons of between-wave factorial structures for Experimentals only. Allowing the number of factors to vary (as the data in table 10.5 show) does not much affect the estimate of common variance, which increases, but only to 52.5 percent. This pattern implies that very little of the between-wave incongruence in factorial structures can reasonably be assigned to the convention of setting the number of factors at seven in most analyses in this chapter. Moreover, the pattern also supports the interpretation that the between-wave incongruence in factorial structures is large enough to suggest gamma effects.

Congruence of within-wave structures, five iterations vs. ninety-nine iterations. As a final test, it seems obvious that the SPSS convention to limit iterations to five had a small impact on this analysis. Specifically, ten sample tests were run which involved all three waves, an N of fifty and thirty-two, and five, six, or seven factors as appropriate. The basic comparison involves determining the congruence of pairs of factorial structures when iterations are cut off at five and when they are allowed to run to a maximum of ninety-nine. The ten resulting estimates of common variance cover a narrow and high

TABLE 10.5
Congruence of Structures with Different Number of Factors, Experimental Cases

	Interclass Correlation	Product-Moment Correlation	Estimated Common Variance
Wave 1 (7 factors) vs. 2 (5 factors)	.7741	.7895	62.3%
Wave 1 (7 factors) vs. 3 (6 factors)	.6852	.7150	51.1%
Wave 2 (5 factors) vs. 3 (6 factors)	.6223	.6631	44.0%

range, from 96.96 to 100 percent, with a grand mean of 98.80 percent. This very high degree of congruence implies that the convenience of limiting iterations to five is not analytically troublesome.

Greater Success by Specifying Kinds of Change

One cannot predict without qualification that OD efforts will be more successful when they routinely begin specifying kinds of change. But that is possible, as was the case cited early in this chapter with an apparent failure that motivated the test for a plural concept of change.

What can we be relatively certain about? Two classes of conclusions will do, for starters. The first comes from good old-fashioned hindsight, for more than a decade has passed since the original argument above was published. The second class of conclusions dates from the original publication, and most of its components still seem quite serviceable.

20/20 Hindsight

The perspective of a decade suggests the usefulness of the effort to test a plural concept of change (Golembiewski 1986). Basically, alpha, beta, and gamma change have become part of the vocabulary of research involved with the study of human change (e.g., Tennis 1989). This is surprising, even astounding. For plural change as a concept is a radical one, which is quite corrosive of established beliefs and practices in both research and application. Agreement does not yet exist about the ways to measure plural change, to be sure, but energetic effort has been applied to the topic and may yet pay off.

The basic distinction between the types of change also has penetrated many of the conventional OD sources of information. Thus, several national conferences of learned societies have featured panels on the change typology. In addition, the basic conceptual distinctions also have become commonplace in the general OD literature—in various textbooks (e.g., Burke 1982), in survey articles intended for professional audiences (e.g., Armenakis 1988), and in other sources.

Why this clear and growing acceptance of a conceptual distinction that is at once a difficult one and also challenges vested interests? The short form of the answer is clear and direct: greater success in OD requires some such distinction, and that point rings true to both scholars and practitioners.

The longer form of a useful working answer has four emphases, which in turn only illustrate a larger possible catalog. First, OD cannot avoid making such a distinction, being involved as it is with choice and change. The plural concept makes general sense, which accounts for its all-but-universal acceptance. Indeed, I know of not even a single criticism of the basic concept (Golembiewski 1989), which stands in sharp contrast to the often-zesty debate concerning ways to measure the various kinds of change (e.g., Armenakis 1988).

Particularly impactful on OD is the basic notion that the results of studies of change are confidently interpretable only under a strict condition: that the existence of non-alpha change *is rejected*. Alpha-only change permits conventional interpretation of results, but non-alpha change poses serious and as-yet-unresolved issues. In concept, this sharply reduces the credibility of interpretations of the results of OD applications. The significance of the notion is widely appreciated, as by a large-scale seller of survey studies. In initial response to the concept of gamma change, the seller commissioned a think tank to do a study, which was critical of the method of measurement but nonetheless seems to have basically accepted the tripartite concept of change. Some employees of the surveying institution later advised clients to test for non-alpha effects.

Second, no counterdemonstration provides a credible basis for rejecting the concept. Rather, the tripartite notion has diffused broadly: into educational and psychological measurement, counseling, management, and the study of opinions among elites (e.g., Chittick, Billingsley, and Travis 1988), among numerous other disciplines, fields, and subfields. This diffusion does not settle matters, but it counts for a great deal.

Third, the basic conceptual distinctions have an intuitive appeal. This is particularly the case in OD, which has often proclaimed its mission to create gamma change—as in the development of new social orders at work, or in generating regenerative interaction to replace the degenerative variety. The basic point gets its sharpest expression in the current emphasis on "transformation" (e.g., Adams 1984), in contrast with incremental development.

Fourth, gamma suits many of the metaphors common in OD. Thus, a facilitator may exult: "Our group went into a new orbit." This refers to achieving a different mode of functioning, of course, and suggests gamma.

The View a Decade Ago

While the data do lead to conclusions that are intriguing—and challenging—

we encourage moderation in interpretation. Most important, the data do seem to indicate that something like gamma does occur in the population examined. Moreover, substantial reasons discourage presuming that patterns in the data are determined by other features—by random causes, a single factorial procedure only, dependence upon the level of N, the basic convention of considering seven factors for each wave, or the convenience of limiting to five the number of iterations seeking to maximize congruence of each structure.

The results above may reflect the impact of factors not considered here, of course. For example, several other ways could have been used to estimate congruence, even though preliminary work with them requires no modification of the present conclusions. Here note only that specialists of goodwill differ profoundly as to what is the most appropriate measure of congruence (Armenakis 1988). However, despite interpretive problems, a major test of an alternative way of determining congruence provides no clear support for the hypothesis that the present results are artifacts of the specific measure of congruence used (Golembiewski, et al. 1976b). Also, the ratio of subjects to items in the present data batch is at best 2.6:1. Normally, this would suggest a question about the results above, but the patent stability of the factorial structures when N is allowed to vary suggests that the problem is not significant. It seems safest to highlight only two conclusions about the preceding analysis.

The analysis implies the real possibility of gamma changes. Essentially, the complex analytic procedures imply that the OD intervention changed in major ways the psychological dimensions that employees used to evaluate their worksite. Not only did the several factorial structures differ substantially between waves, but a number of alternative explanations for those differences also were tested and discarded. Essentially, those two facts constitute our case for the need to distinguish gamma effects.

We do not describe the specifics of the gamma change. For that would involve verbal interpretations of the several factorial structures, which would burden this analysis with massive conjectural detail. Rather, we rely on the summary tactics to indicate the major incongruencies between factorial structures. Our focus was on comparing clusters of factors rather than on interpreting individual factors.

Reaching this point has been trying enough—especially for the reader impatient with statistical complexity—but extensions of this promising line of research will challenge researchers. Thus, it will be exceedingly difficult to establish the existence of gamma, as well as to satisfactorily differentiate gamma from alpha and beta. But the present results suggest strongly that the effort is necessary, since alpha or beta cannot credibly account for the major incongruence in structures reported here.

To the degree that the preceding analysis is close to reality, it has profound implications for experimental research designs in the social sciences, as well as OD. Here we recommend other tests of this analysis, as well as an interim exercise of prudence that can ameliorate our present lack of knowledge about kinds of change. Six themes are especially noteworthy in these regards.

First, this analysis implies that prodigious energies in the behavioral sciences have been applied to the wrong methodological issues. Consider the sophisticated but inconclusive effort directed at the question of how change is to be measured (Cronbach and Furley 1970; Van Meter 1974; and many others). In contrast, this analysis suggests strongly that the first question should be: What kind of change is being measured? Few studies (e.g., Buss 1974) deal with this prior question, however. Most studies seem to assume that only alpha is relevant. That assumption seems clearly inappropriate for successful OD interventions, and the same may be true of many natural-state contrived experiments.

Second, this analysis suggests that one useful strategy for measuring change tests for incongruence in the dimensions of the perceived psychological domains, as by comparing the results of factor analyses before and after an OD intervention. This is relatively simple, and avoids many of the formidable problems in calculating meaningful change scores.

Going one step further will present major complexities, to be sure. It is one thing to estimate statistically the incongruence between two structures, and quite another to label and compare the individual factors in those structures. The first task is mechanical, if involved. The second task is a major art form in behavioral science. Our study took the easier route. It does not deal with the specific changes in individual factors induced by the Flexi-Time intervention. It was a matter of doing the simplest things first, as it were.

Third, this analysis implies a hard message for much OD research. Specifically, interpreting any results of existing research is chancy in the absence of knowledge about types of change, which is seldom available. Even research designs that surpass the usual norms for rigor and care are suspect in this regard.

Fourth, this focus on types of change implies the strategic value of time-series designs, as well as of such variants as time-lagged designs (Campbell 1963). These two kinds of designs may be sketched as follows.

- Time-series design: $O_1 - X - O_2 - O_3 \ldots$
- Time-lagged design: $O_1 - X - O_2 - O_3 \ldots O_1 - O_2 - X - O_3 \ldots O_1 - O_2 - O_3 - X \ldots$

As before, "O" is observation and "X" is experimental intervention. Of course, the explanatory power of both designs is enhanced if controls or comparisons are provided. Beta effects and gamma effects seem far more difficult to isolate in simple $O_1 = X = O_2$ designs.

The awkwardly named "catastrophe theory" or "chaos theory" also may be useful. They deal with *discontinuous change* of various sorts, the kind here called gamma change. Catastrophe theory contrasts with most existing mathematics—which, as in the calculus, deals with *continuous change*—and has received wide coverage even in the mass media (Newsweek 1976).

Fifth, clinical attention might be devoted to subjects as they respond to measuring instruments requiring self-reports. The perception by respondents that they are using "rubber yardsticks" might be variously parlayed into a kind of early-warning system that alerts analysts to beta or gamma changes in experimental design.

Sixth, scaling techniques less sensitive to metric-level assumptions could also be profitably used to seek underlying structures in this type of analysis. Such approaches include smallest-space analysis (SSA) and nonmetric multidimensional scaling.

In short, there is a long trail ahead in this line of research. Hopefully, the first few steps head in a useful direction. In any case, the next chapter will report on work that extends the bare initiative established here: that alpha-only cannot account for the variations in the F-T data set.

Notes

1. This chapter is based on the original report in Golembiewski, Billingsley, and Yeager 1976a.
2. The terminology relates to Rensis Likert's (1967) Profile of Organizational Characteristics. The profile seeks two kinds of self-reports: Now responses, which solicit data about how respondents actually see their organization unit; and Ideal responses, which seek information about how respondents feel their organization should be. The focus throughout this chapter is on purported descriptions of existential states only—that is, on Now responses.
3. To test the possibility that any results are artifacts of a single factor-analytical technology, in addition, this analysis was replicated for four variants: Principal Factoring without Iterations, or PFA-1; Principal Factoring with Iterations, or PFA-2; Alpha Factor Analysis; and RAO, or Canonical Factor Analysis. For a detailed description of the differences between these techniques, see McDonald 1970. All four techniques are conveniently available in the Statistical Package for Social Scientists (SPSS).

   Results will be reported here basically for PFA-2. For evidence of the very substantial congruence of the structures generated by PFA-2 and the three other factorial variants, see Golembiewski, Billingsley, and Yeager 1975.
4. To briefly describe PFA-2, or Principal Factoring with Iterations, the main diagonal of the correlation matrix is replaced with the communality estimates, or squared multiple correlations between the variable and the rest of the variables. The estimates of communality are iteratively improved by factoring again with the calculated communality estimates derived from the preceding solution. This process is

continued until the estimates of communality converge, or until the differences between successive estimates are negligible.

The SPSS program is set for five iterations or less, because the CDC 6400 implementation of SPSS used here capitalizes on the 60-bit accuracy of the 6400's word size. A note on the printout alerts analysts if five iterations do not suffice for absolute convergence.

As a major convenience, most analysis in the text deals with structures for variants which have been iterated five times or less.

5. Specifically, the factorial procedure was PFA-1 followed by Varimax rotation.
6. This convention had several motivators. Primarily, the convention facilitated the convenient replication of the results reported here. In addition, it reduced the potential for error when comparing matrices of larger or smaller size, respecting the advice found in Kaiser, Hunka, and Bianchini 1971, esp. 411–12 and 421. Moreover, the choice of seven factors permits the inclusion in Waves 2 and 3 of several items which load heavily on factors 6 and 7 only. Finally, had the decision been to consider only the first five factors generated by each procedure, substantial portions of variance would have been lost in analyses of Waves 1 and 2. Data concerning the effects of the decision to focus on seven factors will be presented below. For now, note only that the convention was not analytically troublesome.
7. Subjects were randomly eliminated so that five independent subpopulations of thirty-five were isolated for each of the three waves. PFA-1 was then applied to these fifteen subpopulations as well as to the total population (N = 50), and the resulting factorial structures were compared for within-wave congruence.

The results of this severe test strongly imply that variation in N itself does not determine the pattern reflected by tables 10.2 and 10.3. To illustrate with one of the fifteen comparisons:

	Interclass Correlation	**Product-Moment Correlation**	**Estimated Common Variance**
Wave 1, N=35, vs. Wave 1, N=50	.9427	.9437	89.1%
Wave 2, N=35, vs. Wave 2, N=50	.9415	.9427	88.9%
Wave 3, N=35, vs. Wave 3, N=50	.9734	.9737	94.8%

In sum, over 90 percent of the estimated variance in this illustrative case can be considered common in the underlying structures. The average for all subpopulations tested was about 88 percent, which is impressive congruence, especially given the severity of the test.

References

Adams, J. D., ed. 1984. *Transforming Work*. Alexandria, Va.: Miles River Press.

Ahmavaara, Y. 1954. "Transformation Analysis of Factorial Data." *Annals of Science Fennicae, Series B* 881:54–59.

Armenakis, A. 1988. "A Review of Research on the Change Typology." In *Research in Organization Change and Development*, edited by W. A. Pasmore and R. W. Woodman, 163–94. Greenwich, Conn.: JAI Press, Inc.

Ashby, W. R. 1954. *Design for a Brain*. New York: Wiley.
______. 1956. *An Introduction to Cybernetics*. London: Chapman and Hall.
Bennis, W. G., and Shepard, H. 1956. "A Theory of Group Development." *Human Relations* 9:415–37.
Bereiter, C. 1963. "Some Persisting Dilemmas in the Measurement of Change." In *Problems in Measuring Change*, edited by C. W. Harris, 3–20. Madison, Wis.: University of Wisconsin Press.
Bowers, D. G. 1973. "OD Techniques and Their Results in 23 Organizations: The Michigan ICL Study." *Journal of Applied Behavioral Science* 9:21–43.
Burke, W. W. 1982. *Organization Development*. Boston: Little, Brown.
Buss, A. R. 1974. "Multivariate Model of Quantitative, Structural, and Quantistructural Ontogenetic Change." *Development Psychology* 10:190–203.
Campbell, D. T. 1963. "From Description to Experimentation: Interepreting Trends as Quasi-Experiments." In *Problems in Measuring Change*, edited by C. W. Harris, 212–42. Madison, Wis.: University of Wisconsin Press.
Chittick, W. O.; Billingsley, K.; and Travis, R. 1988. "Persistence and Change in Elite and Mass Attitudes Toward U.S. Foreign Policy." Paper delivered at the Annual Meeting, International Society for Political Psychology. New York. 1 July.
Converse, P. E. 1970. "Attitudes and Non-Attitudes." In *The Quantitative Analysis of Social Problems*, edited by E. R. Tufte, 168–89. Reading, Mass.: Addison-Wesley.
Cronbach, L. J., and Furley, L. 1970. "How We Should Measure 'Change'—Or Should We?" *Psychological Bulletin* 74:68–80.
Golembiewski, R. T. 1972. *Renewing Organizations*. Itasca, Ill.: F. E. Peacock.
______. 1986. "Contours of Social Change." *Academy of Management Review* 11:550–66.
______. 1988. *Organization Development: Ideas and Issues*. New Brunswick, N.J.: Transaction.
______. 1989. "The Alpha, Beta, Gamma Change Typology." *Group and Organization Studies* in press.
Golembiewski, R. T., and Carrigan, S. B. 1973. "Planned Change Through Laboratory Methods." *Training and Development Journal* 27:18–27.
Golembiewski, R. T.; Billingsley, K.; and Yeager, S. 1976a. "Measuring Change and Persistence in Human Affairs." *Journal of Applied Behavioral Science* 12:133–57.
______. 1976b. "The Congruence of Factor-Analytic Structures: Comparisons of Four Procedures and Their Solutions." *Academy of Management Review* 1:27–35.
Golembiewski, R. T.; Hilles, R.; and Kagno, M. 1974. "A Longitudinal Study of Flexi-Time Effects." *Journal of Applied Behavioral Science* 10:503–32.
Hamilton, M. 1967. "Comparisons of Factors by Ahmavaara's Method." *British Journal of Mathematical and Statistical Psychology* 2:107–10.
Hampden-Turner, C. W. 1966. "An Existential 'Learning Theory' and the Integration of T-Group Research." *Journal of Applied Behavioral Science* 2:367–86.
Iyengar, S. 1973. "The Problem of Response Stability: Some Correlates and Consequences." *American Journal of Political Science* 17:797–808.
Kaiser, H. F. 1960. "The Application of Electronic Computers in Factor Analysis." *Educational and Psychological Measurement* 20:141–51.
Kaiser, H. F., and Caffrey, J. 1965. "Alpha Factor Analysis." *Psychometrika* 30:1–14.

Kaiser, H. F.; Hunka, S.; and Bianchini, J. 1971. "Relating Factors Between Studies Based Upon Different Individuals." *Multivariate Behavioral Research* 6:409–21.

Likert, R. 1967. *The Human Organization*. New York: McGraw-Hill.

McDonald, R. P. 1970. "The Theoretical Foundations of Principal Factor Analysis, Canonical Factor Analysis, and Alpha Factor Analysis." *British Journal of Mathematical and Statistical Psychology* 23:1–21.

McGee, V. E. 1966. "The Multidimensional Analysis of 'Elastic' Distances." *British Journal of Mathematical and Statistical Psychology*, 19:181–96.

Muhsam, H. V. 1951. "The Factor Analysis of a Simple Object." *Journal of General Psychology* 45:105–10.

Newsweek. 1976. "Beyond Calculus: 'Catastrophe Theory.'" 19 January 1976. 87:54–55.

Pepper, S., and Prytulak, L. S. 1974. "Sometimes Frequently Means Seldom: Context Effects in the Interpretation of Quantitative Expressions." *Journal of Research in Personality* 8:95–101.

Pinneau, S. R., and Newhouse, A. 1964. "Measures of Invariance and Compatibility in Factor Analysis for Fixed Variables." *Psychometrika* 29:271–81.

Rao, C. 1965. "Estimation and Tests of Significance in Factor Analysis." *Psychometrika* 30:93–111.

Ross, R. 1971. "OD for Whom?" *Journal of Applied Behavioral Science* 7:580–85.

Stewart, D., and Love, W. 1968. "A General Canonical Correlation Index." *Psychological Bulletin* 70:160–63.

Tannenbaum, R., and Davis, S. 1970. "Values, Man, and Organization." In *Organizational Frontiers and Human Values*, edited by W. H. Schmidt. Belmont, Calif.: Wadsworth.

Taylor, J., and Bowers, D. G. 1967. *Survey of Organizations*. Ann Arbor, Mich.: CRUSK, Institute for Social Research.

Tennis, C. 1989. "Responses to the Alpha, Beta, Gamma Change Typology." *Group and Organization Studies* in press.

Torbert, W. 1973. "Some Questions on Bowers' Study of Different OD Techniques." *Journal of Applied Behavioral Science* 9:668–71.

Van Meter, D. S. 1974. "Alternative Methods of Measuring Change: What Difference Does It Make?" *Political Methodology* 9:668–71.

Ward, R. T. 1974. "Culture and Comparative Study of Politics, or the Constipated Dialectic." *American Political Science Review* 68:190–201.

Watzlawick, P.; Weakland, H. H.; and Fisch, R. 1974. *Change: Principles of Problem Formation and Problem Resolution*. New York: W. W. Norton.

Zand, D., and Sorensen, R. E. 1975. "Problems in the Measurement of Organizational Effectiveness." *Administrative Science Quarterly* 20:532–45.

11

Surrogate for Kind of Change: Linkages with Psychological Burnout

Earlier chapters provide gentle access to the importance in OD of specifying differences between people, and the time has come to raise the analytic ante. The emphasis here is on burnout in both conceptual and psychological aspects, and that implies challenge enough. Moreover, the ambition here is to link this treatment with two earlier chapters—with the hopeful illustrations of the power of the phase model of burnout illustrated in chapters 5, 6, and 7, as well as with those troublesome issues associated with a triune model of change left hanging in chapter 10.

Some orienting cues are no doubt necessary. Progress often creates problems as well as solves them, and in cases the problems created are more formidable in the short run than those solved. Gamma change has some of this quality even for those familiar with the concept, and a lot of this quality for others interested in what the concept implies for OD and for all human research.

How to move beyond the problems generated by the bare report of the discovery of plural change in chapter 10? This chapter sketches and then tests a way out of the analytical cul-de-sac into which gamma change has propelled alert researchers and intervenors. This chapter extends the earlier introduction to a program of research on psychological burnout, extends it to several analytical conundrums posed by gamma change, and then tests the phase model of burnout for gamma-like features. In a few words, burnout is seen here as a probable measure of a change in state, and promises a relatively easy way to estimate the health of human systems as well as to provide a surrogate measure of gamma change. As such, the focus on phases of burnout does double duty. It will add sophisticated detail about how specifying differences between people can heighten success rates in OD applications. In addition, the focus on burnout may provide a convenient entree to the central measurement issues in OD: What is change, and how do we estimate degrees of different kinds of change?

The approach is direct, if demanding. This chapter builds on chapters 5–7 and 10, and proposes to extend them—first by conceptual analysis, and subsequently by empirical testing.

Please note one introductory caveat. Positioning this chapter here creates some problems of distance from chapters 5, 6, and 7, which constitute some of this chapter's foundations. On the other hand, positioning this chapter after 7 would create a similar distance from chapter 10. The reader's mind can perform the necessary transmigrations; the printed page lacks such flexibility.

A Conceptual Context for Irony VI, Revisited

Conceptually, the basic metaphor is a visual one, in contrast to the statistics of the last chapter. Directly,[1] since change can be reasonably thought of as occurring on "behavioral surfaces," the contours of those surfaces deserve description and analysis. But such attention has been rare (e.g., McGee 1966; Miller and Friesen 1984), even though without attention to change and contours one can speak meaningfully about neither research nor application.

Thus, this chapter has three conceptual sections. First, the properties of a tripartite model of change will be sketched, not only to reinforce some basic distinctions made in chapter 10 but also, more centrally, to explore the fundamental nature of the pluralization. Second, the surface called a "cusp" will help visualize certain properties of the three kinds of change, so as to draw attention to significant implications for theory and application. Third, a useful approach for understanding plural change is given attention: psychological burnout is viewed as a surrogate variable for monitoring the state of individual and collective systems.

These three conceptual emphases seek to influence OD as well as behavioral research. The first emphasis reflects the growing acceptance of plural change, demonstrates its significance and, especially, indicates points of conceptual difficulty. Some graphics concerning psychological space then provide perspective for both significance and difficulty, while a final conceptual emphasis suggests one approach to exploiting the significance of plural change. This deals with psychological burnout, whose testing relative to gamma will constitute the empirical counterpart in this chapter to preceding conceptual elaborations.

Features and Significance of the Basic Change Distinction

Growing opinion supports the radical view that change has plural meanings, as chapter 10 details. Related concepts variously emphasize a similar distinction between degree and state, between magnitude and pattern. Thus Bateson (1942) speaks of levels of consciousness reflected in "learning" and "deutero-learning"; Normann (1971) contrasts "variation" with "reorientation"; and Argyris and Schön (1978) focus on "single-loop" and "double-loop" learning.

Attention here is focused on one contribution to this tradition—a triune concept of change, which permits reliable judgments about the kind of change necessary to account for the variations in time-series data. Conceptually, chapter 10 proposes a well-defined receiver—always the person providing the self-report—and adds a statistical technology to test for differences in the pattern and magnitude of the social-psychological realities reported on by aggregates of observers. In sum, the approach applies an objective technology to assess the degree of congruence of subjective observations by perceivers.

The original research tested the usefulness of certain cutting points for this statistical technology. That research conceptualized three types of change, to review the distinctions emphasized in chapter 10.

- *Alpha change* involves a variation in the degree of some existential state, given a constantly calibrated measuring instrument that taps a constant conceptual domain.
- *Beta change* involves a variation in the degree of some existential state, complicated by the recalibration of some portion of the intervals of the measurement continuum associated with a constant conceptual domain.
- *Gamma change* involves a basic redefinition or reconceptualization of some domain, a restructuring of perceived reality that involves differences in state as well as differences in degree.

The original research focused narrowly on establishing the existence of very "large" non-alpha change, or gamma. Others (e.g., Armenakis and Bedeian 1972) have directed specific attention at beta change.

Conveniently, these conceptual components will be referred to as the tripartite model, which inspired three kinds of reactions. Basically, observers accept the tripartite model but reflect no consensus about how to systematically isolate the types of change. Thus, two observers (Lindell and Drexler 1979, 1980) attacked the factorial approach, with debatable effect (Golembiewski and Billingsley 1980) while leaving the basic conceptual distinctions intact. Other researchers also accept the trinitarian concept of change and use alternative approaches to distinguish alpha, beta, and gamma change (e.g., Armenakis and Zmud 1979; Bedeian, Armenakis, and Gibson 1980; Porras and Singh 1984; Randolph 1984; Randolph and Edwards 1978; Schmitt 1980, 1984; Terborg, Howard, and Maxwell 1980, 1982). More recently, researchers have taken diverse operational approaches to tripartite change, while also accepting its basic distinctions:

- Comparisons in common data sets of various techniques for isolating the

several types of change so as to assess intertechnique consistency (e.g., Armenakis, Randolph, and Bedeian 1982; Randolph 1984; Schmitt 1984)
- Studies with data sets that are less subject to the uncontrollable effects of research in the field—for example, laboratory studies (Armenakis, Buckley, and Bedeian 1984) or simulation methods (Terborg 1984)
- The search for surrogate variables that indicate differences in state between individuals and groups (e.g., Golembiewski, Munzenrider, and Stevenson 1986)
- Conceptual analysis of the academic response to the introduction of tripartite change (e.g., Tennis 1985), which is reflected in some fifty citations making substantive use of alpha, beta, and gamma

In sum, previous work accepts the tripartite model, and also builds on it. But there is a tentativeness about how such variants can be isolated by standard procedures, about how best to proceed (e.g., Armenakis and Bedeian 1972; Armenakis, Randolph, and Bedeian 1982). The fundamental and radical issue—the pluralization of change—has been retained; indeed, it has gone unchallenged (Golembiewski 1989).

The basic agreement is surprising, even astounding, because the tripartite model has profound implications for long-standing and powerful interests in both research and application. Concerning research, the core implication is consequential: unless one first rejects the possibility of non-alpha, *no* confident interpretation is possible about the burgeoning literatures dealing with multiple arenas of change—in laboratory experiments, interventions in organizations, survey/feedback designs, and so on. Concerning applications, moreover, the tripartite model also challenges special interests. For example, consulting and university ventures often rely on multiple observations via surveys—opinion polling, electoral analysis, planned organizational change, and so on. Again, without an explicit rejection of non-alpha change, the results of such efforts cannot be interpreted, which hits a burgeoning industry in a vital spot. The impact of gamma change has been appreciated by some in the consulting and survey businesses (e.g., Porras and Singh 1984; Macy and Peterson 1983, 455–60), who suggest routinely testing for non-alpha effects between observations at two or more points in time. Others in those businesses reacted more defensively: one large survey operation sent materials that were critical of the statistical technology reflected in chapter 10 to a long mailing list of the users of surveys, but even those materials essentially accepted the tripartite model of change.

Despite the growing conceptual acceptance of plural change, research and applications still are *routinely interpreted as if change is alpha-only.* One cannot have it both ways. The resulting interpretations not only confound analysis, but can even have profound implications for the most basic fundaments of our institutions. Consider two illustrations: one focuses on an interpretation of voting studies that has profound implications that might well be cushioned or even destroyed by the tripartite model, and the second perspective focuses on a methodological innovation that promises much but may deliver far less in the absence of specificity about kinds of change.

Non-attitudes among the Citizenry

One fashionable interpretation of survey findings describes differences in political opinions on surveys over a two-year period as "non-attitudes," or cases in which expressing any opinion—however superficially or tentatively held—is said to be preferable to being classified as a person holding no opinion (Converse 1964, 1970). Researchers propose that test-retest comparisons demonstrate that "even relatively central and permanent issues of American political life have no meaning for the voters, that the issues involved do not form a part of the voters' conceptual framework. Hence, *for a large part of the population*, the [survey] answers are essentially random. No real attitudes exist" (Achen 1975, 1219, my emphasis).

Gamma constitutes a rival hypothesis to non-attitudes, and the implications of the two explanations differ radically in philosophical and practical senses. Basically, gamma change implies data-processing capacities in individuals that support representative ideals. In contrast, non-attitudes imply a very different view of the electorate that can corrode democratic ideals. Achen observes:

> Criticism . . . that voters' preferences on public policy matters are unsophisticated or poorly organized, or that they are without influence in the voting decision [are serious but] they stop short of claiming that voters have no policy views whatever, [as does the non-attitude approach].
>
> This last charge . . . is far more disturbing than the others. For it is one thing to argue that voters have difficulty connecting their preferences to particular candidates and particular schools of thought, quite another to claim that the preferences are absent from the beginning. (1975, 1218)

What can conceptual distinctions about change add to the vigorous debate over non-attitudes? Basically, all parties to the debate allow that three alternative explanations can account for low correlations between successive administrations of the same attitudinal items over a two-year interval. According to Stephens (1976, 1224), all observers distinguish:

- "Real change," or a measurable variation in some definite metric
- "Measurement error," or a disturbance imposed on the measurement process by imperfections in the measuring instrument
- "Non-attitudes," or reports by a respondent "who 'blurts something out' at random [to avoid] the embarrassment of admitting to no opinion"

The common view of real change seems myopic, however. Previous discussion suggests that three kinds of real change can be distinguished, and two of those varieties reject non-attitudes when explaining low correlations between administrations of the same attitudinal items at several points in time. A skeletal argument follows (Golembiewski 1978).

The non-attitudes view acknowledges only alpha change, which occurs along relatively stable dimensions of reality defined in terms of discrete and constant intervals. Alpha changes may or may not be random, as established by some test of statistical significance; they may be very large, or very small, or anywhere in between. If alpha-only occurred in the data used to support the non-attitudes view, Converse's interpretation seems a reasonable possibility.

Two kinds of evidence encourage Converse (1970) to conclude that, in effect, alpha-only occurs. He observes low correlations on several items at more than one point in time, and he finds low correlations between different but obstensibly related items at the same time, which encourages him to reject real change as an explanation. Converse may be correct, but he focuses only on differences of magnitude in responses and does not test for any differences in pattern or structure, which alone can establish alpha-only. For him, "real change" means alpha. Of course, measurement error also could "explain" the two classes of events Converse observes.

The argument can be extended to the second type of change. Beta changes involve the recalibration by respondents, between measurements, of some portion of the intervals used to measure a relatively stable conceptual domain. Notice a subtle point. Beta change is *not* measurement error, such as low test-retest reliability. But without explicit rejection of non-alpha change, beta change could be interpreted as measurement error. That is, the notion of measurement error assumes alpha-only, and in that sense it is context bound.

Occurrence of beta change in Converse's data requires two conditions. The low T_1 correlations between ostensibly-similar items would have to be artifactual—due, for example, to real differences between the items. Moreover, low T_1 versus T_2 correlations are compatible with beta change, given its definition as involving recalibration of some portion of the T_2 measurement intervals. Hence, non-attitudes could have a competitor for explaining the low correlations, and a two-year interval provides sufficient time for the development of the valuational differences implied by beta change.

If beta change occurs in Converse's data, non-attitudes provide a faulty and even seriously misleading interpretation. Beta change does not require the assumption that voters' preferences are unsophisticated or poorly organized. Quite the opposite might be the case, in fact.

The concern about the non-attitudes hypothesis is far greater with reference to the third type of change. Gamma involves a quantum shift in dimensions of reality—the redefinition of both the relevant psychological space as well as the intervals used at T_1. In sum, gamma change refers to a shift from *one state to another* and also implies the unreliability of T_1 intervals at T_2.

The irony only requires stating. If gamma change occurs in Converse's data, the non-attitudes interpretation is profoundly wrong. Rather than a lumpen striving to avoid embarrassment, in effect, the low correlations observed by Converse might indicate profound and general shifts among the electorate over the two-year period of observation. Such a shift implies complex *and* patterned decision-making processes, which the non-attitudes interpretation rejects. In sum, gamma change explains the low correlations reported by Converse at T_1 versus T_2 as well as non-attitudes, while simultaneously avoiding a profound metaphysical pathos.

The choice between the two interpretations is consequential. The non-attitudes interpretation implies a view of the electorate that gives little comfort to those holding representative ideals, and may encourage or even legitimate manipulative and authoritarian practices among political elites. "The people" in this view have the characteristics of a mass waiting to march to someone else's purposes—eager enough to please an interviewer, but unreflectively so.

Empirical research relevant to making this crucial technical and philosophical choice has barely begun. But gamma effects have been found in survey data earlier thought to provide conflicting findings (Chittick, Billingsley, and Travis 1988).

Meta-Analysis and the Researcher

The failure to recognize types of change also can limit the usefulness of such attractive techniques as meta-analysis (Hunter, Schmidt, and Jackson 1982), which provides a valuable statistical way of evaluating the regularities in research findings across multiple studies. The approach promises to bring some order, and perhaps even renewed optimism, to the behavioral sciences. There, accumulations of studies involving similar sets of variables often yield bewildering contrasts in findings—some studies show strong positive associations, others imply negative associations, and still others seem to show only random effects.

The babel of findings can inspire two reactions. Discouragement represents perhaps the dominant response, which in extreme forms can inspire the conclusion that nonorderliness and even chaos dominate in nature. The second reaction somehow tries to order the existing diversity, for example, by focusing on differences in concepts or operations as explanations for apparently diverse findings via what may be called "comparative operational analysis" (e.g., Golembiewski 1962) or by more comprehensive theoretical efforts (e.g., Miller and Friesen 1984).

Meta-analysis falls in this second category. In its most developed form, it assesses the congruence of multiple correlational studies of the same variables by considering three contributors to noncomparability: sampling error, measurement error, and variation or restriction in the range of scores (Hunter, Schmidt, and Jackson 1982, 22–47).

Approaches like meta-analysis have multiple attractions but, provisionally, the technique seems to apply only if non-alpha change is rejected. The most developed form of meta-analysis relates to correlations at a single point in time, to be sure. However, to illustrate, testing the efficacy of a particular intervention can involve cross-study comparisons like that envisioned by meta-analysis. The focal question is, does the intervention really work, given the diverse results in available studies?

The basic problem for meta-analysis in studies of change seems clear: any collection of separate studies presumably will include a distribution of alpha, beta, and gamma changes. Consequently, any cross-study comparisons using techniques like meta-analysis will either have to accommodate to such probable differences in kinds of change, or they may avoid artifactual results only by accident.

Despite appropriate tentativeness, one point seems substantial. Meta-analysis seems most compatible with alpha change, to judge by the three contributors to noncomparability encompassed by meta-analysis. For example, measurement error does not seem easily interpretable or even applicable when gamma change has occurred in some interval T_1–T_2. For beta, moreover, no great confidence seems appropriate that T_1 measurement error is meaningfully comparable to that at T_2.

Similarly, the notions of variation in or restriction of scores have a fuzzy application to non-alpha. Beta involves recalibration of a portion of the T_2 measurement range, and no definite predictions are possible about variations in the range of scores. One can make no general judgments except that, if beta change is established, no presently available interpretive guides exist. For gamma, the issue of range of scores has no clear meaning. Generally, one expects that restricting the range of scores will result in lower correlations. In gamma, however, profound changes occur in both the measurement intervals and in the state measured, and those changes probably will swamp any effects due to restricting the range of scores, or at least will cause severe problems in isolating any effects of any apparent differences in T_1 versus T_2 scores.

Cusp Representations of Psychological Space

These two examples of the possible mischief, indeed even the danger, of a conceptual failure to distinguish kinds of change encourage conceptual analysis via visual representations. Metaphorical and statistical expressions of the three kinds of change dominate, with a clear bias toward the metaphorical. Here, the visual *contours* of psychological space are represented by the "cusp," a popular surface in "catastrophe theory," which focuses on nonlinear and sudden changes in systems. In a technical sense, the cusp constitutes that fixed point on a mathematical curve at which a moving point tracing that curve exactly reverses its direction and duplicates its form. For present purposes, the term is used more loosely to refer to that one possible contour for psychological space fully sketched in figure 11.3 that has cusp-like features.

The present visual emphasis has several motivators. It complements suggestive but vague metaphors, and may provide some sense of substance for statistical abstractions. In addition, the visual approach seeks surprise, and possibly serendipity, that may later direct analytic manipulations and experimentation. Finally, some researchers embrace the labels of alpha, beta, and gamma, but with too little appreciation of their intended substance. This visual exercise cum interpretation might tether such exuberance or, even better, inform it.

Three Primitive Notions

The analysis of "space" begins with three conceptual aids to thought, a trinity of primitives. Hence, this chapter distinguishes:

- behavioral surface, or field
- states
- degrees of a state

The present approach assumes that behavior occurs on some "surface" or "field," which implies both security and constraint. "Surface" suggests a set of relationships in space as well as contours, it implies the sense of within-ness and boundaries, and it requires procedures for testing and maintaining the character and extensiveness of within-ness.

Conceptually, a surface or field also has inherent dynamic features, and these can constrain human behavior as well as goad it. The very usage does imply some degree of equilibrium, and this may provide security (or frustration) for actors "on" the surface. However, the concept—as in the cases of undesirable aspects on one's field, or disjunctions between one's field and those of others—also encompasses motivation for search and change. This property has conceptual appeal, since it reduces the probability that surface or field can be used in the ideologically reactionary ways encouraged by so many concepts in the social and behavioral sciences with a bias toward equilibrium.

Simple examples from the physical sciences illustrate these elemental distinctions. As implied, *different states* can characterize a surface or field at different points in time. An enclosed vessel may constitute a field, for example, and material in it may appear in one of four basic states—plasma, liquid, solid, or gas. Differences in degree within that state also are possible, as in degree of pressure or temperature.

At this point in the development of the behavioral sciences, general notions of states must suffice. We do not know the equivalents of the state-influencing properties of liquid in a vessel—pressure, temperature, and so on. But we can estimate reliably and systematically whether a major change has occurred in some collection of behavioral variables. That is, various statistical procedures permit an estimate of the shared variance in T_1 versus T_2 observations of the structure of the major dimensions characterizing some behavioral field. For example, Ahmavaara's (1954) procedure distinguishes factorial structures in terms of both magnitude and pattern, and the proportions of variance shared at any two points in time can serve as indicators of the kind of change which has occurred. One admittedly arbitrary convention (Golembiewski, Billingsley, and Yeager 1967a) provides that, when patterns in T_1 versus T_2 factorial structures share less than 50 percent of the variance in common, the change is considered sufficient to imply change of state in a system, or gamma. This convention proved useful in isolating major breaks or jumps in a range of properties that accompany changes in state.

The present conceptual analysis of the three kinds of change builds on the arbitrary convention of the original research, *for illustrative purposes only* and without prejudgment of what empirical research may reveal later about appropriate cutting points. Conveniently, figures 11.1, 11.2, and 11.3 propose, *only as an illustration of the patterns*, the following criteria for alpha, beta, and gamma change.

- *Gamma change* is assumed when common variance of T_1 versus T_2 factorial structures is less than 50 percent, which suggests a change in state rather than in degree.
- *Alpha change* is signaled by approximately 100 percent common variance at two or more points in time and refers unequivocally to a continuing state or condition.
- *Beta change* is intermediate, and for present illustrative purposes is placed at approximately 50–75 percent common variance.

This approach also distinguishes *degrees* within a state, but with an important difference from various physical systems. Such estimates in the behavioral sciences are context dependent, as when data come from self-reports that solicit responses on a seven-point scale anchored by Strongly Agree to Strongly Disagree on opinional stimuli such as: "I am free to express myself in my organization." "Express myself" can have very different meanings for different individuals at any point in time, of course, and different meanings for the same individual at different points in time or in various places. These meanings can derive from recalibration of some of the intervals characterizing the degree of a state (that is, beta), or from fundamental changes in the structure of the dimension (that is, gamma).

The major confounding feature of behavioral research inheres in the distinction between a difference in degree and a change in state, as exacerbated by the common reliance on self-reports. Hence, confident interpretation of an apparent change in degree between two or more observations over time requires a prior rejection of beta and, especially, gamma change. In the case of gamma, estimates of degree are not meaningful because the T_1 state differs substantially from T_2. If state differences do exist, as estimated by a low proportion of shared variance, changes of apparent degree have no obvious meaning.

Cusp Contours and Visualizing Change

The cusp permits illustrating these three primitives, and it also helps visualize the three kinds of change. The cusp is only one contour that may characterize some behavioral surfaces or fields, and it has a demonstrated usefulness in visualizing major change (Smith 1980); hence the reliance on it here for illustrative purposes, where degree of state will be defined in terms of seven equal-appearing intervals anchored arbitrarily by "Low" and "High" that should be taken to reflect two extreme clusters of aggregated self-reports. Percentage of shared variance in the patterns of behavioral spaces at two or more points defines similar or different states, as noted.

There are disadvantages of the present approach. A particularly troubling lacuna involves the *pace of change* in the interval from T_1 to T_2. For example, consider a system that changes slowly prior to T_1, then speeds up between T_1 and T_2, and subsequently slows down. Illustratively, Starbuck (1973) encourages distinguishing "fast" and "slow" variables, and he provides details for such a case, which remains a challenge for more elaborate syntheses than this one. On initial evaluation, fast variables seem to have the properties of beta or gamma, and Starbuck may have outlined a dynamic model of change where (in effect) today's beta or gamma can become the basis against which tomorrow's alpha (or slow variables) will be judged.

Visualizing alpha change. Figure 11.1 depicts alpha change along a simple behavioral surface (which appears as a plane there but which also forms the base of a cusp whose extensions in figures 11.2 and 11.3 are only suggested in figure 11.1 by broken lines to conserve space). The state in figure 11.1 is identical at T_1 and T_2, or nearly so. Here, observations A and B pose no problems. The degree of the state has increased from 5 to 6.5 equal-appearing intervals, and B is greater than A.

Most of the technology of behavioral science assumes alpha change, and devotes itself to improving the possibility of generating comparable results. Thus, various techniques—randomization of subjects, or the use of control or comparison groups—seek to reduce contamination due to individual differ-

FIGURE 11.1
A Sketch of Alpha

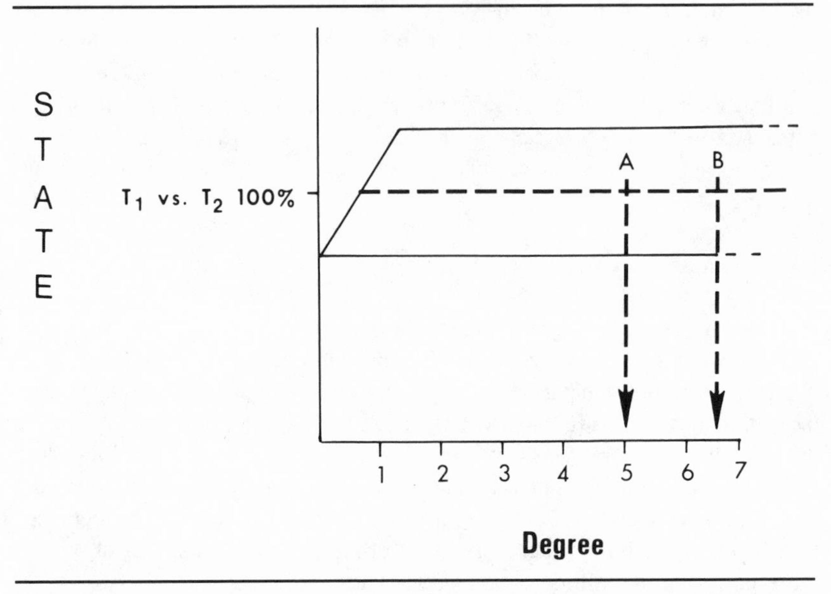

Note: *Determined by shared variance between the patterns of the surfaces extant at T_1 versus T_2

ences, historic or episodic forces, and so on. Moreover, various techniques like test-retest reliability assess the integrity of purported behavioral dimensions. Unless alpha-only is established, however, low test-retest reliability does not yield interpretable data: it may mask a variety of "real change," or it may identify measurement error.

Visualizing beta change. Consider the new college student who chafes under "unreasonable parental controls," and locate that individual on the behavioral space "freedom-coercion." Not uncommonly, that person over the years redefines that space in two ways. Thus the coercion portion of the scale along which an individual estimates degree often gets "stretched." Hence this case of beta change: conditions once rated "often unbearable" can become "sometimes unattractive" or even "acceptable" (Pepper and Prytulak 1974), and as a result T_2 versus T_1 observations show a reduced common variance.

Figure 11.2 sketches one sense of beta change, and that figure suggests severe problems for "normal behavioral science." It depicts two T_2 points—B and B′—which represent progressively greater distances from some point A *along the contour of* the behavioral surface such that B′ is greater than B which is greater than A. Given the usual failure to acknowledge beta change, and given our inability in normal practice to see the contours of the surface sketched in figure 11.2, curious conclusions may result. If one projects B and

FIGURE 11.2
A Sketch of Beta

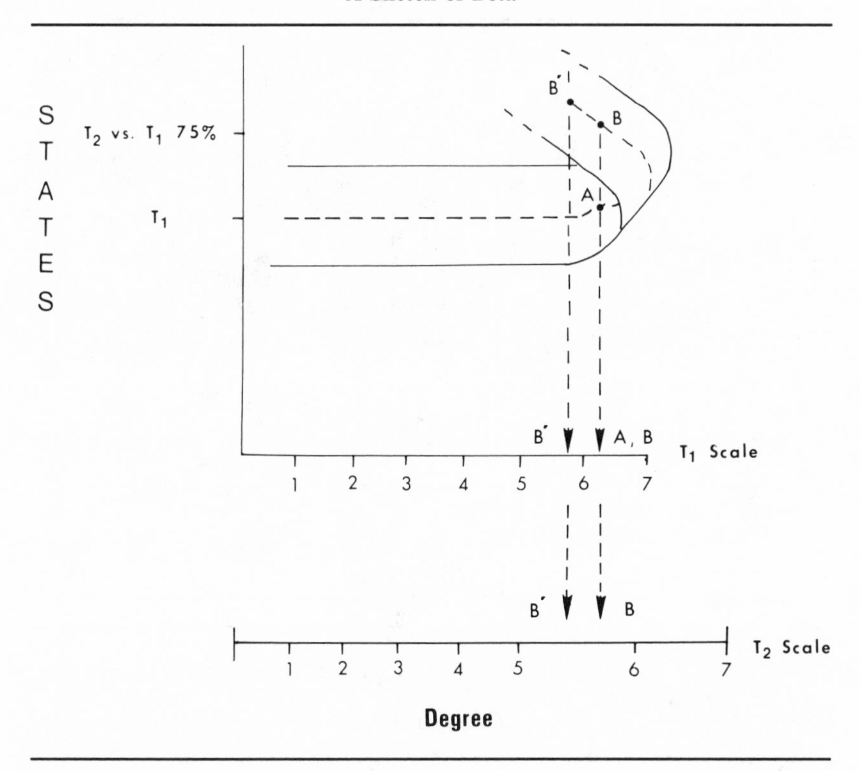

B′ onto the T_1 axis, one would erroneously conclude that 1A is equal to 1B, 1A is greater than 1B′, and 1B is greater than 1B′. An analyst may project B and B′ onto the T_2 scale, alternatively, which in effect happens in the typical research study where beta change occurs in the interval between observations. In this case, 1A is greater than 2B which is greater than 2B′. Neither set of conclusions mirrors the posited reality, of course, and both imply the significance of effective concern about types of change.

Normal behavioral science also might encourage other artifactual conclusions. For example, beta change means a range of substantially different T_1 versus T_2 intervals, whose effects might be interpreted as measurement error. Or the T_2 versus T_1 comparisons might imply to external observers that A is greater than B which is greater than B′, while persons "on" the field would report B′ is greater than B which is greater than A. Precisely this situation led to the search for non-alpha change, in fact. The data viewed as alpha-only suggested "worse" relations, while people in the system reported that things

FIGURE 11.3
A Sketch of Gamma

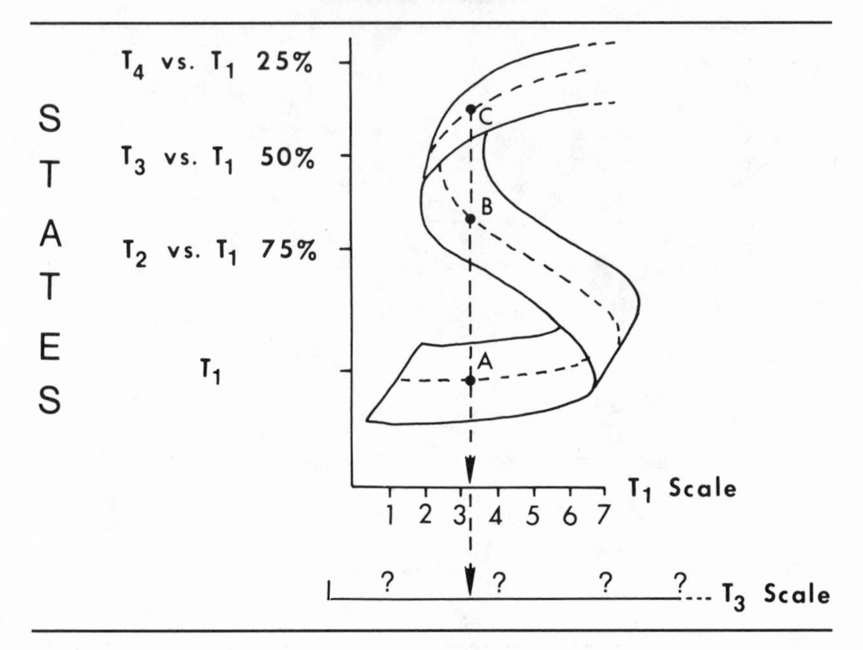

were substantially "better" (Golembiewski, Billingsley, and Yeager 1976a). Ostensibly, those "living on the surface" perceive or feel the difference in kinds of change in ways unavailable directly to external observers relying on survey methods. Parenthetically, this suggests the good sense of speaking with survey respondents as well as processing their self-reports.

Visualizing gamma change. Ease of illustration largely disappears in the case of the third variety of change, and hence figure 11.3 is a pale replica. That figure assumes that several observations of a system in transition are made at different times. After T_1, successive measures capture progressively less of the common variance until 25 percent or less is common to the T_4 versus T_1 measures. At T_2, and perhaps before, one may conclude that the behavioral space has so changed that no meaningful comparisons with T_1 are possible. In addition to profound changes in the field and its contours, gamma change includes redefinition of the intervals used to estimate degree. Hence, the T scales become unreliable—not only in estimating degree, but even in indicating the direction of change. The latter problem affects figure 11.2 in lesser ways, and affects figure 11.1 very little, or not at all.

Patently, differences in either degree or, especially, state will obfuscate comparisons at T_1 or T_2 with earlier observations. In the example in figure 11.3, A is equal to B which is equal to C on both T_1 and T_3 scales. This neglects the contours along which change occurs and grossly misevaluates the actual distances traveled.

Responding Pessimistically to Planned Change

These elementary graphics and their underlying conceptual distinctions also imply a metaphysical pathos, a set of attitudes that encourage pessimism and perhaps even despair. Some researchers will be stimulated by plural change to explicate its properties, even though living with the conceptual distinctions is awesome. So what if you can establish that more than one kind of change exists? And so what if you can validly and reliably measure when non-alpha change occurs? One loses the sense of innocence thereby, but wisdom is less assured than ever. In the short run, gamma change taketh more than it giveth in five senses.

- The original statistical technology for determining gamma change requires a large N, which limits its flexibility.
- Most attention to gamma change focuses on aggregates of individuals, which neglects those many cases in which the individual is the unit of analysis.
- All technologies for determining non-alpha change require major and debatable assumptions.
- Available research fixates on testing for non-alpha change *between* T_1 and T_2, and neglects the tangled issue of T_1 comparisons *with* T_2. For alpha change, T_1 can be considered 0, and T_2 could be + or −. For gamma, "direction" has no obvious meaning.
- The covariants of the new state indicated by gamma change will be poorly mapped until the properties of alternative states are understood sufficiently to develop a taxonomy of states.

The tripartite model has an awkward profile, then. It plainly corrodes old assumptions, but does not yet qualify as constructive in providing new and firm guides for analysis. The stakes are raised in the game of research; once-comfortable rules for interpreting results are less applicable, but the new rules remain uncertain, if rules there will be.

For practitioners or organization interventionists, the pain is greater, if anything. Already badgered with complaints about their know-nothing status being "not rigorous"—but firmly believing that they know when interventions work—their comfort level gets unrelievedly buffeted by notions like gamma change, in a catch-22 sense. Intervenors typically seek non-alpha change—witness the emphasis on "inducing a new culture at work." So beta and, especially, gamma have an intrinsic interest. However, if non-alpha change can be said to occur, the researcher must acknowledge that no specific way presently exists to accomplish two critical analyses. They involve determining in any single case whether that newly induced dimensional space has the intended character—whether the movement has been in the intended direction and, if so, how far—and making the same judgment in comparisons of two or more cases. In effect, common measures finesse this problem, as in assuming alpha-only change which gets charted along (for example) Likert's (1967) four systems of management—with System 4 typically being considered the ideal of intended change, progress toward which may be estimated by successive waves of self-reports.

So gamma change not only introduces complexity but, as in chapter 10, also precludes relative certainty, or at least reduces convenience. Concepts like gamma change can induce pessimism or lack of interest as an unintended by-product of research that seeks to enrich knowledge.

Managing Pessimism re Types of Change

What to do, then? Three points provide some guidance. While not comprehensive, they provide some direction and even hope.

First, some obvious prescriptions apply, although they do not help much in the short run. For example: better to be wary about non-alpha change than wrong about it, even given the problems.

Second, everyday experience contains examples of several kinds of change, and this may embolden us to accept the challenge of understanding plural change so as to use that knowledge to ease transitions. No other viable possibility may exist, to put the point in the boldest terms. Moreover, figures 11.1, 11.2, and 11.3 suggest this single basic strategy, about which we might have to become much more clever in order to be more efficient and effective. One can either follow the contours of a surface, that is, or jump between the folds in the behavioral space. The former is the long way around, and probably also more costly in resources. In common, all leaps involve recognizing the contours of transitional stages, and then using that knowledge to consciously short-circuit the full developmental distance along the surface of the contour.

Third, energetic attention should be directed toward testing ways to bridge the developmental gap between present understanding and eventually satisfactory ways of describing particular beta and gamma changes and their properties. Two examples will be sketched here.

Computer simulations of kinds of change. One such initiative at jumping the developmental gap has not proved fruitful. Efforts were made to simulate the three types of change on a computer, with the eventual purpose of experimenting with the simulations and, hence, of economically learning about the properties of different kinds of change. Analogous to thermodynamic systems, for example, "state variables" might be isolated and continuities or discontinuities in curves expressing them might be developed and manipulated to learn about the properties of the three types of change.

Alpha change constitutes no problem, but about gamma change we learn at great cost only what we already knew: that gamma change means radical redefinition of a structure. We failed to think in "big bang" terms. The initial structure proves very resistant to our incremental operations, which involve randomized applications of various decision rules to individual scores: no change, increases (or decreases) of one-half standard deviation, increases (or decreases) of one or two standard deviations, and so on. Several thousand computer runs proved incapable of generating change in the original structure profound enough to be considered gamma change, as estimated by Ahmavaara's technique (1954).

Burnout as a surrogate for gamma change. A search for surrogate measures of gamma change proves more fruitful. Promisingly, accumulating evidence suggests that the phase approach to psychological burnout may help tap differences in state as well as in degree. This discussion builds on earlier chapters—5, 6, and 7—as it extends them.

Phases of Burnout as a Surrogate for Gamma Change: Conceptual Attractions

Earlier chapters detail the conventions for measuring the phases, but a brief review will be useful. The Maslach Burnout Inventory (MBI) constitutes a paper-and-pencil instrument which defines differences in three domains of burnout (Maslach and Jackson 1982, 1986):

- *Depersonalization*, high scores on whose component items indicate individuals who consider others as things or objects and who distance selves from human relationships
- *Personal accomplishment (reversed)*, low scores on whose component items indicate individuals who believe they are doing well on a task that is worth doing
- *Emotional exhaustion*, high scores on whose component items indicate individuals who are experiencing strain at or beyond their comfortable coping limits, who are "at the end of their rope" in psychological and emotional terms

The phase model adds significant structure to the three MBI domains. It assumes the three domains vary in virulence, in the order presented above, and then uses High versus Low scores on the domains to assign individuals to one of the eight possible combinations of the three domains, each taken twice, as in table 5.1. The High versus Low distinctions rest on norms derived from median splits in a large population (Golembiewski and Munzenrider 1984).

The model does not require that any individual case of full-bloom burnout will progress through each of the eight phases. This full progression seems psychologically awkward, in fact, as in a movement from phase II to phase III. Rather, the phases seem to contain both chronic and acute pathways, following the medical and psychiatric usages. The chronic pathway—phase I to phase II to phase IV to phase VIII—assumes deteriorating conditions at work, beginning with worsening personal relationships. Several acute pathways may exist—for example, phase I or II leading to phase V, as in the sudden death of a loved one, with V perhaps leading to VIII in a difficult grieving process (Golembiewski, Munzenrider, and Stevenson 1986, 206–8).

Phase Model and Differences in State

Two points suggest the usefulness of the phases of burnout as a surrogate measure for differences in state as well as in degree. First, although a major research agenda still requires attention, the evidence strongly supports the usefulness of the phases in isolating significant associations between burnout and a range of variables. Attention has focused on 300 variables (Golembiewski, Munzenrider, and Stevenson 1986; Golembiewski and Munzenrider 1988), which all-but-universally worsen as the phases advance. For example, chapter 5 shows that physical symptoms increase, regularly and robustly, as phase I approaches phase VIII. Similar patterns are found in

- panels of worksite descriptors including, in various studies, sixteen to twenty-two features commonly considered as significant by organization analysts; the descriptors include conventional measures of job tension, participation in decisions at work, job involvement, willingness to disagree with supervisor, two trust scales, and ten Job Diagnostic Survey scales;
- nineteen symptoms of physical distress;
- performance appraisals;
- various measures of group properties; and
- quantitative and qualitative measures of productivity.

This burnout research does not establish gamma differences, but it does encourage explicit testing. The differences in the phenomenal worlds of respondents in the extreme phases seem substantial, and the conceptual sense of extreme phases of burnout implies differences in state rather than merely in degree.

The priority of testing the phases for gamma effects, moreover, is also heightened by a range of advantages available via the use of burnout as a surrogate indicator. Suggestively, the phase model has the following advantages in research and intervention involving gamma change:

- A large N is not required, once surrogate status is established.
- The individual is the unit of analysis, and aggregations of individual scores also are possible—for example, for work units—given the generic problems with any such uses of individual-level data (e.g., Golembiewski 1962, 56–58).
- The technology for measuring an individual's phase of burnout is quite direct.
- Changes in T_1 versus T_2 burnout have a specific direction—that is, phase VIII versus phase I covariants powerfully reflect deficits or deficiencies: the worksite has less-attractive features, more physical symptoms are reported, performance appraisals decrease, and productivity falls.
- The covariants of burnout phases are increasingly known.

Phases as a Surrogate for Gamma: Statistical Tests

So let us get on with testing the phase model for gamma effects. In sum, this section provides evidence supporting the view that the eight-phase model of burnout in fact measures at least one difference in state, rather than mere differences in degree. Comparisons of pairs of factorial structures establish this crucial point, using Ahmavaara's technique. This evidence supports the view that burnout phases can be used as a surrogate estimating gamma change.

Despite the ponderous number crunching, the basic research design has a direct quality. The focus is on how respondents assigned to the various phases conceptualize burnout. Without at least one gamma difference, the phase model cannot be said to measure what it purports to measure: the assumed discontinuum from non-burnout to burnout. Somewhere in the phases, to put the essential point in another way, at least two different states must exist.

The test for state differences in the phases will require three steps. First, the statistical technology will be sketched. Second, the results for the phases will be reviewed. Third, one approach to confirming the analysis also will be illustrated.

A Primer on Statistical Technology

This search for differences in burnout states between those classified in various phases employs factor-analytical techniques, whose resulting matrices will be tested for congruence, using Ahmavaara's technique. (See also chapter 10.) His procedure provides two important outputs: an intra-class correlation coefficient, and a product-moment correlation coefficient. The intra-class correlation indicates the degree to which any two structures are similar in both pattern and magnitude. Product-moment coefficients indicate the similarity in patterning only. The square of either of these coefficients indicates the percentage of variance that any two structures being compared have in common, of course. The two coefficients tend to be similar, but both are reported below. The intra-class correlation coefficient probably provides the more strict estimate of gamma.

As a general indicator, any r^2 in the .50 range will be taken to indicate gamma-like differences. This constitutes a major assumption, but probably a very conservative one. Numerous computer runs have tried to simulate r^2 of .50 or less on Ahmavaara's coefficients, and the task still defies accomplishment. In short, r^2 of .50 or less can be taken to indicate very large differences in comparisons between any pair of factorial structures.

Hence, when two factorial structures approximate 50 percent common variance, this analysis proposes that they are sufficiently different to qualify as non-alpha. To say the same thing, a 50 percent loss in variance in any comparison of two factorial structures seems safely far beyond that attributable to alpha and beta differences. But the 50 percent cutting point remains arbitrary and, if so, it is probably too high rather than too low. Note also a second sense in which the present convention is conservative, if anything. *High* correlation coefficients may be generated artifactually in some cases, but that caveat does not hold for *low* correlations.

Phases and Gamma Differences

Respondents came from a single division of a federal agency, with over fifty offices nationwide. There were approximately 1,590 respondents for present purposes, and the total response rate to the mail-back survey was 55 percent. Other details are available elsewhere (Golembiewski, Munzenrider, and Stevenson 1986, 1–29).

Findings about gamma differences in respondents' structurings of the MBI items follow under two headings. Greater details are available elsewhere (Golembiewski and Munzenrider 1989a and b) for the very serious reader.

Gamma between adjacent phases. Comparisons of the seven intervals between adjacent phases constitute the most severe test of gamma differences, in effect, and this test relates to the basic issue of whether as many as eight phases are useful. No expectations are appropriate, but the present phase model would receive maximum support if all seven tests between adjoining phases indicate gamma differences. Gamma differences for each of those seven paired comparisons would imply changes in state between each phase.

As table 11.1 shows, gamma differences may be said to exist in each of the seven cases of adjacent phases. Put otherwise, individuals assigned to the

TABLE 11.1
Ahmavaara's Analysis of Adjacent Phases (N = 1,595)

Paired Comparisons	Intra-class Correlations r	Intra-class Correlations r^2	Product-Moment Correlations r	Product-Moment Correlations r^2
I vs. II	.44	19.4%	.53	28.1%
II vs. III	.40	16.0%	.49	24.0%
III vs. IV	.62	38.4%	.66	48.6%
IV vs. V	.49	24.0%	.58	33.6%
V vs. VI	.67	44.9%	.73	53.3%
VI vs. VII	.64	41.0%	.69	47.6%
VII vs. VIII	.67	44.9%	.72	51.8%
		x = 32.7%		x = 41.0%

several phases in terms of their responses to the same MBI items have quite different factorial structures in their heads. Specifically, on average, less than 33 percent of the variance is common on the intra-class correlation coefficient, which relates to both pattern and magnitude of the factorial structures. For the product-moment correlations, which refer to similarities in the patterning only, about 40 percent of the variance is shared.

Gamma between other pairs of phases. There are 28 possible paired comparisons of the eight phases, and seven of these comparisons deal with adjacent pairs. Table 11.1 presents data about these adjacent cases, in which congruence should be greatest. Table 11.2 presents summary data on the twenty-one cases not dealt with in table 11.1.

The data in tables 11.1 and 11.2 support two conclusions. First, both tables suggest strongly that gamma differences exist between most pairs of the eight phases. In sum, thirty-eight of the fifty-six coefficients are less than .50, and an additional thirteen are in the .50 to .59 range. Second, the average percentage of shared variance is higher in table 11.2, which defies easy explanation but nonetheless requires no change in our conclusions.

Do these summary data hide any more discrete patterns? The distances between the phases might be revealing, for example, because they permit a test of the crucial possibility that what the present approach sees as gamma effects are merely artifacts of restricting the range of variance by comparing pairs.

The analysis of the coefficients by the several distances between the phases does not support the artifactuality argument, however. Generally, one supposes, the more proximate the phases, the greater the congruence between pairs of factorial structures. The average coefficients suggest only a single major difference in the pattern of "gaps," and that relates (curiously) to the most distant paired comparison. Table 11.3 summarizes the results.

TABLE 11.2
Ahmavaara's Analysis of Remaining Twenty-one Paired Comparisons of Phases

	Intra-class Correlations		Product-Moment Correlations	
Paired Comparisons	**r**	**r^2**	**r**	**r^2**
I vs. III	.75	56.3%	.78	60.8%
II vs IV	.40	16.0%	.53	28.1%
III vs. V	.59	34.8%	.65	42.3%
IV vs. VI	.61	37.2%	.73	53.3%
V vs. VII	.71	50.4%	.74	54.8%
VI vs. VIII	.86	74.0%	.87	75.7%
I vs. IV	.70	49.0%	.73	53.3%
II vs. V	.54	29.2%	.60	36.0%
III vs. VI	.66	43.6%	.69	47.6%
IV vs. VII	.54	29.2%	.60	36.0%
V vs. VIII	.71	50.4%	.74	54.8%
I vs. V	.62	38.4%	.66	43.6%
II vs. VI	.54	29.2%	.61	37.2%
III vs. VII	.52	27.0%	.61	37.2%
IV vs. VIII	.70	49.0%	.77	59.3%
I vs. VI	.70	49.0%	.74	54.8%
II vs. VII	.54	29.2%	.60	36.0%
III vs. VIII	.71	50.4%	.75	56.3%
I vs. VII	.57	32.5%	.63	39.7%
II vs. VIII	.62	38.4%	.67	44.9%
I vs. VIII	.80	64.0%	.82	67.2%
		x=41.8%		x=48.5%

TABLE 11.3
Congruence of Structures of MBI Items

	Distances between Phases in Paired Comparisons						
Mean r^2	**1**	**2**	**3**	**4**	**5**	**6**	**7**
Intra-class correlations (in %)	32.6	44.7	41.4	35.8	42.7	35.0	64.0
Product-moment correlations (in %)	40.4	52.5	46.8	44.3	49.0	42.5	67.0

Phases and Worksite Descriptors

One can assess artifactuality of the gamma differences above in a different way—by comparing respondents assigned to different phases in terms of how they structure psychological space in their responses to a panel of target variables that deal with common worksite descriptors. Conceptually, these target variables seek to be unidimensional. Hence, *if* their factorial structures tend to be congruent—that is, if worksite descriptors reflect differences in

TABLE 11.4
Congruence of Structures of Worksite Descriptors

Mean r^2	Distances between Phases in Paired Comparisons						
	1	2	3	4	5	6	7
Intra-class correlations (in %)	78.8	79.1	79.6	83.3	81.1	82.0	90.3
Product-moment correlations (in %)	79.5	79.4	80.4	83.5	81.7	82.0	90.3

degree only—this will provide some evidence for the unique character of the phase model, even though it cannot dismiss the argument about the artifactuality of the results just summarized.

The twenty-one items to be factor-analyzed in this test of assumedly alpha-only differences come from three scales: Participation in Decisions at Work (White and Ruh 1973), Job Involvement (White and Ruh 1973), and Job Tension at Work (Kahn et al. 1964). The details of the factor analysis are available elsewhere (Golembiewski and Munzenrider 1989b) but, in general, the resulting factors suggest three unidimensional constructs. Consequently, as noted above, the expectation is that individuals assigned to different phases will have similar factorial structures for the three factors descriptive of the worksite.

The findings support the view of non-gamma differences between persons assigned to different phases and the way they psychologically structure the twenty-one items of the three worksite descriptors. To conserve space, the appropriate table is not reproduced here. But the summary in table 11.4 of paired comparisons shows convincingly that at all distances similar and high proportions of variation are shared.

Greater Success by Specifying Kinds of Change, Revisited

This difficult chapter and its immediate predecessor relate to crucial theoretical and applied issues in OD, and they in turn constitute potential keys to unlocking the door to a future of markedly higher success rates. In short, the ability to distinguish types of change is crucial to our ability to measure success along the kinds of contours illustrated above. And ability to measure success sensitive to kinds of change, in turn, will provide the foundation for determining with growing certainty what specific OD designs have which consequences under what conditions. Penultimately, as our familiarity with non-alpha forms grows, so also will we have pictures of various "social contours," and this knowledge may well indicate alternative pathways for growth and development. Ideally, such contours also will highlight shortcuts for getting from A to B.

These comments suggest a heady potential for greater success in OD via developing knowledge about non-alpha change. At the risk of getting too far ahead of existing research and practice, a bit more detail seems appropriate in detailing the advantages of approaching non-alpha change, both directly and by using burnout phases as a surrogate measure.

Some Generic Advantages of Gamma Estimates

Chapters 10 and 11 present a quite-specific foundation for beginning a great-leap-forward. Those chapters propose that gamma change is the goal of OD, and that T_2 versus T_1 differences in the profiles of burnout phases in an organization may provide a key estimate of whether gamma change has occurred. This capability has both tactical and strategic advantages. It promises greater certainty about whether a specific OD application worked, in providing a useful (if general) judgment about non-alpha change. In addition, the accumulation of such studies can provide the grist for theories of greater comprehensiveness, as well as guidance for more effective praxis.

This essential bottom-line reflects a very potent combination. As matters stand now, most observers accept gamma conceptually, but major theoretical and practical problems restrict defining the character and direction of gamma change. Existing approaches do estimate the magnitude of gamma-like changes, but that information is not sufficient to reliably and validly characterize the direction of any T_2 versus T_1 change or difference. Indeed, the acceptance of gamma—without knowledge of character and direction—seems to have contributed to an analytic pessimism. We know enough about what we should know, that is, to make many of us pessimistic about what we do know.

The burnout phases provide a possible way out of this malaise. For differences in the phases imply not only magnitude, but they also specify character and direction—of better and worse, if you will, as in terms of the regular and robust association of the phases with a growing incidence of physical symptoms. (See chapter 5.) This directionality provides useful guidance for both the researcher and the practitioner, especially in pursuit of the accumulating sense of which designs work under what specific conditions.

One cannot yet be specific about all the theoretical and practical stakes involved in chapters 10 and 11, but they seem very big. If gamma exists, and if changes in burnout phases estimate gamma, that is, advances in knowledge can come thick and fast. Basically, the burnout phases provide information useful for differentiating individuals, small groups, and large organizations. Evidence is still incomplete, but the phases co-vary with many defects and deficiencies for individuals (Golembiewski and Munzenrider 1988b), group properties seem to deteriorate as burnout phases escalate from phase I toward phase VIII (see chapter 7), and advanced phases also seem to generate prob-

FIGURE 11.4
Two Ways from A to B

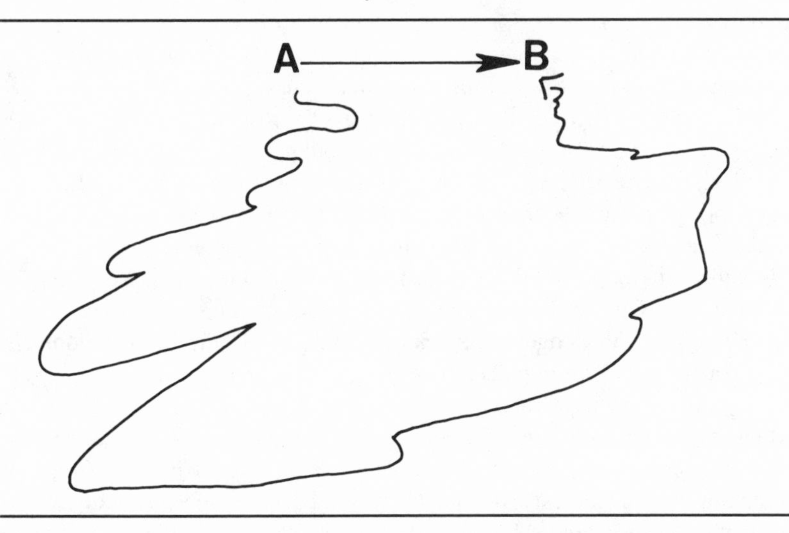

lems for the cultures of large organizations (Janz, Dugan, and Ross 1986). Such multiple differentiation, in turn, will aid both description and prescription in OD, with predictably positive effects on already-substantial success rates.

Let us dwell a bit on how knowledge of behavioral contours may permit quantum leaps in planning and intervening for change. We do not yet have a clear sense of what could happen, given a better sense of the contours of our social and psychological space. Directly, however, the several figures above suggest the basic strategy with which we might have to become much more facile when big change is required and time is short. One can either follow the contours of a surface such as that in figure 11.3 or jump between the folds in the behavioral space. The former is the long way around, and probably also more time-consuming and costly.

A homely example illustrates the virtues of thinking about gamma change and the contours of behavioral spaces, despite the attendant complexities. Consider figure 11.4, which suggests two pathways for getting from A to B, where B refers to a very high probability of a train staying on the tracks and A to a much lower probability.

History is full of examples of taking the long way around, as in the curious but early decision to weld flanges to the *outside of each track* to keep trains from sliding off. Getting to B proved very challenging along this developmental path, which is suggested by the uneven solid line connecting A and B. Why challenging? The welded flanges had the nasty tendency to come loose with wear—curling up and then sometimes impaling the railroad cars and even passengers. A long line of developments could reduce these problems, but only at great cost and effort: tracks could be constantly inspected, welding skills could be improved, the bellies of railroad cars could be made of costly metal rather than of the wood then in common usage, and so on.

A shorter route between A and B existed—"across the open space," as it were—but it took many years to occur to enough people in sufficiently high places. The flange eventually was machined *into the train's wheels,* which not only kept the train on the tracks, but also saved metal and could be done more reliably and with a sharply reduced chance of misadventure.

Many similar opportunities for reducing developmental distances exist. In common, they involve recognizing the contours of transitional stages, and then using that knowledge to consciously short-circuit the full development cycle. In this sense, comprehending gamma can be the platform for great increases in OD success rates.

Finally, for present purposes, coming to grips with tripartite change provides an alternative to analysis by metaphysical pathos, as it were. Consider the non-attitude hypothesis. It leaps from some data, to be sure, but (perhaps prematurely) gets extended into a kind of pessimistic world view about people and politics. The sociologist Gouldner alerted us to the tendency to overgeneralize from a spot of evidence or experience, to create a metaphysical pathos that transcends and even engulfs its origination and originators. Gamma change provides one test of the non-attitude hypothesis, which should precede the spread of a pessimistic world view. Indeed, a finding of gamma change could generate a heightened optimism about our political processes.

Something of the same sort is possible in OD. Its initial world view was upbeat and optimistic, and so overexuberant as to lead otherwise-sound observers to predict some wondrously improbable things, such as "the coming death of bureaucracy" (e.g., Slater and Bennis 1964). Basically, this OD world view has persisted, even if its cloth has been cut to fit the uncomely shape of some powerful realities (e.g., Bennis 1970). Concepts like gamma will significantly influence, if not determine, whether OD's world view can remain realistically optimistic about people and their organizations. Alternatively, substantial success rates and all OD may increasingly fall victim to the corrosiveness of a despair about comprehending successive challenges to both its values and technology. As OD aficionados have long proposed, one who isn't learning is already dead.

A Specific Concern about Gamma Effects

A central question still must be posed, finally, advantages notwithstanding. Is the very measurement of phases subject to plural change even as it is here proposed as a surrogate measure of gamma change? The answer is yes, but with two qualifications that substantially moderate the adverse impact of this apparently serious affirmation. In sum, the qualified response diminishes, but does not destroy, the usefulness of burnout as a surrogate measure.

Although non-alpha might occur in self-reports concerning burnout, the present reliance on High versus Low distinctions in assigning phases serves as a buffer. Let us take the easier of two cases first. Should beta change occur between successive burnout measurements, the high probability is that this would not impact essentially on phase assignments. After all, beta change seems more likely to occur in "elongations" of portions of purported continua, and this typically would mitigate effects on the High versus Low distinctions which determine assignments to phases.

The case for gamma in burnout measurements presents greater difficulties, and must be conjectural. A minimal position seems reasonable, however, as a first approximation. Burnout seems to be a bottom-line measure: what constitutes too much will vary not only between individuals, but probably also for an individual at several points in time; but whenever too much exists, the phase model proposes that deficits or deficiencies will occur. So the present measurement approach to phases permits different triggers for specific individuals, but the effects of that differential triggering seem similar in state if perhaps different in degree. From one point of view, then, the phase model's focus on "too much-ness" rather than "what-ness" constitutes a buffer against profound gamma-like differences in the dimensions in terms of which individuals make that assessment. Put another way, the phase model focuses on the degree of strain relative to coping capacities, independent of the stressors or the character and quality of the coping process.

Note

1. An early version of the first three emphases in this chapter appears in Golembiewski 1986.

References

Achen, C. R. 1975. "Mass Political Attitudes and Survey Response." *American Political Science Review* 69:1218–31.

Ahmavaara, Y. 1954. "Transformation Analysis of Factor Data." *Annals of The Academy of Science Fennicae, Series B* 881 2:54–59.

Argyris, C., and Schön, D. A. 1978. *Theory in Practice*. Reading, Mass.: Addison-Wesley.

Armenakis, A. A., and Bedeian, A. G. 1972. "On the Measurement and Control of Beta Change: Reply to Terborg, Maxwell, and Howard." *Academy of Management Review* 7:296–99.

Armenakis, A. A., and Zmud, R. W. 1979. "Interpreting the Measurement of Change in Organizational Research." *Personnel Psychology* 32:709–23.

Armenakis, A. A.; Bedeian, A. G.; and Pond, S. B. III. 1983. "Research Issues in OD Evaluation." *Academy of Management Review* 8:320–28.

Armenakis, A. A.; Buckley, M.; and Bedeian, A. G. 1984. "Conditions Affecting Time Order Error in Temporal Survey Research: A Laboratory Investigation." Paper presented at the Annual Meeting, Academy of Management. Boston.

Armenakis, A. A.; Randolph, W. A.; and Bedeian, A. G. 1982. "A Comparison of Two Methods for Evaluating the Similarity of Factor Analytic Solutions." *Proceedings*. Southwestern Academy of Management Meeting.

Bateson, G. 1942. "Social Planning and the Concept of 'Deutero-learning' in Relation to the Democratic Way of Life." In *Science, Philosophy and Religion: Second Symposium*, 81–97. New York: Harper and Bros.

Bedeian, A. G.; Armenakis, A. A.; and Gibson, F. 1980. "The Measurement and Control of Beta Change." *Academy of Management Review* 5:561–66.

Bennis, W. G. 1970. "A Funny Thing Happened on the Way to the Future." *American Psychologist* 25:598–603.

Chittick, W. O.; Billingsley, K.; and Travis, R. 1988. "Persistence and Change in Elite and Mass Attitudes Toward U.S. Foreign Policy." Paper delivered at the Annual Meeting, International Society for Political Psychology. New York. 1 July.

Converse, P. 1964. "The Nature of Belief Systems in Mass Publics." In *Ideology and Discontent*, edited by D. E. Apter, 206–61. New York: Free Press.

______. 1970. "Attitudes and Non-Attitudes: Continuation of a Dialogue." In *The Quantitative Analysis of Social Problems*, edited by E. R. Tufte, 168–89. Reading, Mass.: Addison-Wesley.

Golembiewski, R. T. 1962. *The Small Group*. Chicago, Ill.: University of Chicago Press.

______. 1986. "Contours of Social Change." *Academy of Management Review* 11:550–66.

______. 1989 "The Alpha, Beta, Gamma Change Typology." *Group and Organization Studies* (in press).

Golembiewski, R. T., and Billingsley, K. 1980. "Measuring Change in OD Panel Designs: A Response to Critics." *Academy of Management Review* 5:97–104.

Golembiewski, R. T., and Munzenrider, R. F. 1984. "Phases of Psychological Burnout and Organizational Covariants." *Journal of Health and Human Resources Administration* 46:233–49.

______. 1988a. "Burnout as Indicator of Gamma Change, I: Methodological Perspectives on a Crucial Surrogacy." *Journal of Health and Human Resources Administration* 11:218–48.

______. 1988b. *Phases of Burnout*. New York: Praeger.

______. 1989a. "Burnout as Indicator of Gamma Change, II: State-like Differences between Phases." *Journal of Health and Human Resources Administration* in press.

______. 1989b. "Burnout as Indicator of Gamma Change, III: Differences of Degree in Worksite Descriptors." *Journal of Health and Human Resources Administration* (in press).

Golembiewski, R. T.; Billingsley, K.; and Yeager, S. 1967a. "Measuring Change and Persistence in Human Affairs: Types of Change Generated by OD Designs." *Journal of Applied Behavioral Science* 12:134–40.

______. 1976b. "The Congruence of Factorial Structures: Comparisons of Four Procedures and Their Solutions." *Academy of Management Review* 1:26–35.

Golembiewski, R. T.; Munzenrider, R. F.; and Carter, D. 1983. "Phases of Progressive Burnout and Their Worksite Covariants." *Journal of Applied Behavioral Science* 19:461–80.

Golembiewski, R. T.; Munzenrider, R. F.; and Stevenson, J. 1984. "Physical Symptoms and Burnout Phases." In *Organizational Policy and Development*, edited by R. Moise, 71–86. Louisville, Ky.: Center for Continuing Studies, University of Louisville.

______. 1986. *Stress in Organizations*. New York: Praeger.

Hackman, J. R., and Oldham, G. R. 1980. *Work Redesign*. Reading, Mass.: Addison-Wesley.

Hunter, J. E.; Schmidt, F. L.; and Jackson, G. B. 1982. *Metaanalysis*. Beverly Hills, Calif.: Sage Publications.

Janz, T.; Dugan, S.; and Ross, M. S. 1986. "Organization Culture and Burnout." *Journal of Health and Human Resources Administration* 9:78–92.

Kahn, R. L.; Wolfe, D. M.; Quinn, R. P.; Snoeck, J. D.; and Rosenthal, R. A. 1964. *Organizational Stress*. New York: Wiley.

Likert, R. 1967. *The Human Organization*. New York: McGraw-Hill.

Lindell, M. K., and Drexler, J. A. Jr. 1979. "Issues in Using Survey Methods for Measuring Organizational Change." *Academy of Management Review* 4:13–19.

______. 1980. "Equivocality of Factor Incongruence as an Indicator of Types of Change in OD Interventions." *Academy of Management Review* 5:105–8.

Macy, B. A., and Peterson, M. R. 1983. "Evaluating Attitudinal Change in a Longitudinal Quality-of-Work Intervention." In *Observing and Measuring Organizational Change: A Guide to Field Practice*, edited by S. Seashore, E. E. Lawler III, P. H. Mirvis, and C. Cammann, 453–76. New York: Wiley Interscience.

Maslach, C., and Jackson, S. 1982, 1986. *Maslach Burnout Inventory*. Palo Alto, Calif.: Consulting Psychologists Press.

McGee, V. E. 1966. "The Multidimensional Analysis of 'Elastic' Distances." *British Journal of Mathematical and Statistical Psychology* 19:181–96.

Miller, D., and Friesen, P. H. 1984. *Organizations*. Englewood Cliffs, N.J.: Prentice-Hall.

Normann, R. 1971. "Organizational Innovations." *Administrative Science Quarterly* 16:203–15.

Pepper. S., and Prytulak, L. S. 1974. "Sometimes Frequently Means Seldom: Context Effects in the Interpretation of Quantitative Expressions." *Journal of Research in Personality* 8:95–101.

Porras, J. I., and Singh, J. V. 1984. "Alpha, Beta, and Gamma Change in Modeling-Based Organization Developed." Mimeograph.

Randolph, W. A. 1984. "A Comparison of Two Approaches for Measuring Organizational Change." Paper delivered at Annual Meeting, Academy of Management. Boston. 9–11 August.

Randolph, W. A., and Edwards, R. G. 1978. "Assessment of Alpha, Beta, and Gamma Changes in a University-Setting OD Intervention." *Academy of Management Proceedings*: 313–17.

Schmitt, N. 1980. "The Use of Analysis of Covariance Structures to Assess Beta and Gamma Change." *Multivariate Behavioral Research* 17:343, 358.

______. 1984. "Comparison of Three Techniques to Assess Group-Level Beta and Gamma Change." Paper delivered at Annual Meeting, Academy of Management. Boston. 9–11 August.

Slater, P. E., and Bennis, W. G. 1964. "Democracy Is Inevitable." *Harvard Business Review* 42:51–59.

Smith, W. C. 1980. "Catastrophe Theory Analysis of Business Activity." *Management Review* 69:27–28 and 37–40.

Starbuck, W. H. 1973. "Tadpoles into Armageddon and Chrysler into Butterflies." *Social Science Research* 2:81–109.

Stephens, S. V. 1976. "A Reanalysis of Achen's Critique of the Converse Model of Mass Political Belief." *American Political Science Review* 70:1224.

Tennis, C. W. 1985. "The Alpha, Beta, and Gamma Change Technology: The Response of an Invisible College." Unpublished ms.

Terborg, J. R. 1984. "An Empirical Investigation of Two Techniques for Measurement of Alpha, Beta, and Gamma Change at the Individual Level of Analysis." Paper delivered at Annual Meeting, Academy of Management. Boston. 9–11 August 1984.

Terborg, J. R.; Howard, G. S.; and Maxwell, S. E. 1980. "Evaluating Planned Organizational Change: A Method of Assessing Alpha, Beta, and Gamma Change." *Academy of Management Review* 5:109–21.

Terborg, M. R.; Maxwell, S. E.; and Howard, G. S. 1982. "On the Measurement and Control of Beta Change: Problems with the Bedeian, Armenakis, and Gibson Technique." *Academy of Management Review* 7:292–95.

White, J. K., and Ruh, R. A. 1973. "Effects of Personal Values on the Relationship between Participation and Job Attitudes." *Administrative Science Quarterly* 18:506–14.

Zmud, R. W., and Armenakis, A. A. 1978. "Understanding the Measurement of Change." *Academy of Management Review* 3:661–69.

Postscripts about Multiple Ironies

12

Tactics and Strategies for Reducing Ironies

This book highlights several ironies, but each and all for only a trinity of purposes. Both for convenience and because of their content, these purposes may be labeled

- the sense of this effort
- the belief underlying this volume
- the conviction of this volume

The basic *sense* of the volume is that OD intervenors are coping tolerably well, even with the several gaps and unclarities in theory and philosophy. The success rates detailed in chapters 1 and 2 provide support for this sense of the volume, not only in a batch of OD applications representing economically developed settings but also in a batch deliberately restricted to what are called Third World settings, if loosely.

These success rates are tolerably good news, although they may surprise some observers. For they suggest that ODers who care enough about their practice to write about experiences—whether for publication or just for a record to learn from—are able to make the subtle and multiple adjustments at the many points at which the arts of consultation have to transcend what is known rigorously and scientifically.

More basically, however, this book seeks to use today's praxis not as a place to rest but as a platform from which to leap toward greater comprehensiveness and greater success rates. More important than the *sense*, then, the *conviction* of this book is that we need not simply reconcile ourselves and our clients to the present level of achievement, attractive though that general record now seems. We should do better, and clients should expect us to do better, even though our average performance at this time isn't at all bad.

Penultimately, the *belief* underlying this volume is dual—not only can we reduce the surprises in OD, but proximate ways and means for doing so are conveniently at hand. Ironies in OD praxis may be all well and good, but we need greater specificity and precision in what we recommend and why. The eleven chapters preceding this one do the heavy work of acting on this belief: they specify some convenient ways and means of doing better than average. These chapters do not exhaust these ways and means, but the sampler is representative of what can be done, why, and how.

The alternatives to reducing surprises—especially the unpleasant ones—are not attractive. The major consequences feature a substantially stagnant central core of concepts and ideas, along with overreaching extensions beyond that once-solid base. In short, these alternatives risk allowing OD to fall in on itself, as it were, with the old foundations progressively less able to support the weight of burgeoning practice. This suggests a meta-irony: what appears to be bustling activity on the surface of things could in point of fact be coupled with an increasingly inadequate theoretical infrastructure, and this means growing trouble not only in the present but, especially, in the near future.

So this book goes about acting on this *sense*, motivated by that *conviction*, both inspired by a *belief* that we not only can, but must, do something more because the ironies are not likely to take care of themselves. The spirit of this volume is upbeat and even optimistic—when the prescriptions are straightforward and available (as in chapters 8 and 9), when they are subtle and off in some future (as in chapters 10 and 11), and when those prescriptions are somewhere in-between (as in the other seven chapters).

What are the odds that the surprises can be reduced? This chapter proposes that those odds are pretty good, as it goes about detailing a skeletal agenda for OD.

The ironies may well bury OD, of course. But ODers seem to be coping with them well enough for the present, and substantial enhancements of OD praxis do *not* seem to require a great leap forward. They seem readily available, at least in sufficient part.

Three Reactive/Proactive Classes

This volume can only illustrate how to go about acting on this trinity of sense, conviction, and belief, but the several illustrations have real substance to them. Let us summarize, with a concern about repetition but with an absolute fear that some important things will not get due attention.

Conveniently, we identify three classes of responses that do something reactive about the ironies, or even proactive. The timeframes of these classes are substantially identified by their labels: immediate plug-ins or short-run efforts; intermediate-range amelioratives; and long-range or even far-out thrusts.

Immediate Responses

In the very short run, this volume suggests several reasonable ways to reduce ironies in OD, right now. For present purposes, consider only three immediate responses: taking advantage of as-is plug-ins, inducing appropriate expectations, and making changes in the packaging of OD applications.

Taking advantage of as-is plug-ins. Directly, a number of the chapters detail opportunities that require little or no further development before being put into general use. Indeed, chapters 4 through 9 can go now, more or less as-is.

The point of as-is applicability may be established briefly and conveniently. The focus is on chapters 4, 8, and 9.

- Chapter 4 requires only a minor technical adjustment in the way most surveys are processed, although the ethical and philosophic issues definitely breed careful review. Performance appraisals constitute only another breakout variable that can be used to search for patterns in survey data and, in practice, this requires the same kind of analysis as that applied to the demographic variables typically included in surveys—age, sex, and so on. As chapter 4 suggests, however, performance appraisals may be a *critical breakout variable*.
- Chapters 8 and 9 similarly present as-is opportunities, and both seem to be associated with high success rates. Flexi-Time applications in the hundreds have been written about, and one has to persevere to find an overt failure. But only small fractions of the work force are covered, even now. The demotion design has been applied several times to my knowledge, and the effects have been all-but-uniformly like those in the original application detailed in chapter 9.

It requires only a little more of a stretch to see how the thrust of chapters 5, 6, and 7 can be brought into direct play in OD applications, in three distinct senses. First, elementally, chapter 5 illustrates how the phases of burnout are associated directly with important deficiencies or deficits, and measuring the phases can provide important data in a profile of an organization's climate and culture as well as a profile of its individual members. The phases may provide a revealing measure, as well as a convenient one. To suggest the point, Janz, Dugan, and Ross (1986) report a very high correlation (-.82) between a summary measure of an organization's culture and the percentage of employees in the three most advanced phases of burnout. Other observers report that performance appraisals fall as burnout phases approach VIII (Golembiewski and Munzenrider 1988, 85–93); and mortality levels in health-care settings have been associated directly with the proportions of staff in advanced phases, this author has heard from reliable sources. See also Golembiewski 1987, where an entry design based on phase assignments as a key socio-emotional indicator is elaborated.

Second, and a bit more expansively, chapter 6 shows how something useful may be done about reducing one mode of advanced phases of burnout—the active mode, in the present vocabulary. The larger job remains to be done—

dealing with the (probably) more numerous cases of a passive response to advanced burnout. Most demanding will be the obvious challenge: inducing worksite features that inhibit movement away from phase I, and which also restrict active-to-passive migration.

Third, even much-broader initiatives detailed in this volume seem actionable, *now*, at least in part. Consider chapter 7.

- Chapter 7 seems to present far more opportunities than difficulties in as-is applications. Specifically, different designs seem appropriate for those in advanced phases of burnout than for those with modest degrees of that dis-ease. Mass team-building projects are in increasing vogue nowadays, for example, and differentiating burnout may be very helpful in fitting one of several designs to specific teams rather than—as is almost always done—using a single design for all teams. A one-size design no more fits all organizational teams than one-size socks fit all feet.

Conveniently, teams seem to have an affinity for extreme scores on burnout. Although burnout is an individual property, the typical group tends to have an affinity *either* for those in advanced phases *or* for those persons experiencing little burnout. There seem to be few groups that are substantially mixed, when it comes to phase assignments (e.g., Golembiewski and Munzenrider 1988, chap. 6). This affinity implies that the OD designer can have his cake and eat it too, in the sense of taking individual burnout into account and yet dealing essentially with groups rather than with isolated individuals.

What keeps ODers from acting on such easy as-is opportunities, and in large numbers? The hopeful (or even impertinent) short answer is that perhaps more *will* be done after people read this book. Much of the material has been published elsewhere over the years, but this reworked reappearance between two covers might leverage the impact of the individual chapters. That is my hope, in any case.

Of course, this short answer will not do, for the question poses complex issues in the dissemination and diffusion of knowledge. In sum, chapters 4 through 9 do not constitute a slam-dunk in every sense.

For example, consider chapter 4, which poses no technical problems but which does require that ODers reevaluate long-standing preferences—some matters of mere convenience, and others determinedly philosophical and deep in a person's being. Technically, chapter 4 requires a bit more sophistication in data processing than usual, but the techniques are nonetheless well within the capabilities of widely available canned programs for personal computers and micros. These are everywhere nowadays. Conceptually, there are two tendencies at odds in that chapter: the technical search for the highest-quality data available, and the populist empowerment of all respondents by assuring that their voices are safely heard, especially in large aggregates. The view in chapter 4 is that, at least in the long run, the second goal will be achieved only as the first goal is increasingly met. So investing in a little additional data processing constitutes a cheap price and a tolerable risk, in the present view. The risk will be most manageable in regenerative-interaction systems, which is what OD is about in its most essential sense.

Some reasonable people see the situation in another light, even some who have the data processing skills. They want to reduce specialist inputs in the surveying process, thereby increasing ownership and involvement by nonspecialists. Moreover, they want to maximize participation by absolute anonymity. The intent is a radically populist kind of action research, with maximum involvement and participation of "just people." These goals reduce the probability of—but do not eliminate—analyses like that illustrated in chapter 4.

This other view is seen as too limiting, as a general rule, even though I understand and applaud the insistence on the argument under certain repressive conditions (e.g., Brown and Tandon 1983). What may seem to be harsh medicine to some is viewed here as in the enlightened self-interest of ODers, in addition to being in the long-run interest of others.

Think about the choices for a minute, in response to a selective barrage of questions. Who will pay good money and spend precious time to generate data that may be unrevealing, if not absolutely misleading? Only the uninformed, over the long run; or perhaps the manipulator using a survey as a public relations effort, with no serious intent to act on the data. Apart from earning a fee, what virtues inhere in having such clients? And even considering the fee, what is the impact on the derivative credibility of OD practice and practitioners, at least over the long run? Moreover, no one will be served by potentially misleading data. And whom will such faculty data empower, in more than a temporary and ephemeral sense? In the long run, at least, probably neither clients nor respondents.

Indeed, one might argue that pseudo-empowerment is the worst outcome of all, not only lacking substance but involving a cruel raising of unfounded hopes.

Inducing appropriate expectations. Immediately, also, OD ironies can be moderated by using our existing base of knowledge to create appropriate expectations. For openers, this discussion suggests three approaches to a reasonable setting of expectations.

To begin, chapters 1 and 2 will help create some realism about overall success rates. Moreover, motivation to do better than average comes from all of the chapters, this author hopes. This may seem to be a motherhood-and-apple-pie recommendation, but it has a dual edge. Noting tolerable success rates may seem like so much horn-tooting, but the claim can become a standard which the client expects the ODer to achieve or surpass. These dynamics can be powerfully useful. Unrealistic assessments of success rates do no one any long-run good. The estimates in chapters 1 and 2 are high and set no easy standard.

The second approach is that chapters 10 and 11 also help set expectations in sophisticated and critical senses. OD applications often seek gamma change—or changes in state rather than in degree—and the two chapters provide a sense of what that direct statement implies for evaluating OD applications. It does no good to use alpha-change conventions for assessing gamma. Indeed, one can be seriously misled. Moreover, we suspect that failure to recognize gamma results in classifying more applications as failures than successes. This is an elemental, if speculative, sense in which learning from chapters 10 and 11 can increase OD success rates.

Now, this point may seem like a hard sell for both consultant and client, but it has its clear virtues. The data-processing costs and skills have to be taken into account, but only the determination of kind of change permits an informed judgment about whether or not an intervention worked. Indeed, the discovery of gamma was inspired by a case in which the numbers indicated an intervention failed even as participants saw success. When alpha-only was assumed, the intervention seemed to be a definite failure. But gamma change seems to have occurred, and that required a reevaluation of effects. A "big bang" change occurred, given a plural change view of the effects, while a conventional view indicated no intended change—indeed, the data suggested a regression.

So both client and intervenor have a real interest in gamma change, independent of the longer-run benefits that awareness of it may generate. Without testing for gamma, neither client nor intervenor will know whether an intervention worked. Only fads do without testing for their effects, and that only because, generally, fads soon do themselves in. We can all be thankful when that does not take very long. We should adjust our thinking so as to make it occur sooner.

Even if reasonable, this recognition of gamma will seldom come easily. One large commercial survey operation may be prototypic. The initial reaction to gamma change was to fund a sizeable study by a think tank to investigate the concept, perhaps even to deep-six it. The motivation may only be guessed at, but gamma did challenge the survey organization's normal way of doing business. The second-look view? The later reaction was to recommend that clients consider using a routine test for gamma.

The third approach is that chapters 5 through 7 provide a direct message about appropriate expectations. OD designs should have higher success rates when they fit the contexts in which they are applied.

Enough said, in general. Chapters 5 and 7 focus on one aspect of possible differences between individuals and groups, and chapter 6 seeks to extend the core insight. (See also the discussion of chapter 6 under the heading "Intermediate-Range Initiatives" in this chapter.)

Making changes in OD packaging. Finally, for the present short list of immediate ways to reduce ironies in OD, intervenors might well change some policies and procedures. For example, some OD contracts might well carry a 5 or 10 percent add-on to advance the science and the art, in addition to the resources necessary for the specific objectives sought. Third parties might well specialize in putting such add-on funds to good use, providing at once an objective evaluation of an intervention and tests or even extensions of existing theories.

Such a policy would not only add to our knowledge base, and in that sense "put something back in the pot" to acknowledge a debt to the earlier investments of others, but it would also "pass on the favor" to future ODers. In addition, the use of third parties has methodological advantages—or at least avoids implications of direct self-interest in cases where OD intervenors do their own research.

One can also conceive of policy making that constitutes far more of a stretch. Consider what might be called the Fund for Displaced ODers. The idea is not a new one, and similar institutions exist for such an unlikely gaggle of professionals as chemists, pastors, and federal officials. The core dilemma is common: what of those professionals who are tempted, or even ordered, to violate "standards of acceptable conduct" lest they lose their jobs or otherwise get punished?

The purpose of the fund would be to provide support for those ODers who are in trouble with their employing agency for doing the proper thing. Such a fund could reduce the probability that individuals will cave-in to repressive forces and, in the longer run, also might reduce the likelihood that some employers would try to apply muscle to their employees. For example, a person serving in an OD role might get some information, given in confidence, which some management group wished to track down to its source. To tell might save the ODer's job, but at great personal cost to self and perhaps others. If ODers were not left to face that music on their own, matters might be improved all the way around (e.g, Golembiewski 1986b).

Intermediate-Range Initiatives

Ironies does not exist only in the immediate present. Several of the chapters suggest targets that will not be attainable in the very near future, and yet do not have Star Wars time frames. A trinity of such intermediate targets gets some attention. Discussion deals with, in turn, exploring the issue of the fit between design and context, avoiding the reputation and reality of OD as a "mature product line," and enhancing OD's foundations.

Fit between design and context. Chapters 2, 3, and 6 deal with the central issue of the degree of fit or congruence between specific OD designs and various contexts of application, though in different ways. Chapters 2 and 6 got some earlier attention, so let us focus here on chapter 3.

Chapter 3 deals with the issue of an "optimum prior discrepancy" in OD, which typically requires that people "unfreeze" as a first step in increasing their consciousness about the appropriateness of choice or change. Various discrepancy-highlighting approaches have been used in OD—feedback in a supportive context like a sensitivity training group, the sharing of 3-D images for purposes of directing confrontations, and the use of surveys to contrast what respondents report with what they prefer or believe to be the case.

Clearly, however, some degrees of discrepancy can be too much, and others too little. Greater clarity about which degree of discrepancy is appropriate under what conditions seems like a high-priority item for the research agenda of the near future.

Chapter 6 enlarges the focus to deal with the fit between specific designs and various individual and group contexts. That chapter highlights the generic issue of which designs seem most appropriate under which specific environmental contexts or conditions (e.g., Bowers and Hausser 1977; Miller and Friesen 1984). This catalog poses a real challenge for intermediate-range initiatives.

The specifics can be troublesome in cases, for we have few taxonomies for describing significant contexts. Moreover, useful taxonomies probably will be quite detailed—for example, some studies indicate there may be twenty or so distinct types of small work groups (e.g., Bowers and Hausser 1977), and a dozen or so "organizational archetypes" (e.g., Miller and Friesen 1984).

But whoever said that nature promised us a rose garden? Certainly no credible argument can be made today for using simple and single interventions just because it is more convenient that way, whatever can be said of the earliest start-up days. The two initial chapters on success rates imply that ODers do a tolerably good job of establishing the fit of design to context, in general. Nonetheless, this is no place to stop. The effort no doubt will require major tooling-up, and results may come slowly. But as we gain experience about the more precise tailoring of designs to the major varieties of contexts, so also will success rates increase. This provides powerful motivation for proceeding, posthaste, to test where we have good theoretical reasons for believing we have a handhold on some strategic differences in context, as in chapters 6 and 7.

To be sure, neglecting such differences in context seems easy to do for certain designs, as in the cases of flexible work hours (chapter 8) or demotion (chapter 9). They seem to work in almost all cases. But even this understandable tendency to go with apparent winners must be resisted, lest we get into bad and irreversible habits.

Some tolerably-precise sense of fit exists, in fact, and although this is not the place for details some sense of the possible can be communicated economically. For example, chapter 7 provides a working idea of a reasonable fit in cases of advanced phases of burnout, and especially those in the passive mode. Here, low-stimulus designs seem appropriate, if only because individuals so classified are at their comfortable coping limits, if not beyond them. Low-stimulus designs include flexible work hour programs, job rotation, and mild role negotiation. High-stimulus designs for learning include interpersonal confrontations, sensitivity training, and so on, and these seem more applicable to cases in which individuals are active copers, as was the case with most of the organization members considered in chapter 7.

But the illustrations cannot dominate here. Interested readers can consult more elaborate reviews of the fit of OD designs to conditions at specific sites (e.g., Golembiewski 1989). See also tables 2.4, 6.4, and 7.1 for introductions to a detailed view of the fit of OD designs.

In short, really satisfactory solutions to anything will involve major progress on everything. This need not be intimidating, but it might well be. Directly, we do not have to do everything at once. But no harm exists in taking a global view of what would constitute major enhancements of OD.

This does not mean that we should proceed, willy-nilly. Indeed, two intermediate-run priorities seem clear enough: expand the conceptual boundaries of OD practitioners and their theories, and deepen the foundations of OD, especially in small-group analysis. In turn, the two subsections below focus on these priorities.

Avoiding the "maturing product" label and reality. OD will be well served by an expanding periphery, although not an exploding one, as well as by that solid central core rooted in process analysis and the values associated with the laboratory approach to education (e.g., Golembiewski 1979, vols. 1 and 2). Basically, this expanding periphery requires a growing set of testable and tested designs for specific learning purposes, and it also implies growing knowledge about the set of contexts in which those designs are applicable. Progressively, the expanding periphery implies such integrative thrusts:

- from interaction designs to structural and policy designs
- from affluent contexts to impoverished settings
- from growth to cutback or stagnation
- from high-technology industrial settings to rural subsistence settings
- from executive and managerial levels to workaday world at bench, shop, and assembly-line levels
- from a fixation on management and executives to collaboration between all stakeholders: labor unions, management, consumer groups, and so on
- from work settings to family and leisure settings
- from organizational problem solving and conflict resolution to issues of national and global peace

- from North American and Western European to global settings

Of course, several of the chapters above illustrate such thrusts for OD. For example, chapter 2 looks at applications in Third World countries, chapter 8 focuses on policy rather than interaction, and chapter 9 deals with the darker side of collective life, while most OD developed in a context of growth and expansion.

One must nurture such initiatives, and not merely announce them. Why? The motivation for the ODer is enlightened self-interest. Krell (1981) has usefully pointed up the several self-defeating features of maturing product lines, and these must be avoided and managed: overstatements of efficacy, spurious or at least superficial differentiation of products and services, cannibalizing the research of the past rather than investing in the research of the future, and so on. Only an expanding periphery will help avoid these dire concomitants of a maturing product line.

Investing in and expanding OD's foundations. In both tactical and strategic senses, movement toward intermediate-range initiatives will rest upon a concerted research push on small-group analysis which, in many ways, is at the heart of the OD technology. If this is an essentially correct statement, much work will need doing.

The point is that small-group analysis must be reinvigorated. Consider the oft-heard question, whatever happened to small-group analysis (Lakin 1979)? My answer may be a bit less common:

> The problem of small-group analysis is that it succeeded in inspiring applications substantially before a satisfactory research map was charted. This is not the worst problem to have, since problems there will be. It is merely a fact that what we learned in small group analysis through the 1960s was so powerful, however incomplete, that it fueled decades of applications.

So we can answer that small-group analysis is not somehow lost or forgotten. It is manifest in much applied behavioral science, and especially in OD. In fact, it succeeded too well, too fast.

Although not lost or woebegone, then, small-group analysis was and is stuck. At first, it was quite a comfortable stuckness, given the heady and even intoxicating advances in applications that resulted from the beachheads begun in the 1930s and 1940s (e.g., Golembiewski 1962). Of late, the stuckness is far less comfortable, and even downright uncomfortable at times. Consider this contrast. At one time, the achievements of small-group analysis permitted applications, even encouraged them. Increasingly, gaps in our knowledge of small groups act as constraints against the reach and grasp of applications.

Try an easy example. It is not extravagant to conclude that some groups are highly personable or even "warm," while others can have an atmosphere or climate that is "stiff," "cold," or even defiantly counterpersonal. Reasonably, then, the same design may not be equally appropriate for groups of these two kinds. Let us grant that the sophisticated OD intervenor working with one or a few groups might well adjust to such differences, even if semiconsciously. The rub? ODers have begun working, in earnest and often, simultaneously with several or even many groups, and that trend no doubt will intensify, if only to make more cost-effective use of expensive OD services. Hence, the contemporary OD intervenor stands in growing need of supports from theory and technology. Differences between groups require both prior measurement and classification, and here small-group analysis is no longer adequate.

How to get small-group analysis unstuck? Chapter 6 proposes one approach, which seems quite generally applicable. It seeks to relate the choice of designs to differences in prevailing crises or presenting conditions in groups, as well as to differing distributions of the burnout phases of a group's members. Similarly, chapter 7 suggests direct covariation between group properties and burnout, with significant implications for both theory and practice that have been confirmed by other research (Golembiewski and Munzenrider 1988, pp. 45–59, 148–64). These findings suggest reasonable ways to get at burnout by restricting the development of group properties that seem associated with the advanced phases—low cohesiveness, high supervisory pressure and punitiveness, and so on. Conveniently, for example, the small-group literature tells us much about how to induce high cohesiveness, which seems to be a function of member liking, prestige of task, and prestige of membership, (e.g., Golembiewski 1962, 149–70). These two approaches are illustrative only, of course, but they do suggest the character and consequence of the needed initiatives.

Of course, OD is not only small-group analysis, as central as that area of inquiry is and will remain. For one thing, OD needs a taxonomy of organizations at least as much as a taxonomy of groups. Here again, the research literature contains glistening suggestions (e.g., Miller and Friesen 1984), but no tried-and-true solutions.

The Longer-Run View

The description above somewhere changes its time line from the intermediate to the long run, to be sure. Workable small group and, especially, organizational taxonomies no doubt are not around any foreseeable analytical corner, and the same certainly seems true of the practical application of the focus of several chapters in this book (for example, 10 and 11).

Briefly, this section tries to pinpoint this transition toward long-run research objectives in terms of two emphases—the need for configurational analysis, and for a related Manhattan Project in the organizational sciences. Both emphases appear elsewhere (Golembiewski 1986a), and are modified somewhat for present purposes.

Toward configurational analysis. Much organizational analysis and prescription reflect an apparent irony. The more work concentrates on a research area, the less we seem to know. That is, initial studies may isolate robust patterns of relationships, and follow-on work sometimes replicates the initial results. Typically, however, cases of random variation and contrary results soon come to dominate what were once promising research initiatives. And the search typically moves on, quickly, in search of the next focus for inquiry.

This tendency tests one's confidence in ever coming to a firm grip with nature, and examples clearly abound. Consider the early excitement about the ratio of administrative (A) to production (P) employees as organizations increase in size, which suggested the general rule that A increases at a faster rate as P grows linearly. Organizations can also struggle to support their own weight, or even break down. The general reader was titillated by popular treatments, such as Parkinson's Law which (roughly translated) proposes that work expands to fill the time of whatever staff is available. Moreover, those laws propose, staff increases whether the work increases, decreases, or remains constant. That motivated many a chuckle.

No doubt the greatest research excitement attended Haire's (1959, 272–306) reliance on biological models to explain line and staff growth, but that reaction was soon dulled by the impact of contrary findings. Less than a decade later, twelve A:P studies provided diverse fodder for a review article (Rushing 1967): four studies showed no significant difference in the A:P ratio in organizations of different sizes, two studies showed increases in the ratio, and six found decreases. Subsequently, Pondy (1969) suggested that interindustry differences argued against any general rule; and Child (1973) completed the regression by proposing that, in any case, A was too heterogeneous to permit a coherent test of the relative rates of growth with P.

The pattern gets repeated, time after time, in many areas. The results of the decade-long fascination with bureaucratization and centralization spearheaded by the Aston group can be written in similar terms (Miller and Friesen 1984, 13–14). Hence, some observers note the boom-and-bust quality of many areas of behavioral and organizational research. Less-respectful souls refer to "this year's sheep dip," a view not only discouraging cumulative research but encouraging cynicism.

But the irony seems only apparent, and hence pessimism may not be appropriate about coming to grips with organizational phenomena. Mini-histories like that sketched above should be expected, in short. It would be astounding were they not to occur, in fact, given the general approach to research design.

Consider the situation in organization analysis described by Miller and Friesen (1984, esp. 15–17), who emphasize that researchers tend to assume that an organization is an organization. From there, conflicting results are only a matter of time.

Mintzberg's (1979) five structural configurations suggest why this outcome is all but foreordained, so fragile is the core assumption about homology. He distinguishes simple structure, machine bureaucracy, professional bureaucracy, a divisionalized form, and *ad hocracy*. Miller and Friesen understate the patent implications of these configurations for organizational analysis and praxis:

> Now, assuming . . . that at least a good proportion of organizations tended to adopt them or some other configurations of their structural parameters—what would happen if different kinds of organizations were mixed in research samples and then relationships gauged . . .? We believe that we already have the answers in the [mini-histories sketched above]. (1984, 14–15)

Specifically, a machine bureaucracy might well tend toward advanced centralization, while a professional bureaucracy might generally favor decentralization, or even chaotic localism. Both might be efficient, for their time and place.

The implied lesson is at once simple and daunting. Apparent contradictions in existing research will be reconciled, if at all, only after differentiating organizational configurations.

Hence the centrality in organization research and applications of "configurational analysis," which seeks some manageable number of sufficiently distinct clusters of multiple attributes. These may be used, in turn, to guide the search for consistent subsets of covariants. Of course, the persevering reader will conclude that *Ironies in Organizational Development* is in effect an effort to start some reasonable next steps for configurational analysis in OD. You bet!

The last words definitely will not be written here concerning configurational analysis, but four points seem safe enough. First, the approach seems to be a reasonable way to test stuckness or even despair born of conflicting research results. For example, small-group analysis has treaded water for a decade or more, and no small part of that record rests on a failure to distinguish families of similarly and differently configured groups (Lakin 1979). Consider only a simple illustration. What kind of intervention or design is best for team building? One approach reasonably proposes that this choice will depend on the characteristics of a specific team, and also details statistical procedures capable of generating distinct clusters of group properties (Bowers and Hausser 1977).

Second, despite the resounding triumph of "contingency theory" and its compatibility with configurational analysis, few have become contingency-ists in more than verbal terms. This elemental point gets support from Miller and Friesen's (1984) effort to develop a census of empirical configurations in the literature. They report: "One of the most surprising results of this survey is the very small number of taxonomies that have been generated" (1984, 35). So the critical item is also a rare one.

Third, configurational analysis will depart in significant particulars from typical research. Illustratively, the work by Miller and Friesen (1984, 18–19 and 34–36)

- deals with many qualities simultaneously to build "a detailed, holistic, integrated image," while most existing research is bivariate;
- analyzes data so as to seek natural clusters of attributes, without the common assumptions that relationships are linear and causation unidirectional;
- differences—for example, in time, process, situation—are taken into account whenever possible, while most available research fixates on a single point in time;
- uses anecdotal data to test the applicability of the configurations, while existing work typically distances the researcher from the context, as in the reliance on questionnaires.

Similar work has been done by Owens (1971) with the properties of individuals, which led him to isolate nearly two dozen Bio-Data Subgroups for classifying persons.

Fourth, two varieties of configurational analysis may be distinguished, at least. The work by Miller and Friesen (1984) illustrates the reliance on statistical procedures that permit reliable judgments about the number of separate domains necessary to encompass differences or similarities in some range of indicators. These researchers define a panel of ten archetypes—some characteristic of successful firms, and others of the unsuccessful. The latter include the archetypes Impulsive and Stagnant, while the former include the archetypes Dominant and Niche Innovator. In addition, Miller and Friesen suggest certain transitional patterns sensitive to environmental changes, identifying "likely destinations" (1984, 133–50) into which specific archetypes may transition. (See also Miller and Friesen 1977, 1980, and 1982.)

A second variety of configurational analysis may be labeled "clinical" and is illustrated by the five "neurotic organizational styles" proposed by Kets de Vries and Miller (1984, esp. 24–25). They key on the personal characteristics of executives, and particularly on the "shared fantasies" that may develop in collectivities exposed to the operating biases and life experiences of particular executives. The analysts induce from their observations these neurotic styles: Paranoid, Compulsive, Dramatic, Depressive, and Schizoid.

These and all other examples of configurational analysis share two significant commonalities. Both have to stand up to empirical test—to determine whether they isolate consistent patterns of covariants and permit successful predictions. As with the statistically derived typology, moreover, the neurotic styles are intended to isolate patterns in organizations. Not surprisingly, since the two books most central to the discussion above share a coauthor, the neurotic styles are tentatively associated with several of the archetypes (e.g., Kets de Vries and Miller 1984, 214–15). Specific interventions would be suitable for different combinations, in general.

Toward a Manhattan Project in organization analysis and praxis. These days of cutbacks in research grants may seem to be a curious time to make the following point, but some things require periodic even if brief emphasis lest we forget their salience. The need for a kind of Manhattan Project for the organizational arts and sciences grows, with the alternative being a growing sense of analytic circularity and even conceptual stuckness. Readers may need reminding about the original Manhattan Project, whose then-unprecedented scale permitted solving problems in atomic theory that led to a quantum leap—to risk a play on words—in what was known about physics, and in what could be done with that knowledge to create both boon and bane for humanity in atomic energy.

The argument is direct, even if the conclusion is intimidating. As noted, part of our legacy of conflicting findings derives from the lack of configurational analysis. Given the probable inclusion in any research area of units of analysis with different characters and characterizations, the research babel of findings is not surprising. Rather, it is inevitable, except by great good fortune. No obvious reasons encourage one to anticipate that organizations configured as Impulsive will share a range of covariants with those labeled Stagnant. Similarly, "neurotic organizations" might well share some deficiencies in processes and products, but Dramatic and Depressive variants no doubt would differ across broad realms of phenomena.

But no narrow success for configurational analysis can be envisioned, given research tools and traditions as they tend to be. As Miller and Friesen emphasize, internal elegance and parsimony will suffice for neither analysis nor, especially, for applications. Rather, any configurations will be useful to the degree that they enhance our knowledge about external relationships and covariants—that is, to the degree that they co-vary consistently with clusters of relationships in nature.

Establishing these covariants for configurational analysis no doubt will require a change in the scale and character of research. Patently, such work will need to cope with the welter of operational definitions common in research about ostensibly similar conceptual targets. Fortunately, considerable conceptual and operational clarification has been achieved in some areas. For example, "cohesiveness" seems in tolerably good shape, and has been for some time; and substantial closure has occurred concerning the relative usefulness of the multiple ways of measuring the facets of "satisfaction." Generally, however, multiple operations are used to measure "the same" conceptual domains, and those operations have probably variable congruencies and have seldom been analyzed in the required detail. For rare expectations, see March 1956, Christie and Geis 1970, and Altemeyer 1981.

No wonder, then, that the research findings in an area are typically inconsistent. Again, from the present perspective, we should expect inconsistency and even contradiction between results. Techniques like meta-analysis may help some (Hunter, Schmidt, and Jackson 1982), but no technique can replace the laborious, ponderous, and (yes!) unglamorous work of what may be called "comparative operational analysis."

Now, what does all this have to do with a Manhattan Project? An introduction to some economics of the research appropriate for configurational analysis cum relational testing implies the puniness of even the most comprehensive contemporary research designs. Consider that Bowers and Hausser (1977) isolate twenty-three types of work groups, and use them to assess the efficacy of targeting five interventions. Even if nature were so cooperative as to generate equal distributions of the types, the design matrix already has 23-by-5, or 115, cells, and even five entries per cell would require 575 work groups under the improbably favorable condition posited here.

Determined relational analysis sharply escalates the scale of the required optimum research enterprise, in short. Appropriate confidence in results would be heightened if a range of variables were included in a design and simultaneously applied to *one* known population. These variables populate at least the five panels shown in figure 12.1.

Only a very large-scale design would suffice, patently. Huge increases in scale also will result from two elemental data: that multiple operational definitions are in common use for many of the relevant variables, and that at present no substantial evidence permits a grounded choice between most alternative operational definitions.

Note a final point. The unlikelihood of the magnum approach—and, perhaps, the basic stuckness of organization analysis—has encouraged an emphasis on N = 1 designs. These may be helpful, of course, but emphasis now on N = 1 designs basically puts matters the wrong way around. The contribution of N = 1 designs would be enhanced *if* a substantial set of conceptual-operational pairs were in hand and thus constituted a common vocabulary for such research. So, N = 1 designs are understandable but, in the present view, they may do more to perpetuate than to solve the problems of organizational designs. In brief, N = 1 designs seem more able to profit from a Manhattan Project in the social sciences than to provide a foundation for it.

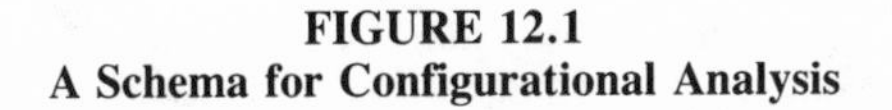

FIGURE 12.1
A Schema for Configurational Analysis

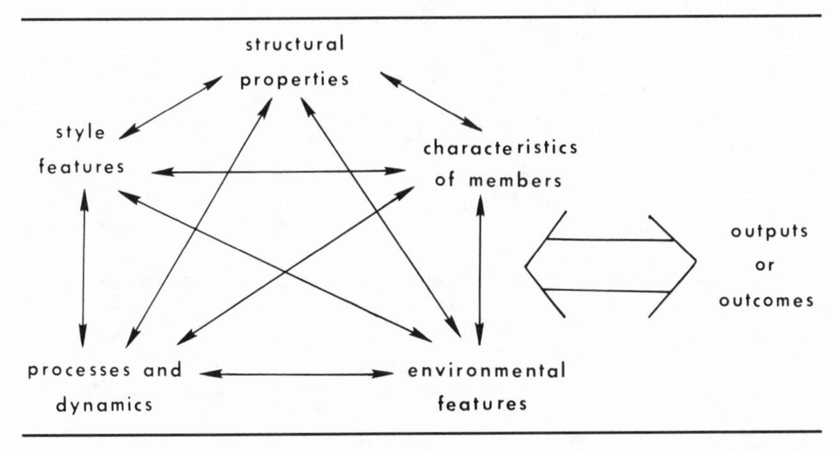

References

Altemeyer, R. A. 1981. *Right-Wing Authoritarianism*. Winnipeg, Canada: University of Manitoba Press.

Bowers, D. G., and Hausser, D. L. 1977. "Work Group Types and Intervention Effects in Organizational Development." *Administrative Science Quarterly* 22:76–94.

Brown, L. D., and Tandon, R. 1983. "Ideology and Political Economy in Inquiry." *Journal of Applied Behavioral Science*, 19:277–94.

Child, J. 1973. "Parkinson's Progress." *Administrative Science Quarterly* 18:328–49.

Christie, R., and Geis, F. L. 1970. *Studies in Machiavellianism*. New York: Academic Press.

Golembiewski, R. T. 1962. *The Small Group*. Chicago, Ill.: University of Chicago Press.

______. 1979. *Approaches to Planned Change*. New York: Marcel Dekker.

______. 1986a. "Organization Analysis and Praxis." In *Review of Industrial and Organizational Psychology*, edited by C. L. Cooper and I. Robertson, 279–302. London: John Wiley and Sons.

______. 1986b. "The Fund for Displaced ODers." *Organization Development Journal* 4:12–13.

______. 1987. "Is OD Narrowly Culturally Bounded?" Paper presented at the Annual Meeting, Academy of Management. New Orleans. 9–11 August.

______. 1989. "OD Applications in Non-Affluent Settings." In *Research in the Sociology of Organizations*, edited by S. B. Bacharach and R. Magjuka. Greenwich, Conn.: JAI Press.

Golembiewski, R. T., and Munzenrider, R. F. 1988. *Phases of Burnout*. New York: Praeger.

Haire, M. 1959. *Modern Organization Theory*. New York: Wiley.

Hunter, J. E.; Schmidt, F. L.; and Jackson, G. B. 1982. *Meta-Analysis*. Beverly Hills, Calif.: Sage.

Janz, T.; Dugan, S.; and Ross, M. S. 1986. "Organizational Culture and Burnout." *Journal of Health and Human Resources Administration* 9:78–92.

Kets de Vries, M. F. R., and Miller, D. 1984. *The Neurotic Organization*. San Francisco: Jossey-Bass.

Krell, T. C. 1981. "The Marketing of Organization Development." *Journal of Applied Behavioral Science* 17:309–23.

Lakin, M., ed. 1979. "What's Happened to Small Group Research?" *Journal of Applied Behavioral Science* 15:265–373.

March, J. G. 1956. "Influence Measurement in Experimental and Semi-Experimental Groups." *Sociometry* 19:260–71.

Miller, D., and Friesen, P. H. 1977. "Strategy-Making in Context." *Journal of Management Studies* 14:259–80.

______. 1980. "Archetypes of Organizational Transition." *Administrative Science Quarterly* 25:268–99.

______. 1982. "Structural Change and Performance." *Academy of Management Journal* 25:867–92.

______. 1984. *Organizations: A Quantum View*. Englewood Cliffs, N.J.: Prentice-Hall.

Mintzberg, H. 1979. *The Structuring of Organizations*. Englewood Cliffs, N.J.: Prentice-Hall.

Owens, W. 1971. "A Quasi-Actuarial Basis for Individual Assessment." *American Psychologist* 26:992–99.

Pondy, L. R. 1969. "Effects of Size, Complexity and Ownership on Administrative Intensity." *Administrative Science Quarterly* 14:47–60.

Pondy, L. R.; Frost, P. J. ; Morgan, G.; and Dandridge, T. C., eds. 1983. *Organizational Symbolism*. Greenwich, Conn.: JAI Press.

Pugh, D. S.; Hickson, D. J.; and Hinings, C. R. 1968. "An Empirical Taxonomy of Structures of Work Organizations." *Administrative Science Quarterly* 14:115–26.

Rushing, W. A. 1967. "The Effects of Industry Size and Division of Labor on Administration." *Administrative Science Quarterly* 12:273–95.

Appendix

A Description of Ahmavaara's Procedure for Comparing Factorial Structures

Overall, the first seven factors generated by each factor-analytic application are taken to constitute a seven-dimensional subspace of the total space encompassed by the eighteen variables. Since the variables used to derive each factor matrix are the same and the individuals are the same, each matrix defines a separate subspace in the same overall space.

The procedures for comparing factorial solutions for a common data set can be described briefly. Note that the approach is generally the same whether the comparison of pairs of structures is between wave or within wave. The former compares the congruence of the factorial structure generated by the same procedure in each of two waves of self-responses; the latter compares the two structures generated by pairs of alternative factorial procedures within a single wave of responses.

Ahmavaara's (1954) method of rotating one factor matrix into the space of another in order to compare them was utilized since it efficiently reduces the noise inherent in prior rotations of either matrix. Convincing evidence strongly implies the special usefulness of Ahmavaara's procedure, compared to a substantial number of alternative procedures that might have been used (Pinneau and Newhouse 1964). To suggest that usefulness, Hamilton notes that Ahmavaara's method is "the simplest, neatest and most elegant [but] it has been little used and little referred to" (1967, 107).

Ahmavaara's procedure begins with the development of a transformation matrix L of the matrices being compared, X being the "problem" and Y the "target" matrix, respectively. Ahmavaara describes L in these terms:

> The columns represent the common factors of the matrix Y, the order being the same in L as in Y. On the other hand, the rows of L represent the common factors of X, the order of factors again the same in L as in X. The elements of L then indicate the cosines of the angles between the factors of the different studies or, more accurately, between the vectors representing these factors. Consequently, if some element of L is exactly equal to unity, the respective factors of the two studies are identical. (1954, 56)

Factor vectors of the same size are created by recalculating L in normalized form.

Subsequently, a check matrix C is derived by multiplying each element of

L by its corresponding element in X, the problem matrix. This is the best least-squares fit of the first matrix into the second.

Finally, the inter-class correlation and product-moment correlation coefficients between the check matrix C and the target Y are computed. These coefficients are critical in the analysis discussed in chapters 10 and 11. The inter-class correlation indicates the degree to which the two structures are similar in both pattern and magnitude. Product-moment coefficients indicate the degree of similarity in patterning only, and the square of these coefficients indicates the percentage of variance that the two structures being compared have in common.

References

Ahmavaara, Y. 1954. "Transformation Analysis of Factorial Data." *Annals of Science Fennicae, Series B* 881:54–59.

Hamilton, M. 1967. "Comparisons of Factors by Ahmavaara's Method." *British Journal of Mathematical and Statistical Psychology* 2:107–10.

Pinneau, S. R., and Newhouse, A. 1964. "Measures of Invariance and Compatibility in Factor Analysis for Fixed Variables." *Psychometrika* 29:271–81.

Author Index

Subject Index